PENGUIN BOOKS

ENGLISH POETRY 1918–60

Kenneth Allott was born in 1912 and educated at various schools and at the universities of Durham and Oxford. After the war he taught at Liverpool University, where he became A.C. Bradley Professor of Modern English Literature. He died in May 1973.

During the 1930s Kenneth Allott was a regular contributor to *New Verse* and published two volumes of poems, which have been reprinted as *Collected Poems*. Among his later publications were the large annotated edition of Matthew Arnold's poetry (1965), a volume of selections from Browning's poems (1967), and a symposium of essays on Arnold, which he edited and to which he planned to contribute a long chapter on Arnold's poetry. This was left unfinished at his death, but was completed by his wife and published in 1975. Miriam Allott succeeded her husband in the Chair at Liverpool University, which she held from 1974 until 1981. She took over most of his unfinished literary projects, and also established a Kenneth Allott Lecture at Liverpool University, to be given every year by a practising poet or someone concerned with modern poetry. The first lecture was delivered in 1978 by Seamus Heaney.

The present collection of poems, first published in 1950 under the title *The Penguin Book of Contemporary Verse*, has frequently reprinted and remains one of the best known and most constantly used anthologies of modern poetry.

ENGLISH POETRY
1918–60

SELECTED WITH AN
INTRODUCTION AND NOTES BY

Kenneth Allott

PENGUIN BOOKS

PENGUIN BOOKS

Published by the Penguin Group
Penguin Books Ltd, 27 Wrights Lane, London W8 5TZ, England
Penguin Books USA Inc., 375 Hudson Street, New York, New York 10014, USA
Penguin Books Australia Ltd, Ringwood, Victoria, Australia
Penguin Books Canada Ltd, 10 Alcorn Avenue, Toronto, Ontario, Canada M4V 3B2
Penguin Books (NZ) Ltd, 182–190 Wairau Road, Auckland 10, New Zealand

Penguin Books Ltd, Registered Offices: Harmondsworth, Middlesex, England

First published as *The Penguin Book of Contemporary Verse* 1950
Second edition 1962
Reprinted under the present title 1982
7 9 10 8

Printed in England by Clays Ltd, St Ives plc
Set in Monotype Fournier

The dates of poets given in the Contents are periodically revised. However, given that the editor has confined his selection to poetry written between 1918 and 1960 the biographical/bibliographical information given in the text remains unchanged from the time of writing (December 1961). As such, it provides the most useful guide to the editor's choice and to the state of English verse at that date.

Contents

Prefatory Note

THIRTY–FOUR years have passed since the spring of 1948 when Kenneth Allott first began to assemble material for the anthology which after its publication in 1950 became familiar to many generations of readers as *The Penguin Book of Contemporary Verse*. Its sucess can be measured by the fact that it was reprinted seven times during the next ten years, published in a revised and enlarged edition in 1962 and reprinted in its new form a further eleven times between 1963 and 1980. Work on a projected new edition, to represent developments in the 1960s, was interrupted by the editor's death in 1973. The book nevertheless is still widely in demand and the time has duly arrived for yet another reprint. The historical cut-off point, then, is obviously no impediment to the book's usefulness and popularity, its special features having in any case long since established it as a classic of its kind. All the same, though nothing else is changed, it is clear that the original title will no longer do. The new title, *English Poetry 1918-60*, is at least in keeping with the editor's account of the book in his 1962 introduction. As he said then, 'the word "contemporary" in the old title, which is retained for familiarity's sake, is already an umbrella with absurdly long spokes when it has to provide cover both for Yeats, Eliot, Dylan Thomas, and other contemporaries, and for the poets who have established themselves since the nineteen-fifties . . . The character of the anthology can be simply indicated. It is a representative collection of English verse written between 1918 and 1960.' So the present title is all the more a fair and just substitute now that we have travelled on so much further in time. Even so, literature being resistant to the most liberal of taxonomies, some qualifications need to be made and we should note the editor's reminder in 1962 that several poems appeared before 1918 – though their impact might have been felt later – and that 'English verse' meant 'written by English poets', not 'written in English'. His regret in 1952 at the omission of American and Commonwealth poets was mitigated by 1962 because of the publication in the interval of

Penguin anthologies of American, Australian, Canadian and New
Zealand verse, a list which has been still further extended since then.

Now that we have gained this longer historical perspective and
learnt a good deal about the way in which the book has been used
and enjoyed, we might add a further gloss on that editorial descrip-
tion. The anthology's 'representative' nature has had a dual appeal
for many readers because it remains obedient to the task of reflec-
ting the period's 'main movements of mind' while yet preserving
the individual flavour of a lively personal taste. The use of succinct
introductory commentaries to combine biographical thoughts
about the poems was something of an innovation at the time and
prompted mild controversy for a while (the 1962 introduction
glances at this). But over the years these commentaries have come
to be looked on as extremely useful guides, especially by new readers
and, indeed, new writers of poetry, for many of whom the book
provided what was virtually their first substantial introduction to
the subject. The underlying critical principle is the need to look
directly at the object while recognizing that if the observer cannot
entirely 'get himself out of the way' he should deal no less honestly
with the movement of his own predilections. (This critical allegi-
ance will hardly surprise anyone who remembers that the editor was
an Arnold scholar as well as being a poet himself.)

To help us to arrive at our own judgements about the broader
critical and historical perspectives, and the critical insights which
seek to illuminate them, the book offers us, then, its wide range of
poems, the commentaries which introduce them and the prefatory
essay which sets out to place the poets and their work by surveying
'the poetic "weather" of each of the last four decades'. For the
present writer the interest of these meteorological readings has
been added to recently by re-reading the correspondence associated
with the 1952 and 1962 editions, itself a record of considerable
historical and personal interest (part of it originates with writers of
earlier years – Siegfried Sassoon, Roy Campbell and Bernard
Spencer among them – who are no longer alive). One of its striking
features is the remarkable congruity of interest and concern linking
editor and contributor, whatever their differences over incidental
judgements. With a few notable exceptions, there is even much

pleasurable agreement about the work chosen to represent an author's most characteristic achievement. Furthermore, letters from those who took time to analyse what seemed to be happening in contemporary poetry, and to weigh their own part in it, take their place beside the editorial commentaries as documents which have stood up well to the test of the years. This is true of various Movement poets of the 1950s, who charted other movements and counter-movements, from the literary revolution in T.S. Eliot and Ezra Pound, through the 'social' 1930s (a more varied decade than some simplifying popular misconceptions currently allow) and the 'apocalyptic' 1940s, to their own demurring period, whose creative climate the editor identifies sympathetically with the carefully neutral tones of what he calls the 'unenthusiastic imagination'.

How he would have reported upon the climatic conditions of the 1960s and 1970s is a matter of speculation but we can make an informed guess since the supplementary material in the 1962 edition tells us that he had read the signs of the coming decade with a shrewd weather eye. Many of his new names were only then beginning to establish themselves but are now familiar everywhere. We can be pretty sure that there would have been revisions and extensions in the selections from, let us say, Ted Hughes, Geoffrey Hill, Sylvia Plath and Thomas Kinsella, who would certainly have been accompanied in a new edition by several of his countrymen, especially Seamus Heaney for whose early poems the editor had a strong feeling long before the publication of *North* and *Fieldwork*. Probably the best hint of a long-range forecast comes at the close of the 1962 introduction which glances at the 'centrifugal forces' spinning the *New Lines* poets 'further and further from a common centre now that the bug-eyed monster of the neo-romantic poem has been scotched'. Far enough away indeed, a 1982 introduction might have added, for there to be no longer any one prevailing weather, only a climate which fosters diversity, a wide choice of styles, the expression of many different voices. A new book of contemporary verse would have brought this home to us. As it is, *English Poetry 1918–60*, its virtues tested and tried, will remain an invaluable guide helping us to understand how it all came about.

March 1982   MIRIAM ALLOTT

Introduction

I

THIS collection now contains 175 poems by 86 poets and ranges chronologically from W. B. Yeats, who was born in 1865, to Geoffrey Hill, who was seven years old when Yeats died in 1939. The youngest generation, of poets still under twenty-five, many of whom have not yet produced a book, is unrepresented; and perhaps the word 'contemporary' in the old title, which is retained for familiarity's sake, is already an umbrella with absurdly long spokes when it has to provide cover both for Yeats, Eliot, Auden, Dylan Thomas, and their contemporaries and for the poets who have established themselves in the nineteen-fifties. Small changes were made in several earlier reprints of the anthology, which was first published in 1950, but the present edition is the first to add a considerable number of poems to the original collection and to attempt to bring up to date the commentaries accompanying the individual selections. Nearly a third of the poems now assembled are new. A few of the additional poems are by poets already represented – I have seized the opportunity to include Part II of T. S. Eliot's *Little Gidding* (which I was unable to use in 1948) and to add later pieces by W. H. Auden, Roy Fuller, Norman Nicholson, and a few others – but four out of every five of the new poems are by poets whose work was either unpublished or virtually unknown at the beginning of the last decade.

The character of the anthology can be simply indicated. It is a representative collection of English verse written between 1918 and 1960. This statement is not quite accurate to the letter. There are several pieces composed earlier than 1918 – pieces, for example, by Isaac Rosenberg and Edward Thomas – but even here the impact of the poems on readers came somewhat later. It should be explained that English verse means 'written by English poets', not verse in English. In 1948 I thought it necessary to apologize for the omission of American poets (and, to be logical, I should have added Commonwealth poets), but the publication of Penguin anthologies of American, Australian, Canadian, and New Zealand verse in recent years happily makes that apology superfluous. It would obviously be impossible to bring all the poets now writing in English together within the covers of a single volume, and most people are far more aware than they used to be that poets from the United States and the countries of the Commonwealth have strong national accents. I have not been absolutely consistent. I have excluded neither the poems written by T. S. Eliot before he became a naturalized Englishman, nor those written by W. H. Auden after he became an American citizen; and I have claimed Sylvia Plath as English because she married an English poet and settled in this country, although she was born in Boston and the main literary influence on her work is that of John Crowe Ransom. Similarly, I suppose it is inconsistent to include Arthur Waley's translations from the Chinese while ruling out all other translations for reasons of space, but I feel that Mr Waley's translations are original poems for the English reader. For practical purposes, then, this is an anthology of the poetic work of the twenties, thirties, forties, and fifties in England.

In choosing the poems and compiling the commentaries I have kept specially in mind two classes of readers: the large class for which poetry of any kind is only occasional reading; and the smaller one of those already interested in contemporary poetry who find it hard to keep up with and impossible to buy the many books of verse published today. For this second class the situation is certainly no easier than it was in 1948 – prices are high, booksellers outside London and a few university towns are just as unwilling to stock their shelves speculatively with new poetry, and many of the fifties poets have published their early work from small or semi-private presses. For the sake of the audiences described I have made my commentaries full and informative in a popular way. The usual biographical facts are given, but I have gone beyond this in supplying bibliographical information about a poet's publications, or in listing studies of his or her work. The idea behind all such editorial helps is that an anthology justifies its existence only if it encourages the reader to move on from the packaged tour to independent travel, and that he is more likely to do so if he is given directions. I think that most of the information will be useful to some reader. (This was no more than a pious hope when I first wrote it, but the adoption of a similar type of commentary in certain other anthologies suggests that the hope was a reasonable one.) I have also committed myself in the commentaries to saying what I felt about the work of particular poets. This may be to invite the contempt of those who do not recognize the difficulty of giving summary judgement on a writer in a few lines, or who deny the use of such judgements altogether. For the sake of the readers I particularly had in mind that risk seemed worth taking, and for my own sake I was glad not to have to pretend that I had no preferences.

Sometimes my guess at a poet's importance is suggested by the amount of his work that I include. There is more work by Yeats, Eliot, Graves, and Auden than by other writers in the earlier part of the anthology, and more work by Philip Larkin and Donald Davie than by their contemporaries in the new supplementary part, and these facts coincide with my opinion that the poets named are respectively the most important in the metropolitan and suburban areas of this collection. Of course this mechanical kind of estimate cannot be applied to the anthology as a whole. The sorting-out process of time has operated most severely on the earlier decades, so that I have been less and less selective about mere inclusion as I approached the present. Against this, as far as the additional poems in this edition are concerned, economic reasons have stood in the way of representing a few poets as they deserve. With a longer purse I should have included more poems by Larkin, Davie, Amis, Tomlinson, Gunn, Kinsella, and Ted Hughes. So much for the inclusions. Exclusions are more difficult to discuss tactfully, but I have read conscientiously, and if there are some obvious omissions, they are not inadvertent.

Finally, within the general aim of printing what I consider to be good poems, I have found room for a few pieces either because they are typical of a particular time or temper (Aldous

Huxley, Christopher Fry), or because their authors appear to have exercised an influence (Charles Williams) or to have large and deserved reputations in other branches of literature (James Joyce, Wyndham Lewis, Herbert Read). Further, when a poet is represented by three or four poems I have not felt bound to choose his best work exclusively – sometimes it has seemed better to illustrate his development or his poetic variety, or to print a poem by him that comments usefully on other poems (see, for example, Davie's 'Remembering the Thirties'). To determine when such considerations should be allowed to qualify a choice based simply on merit is probably the anthologist's biggest headache.

II

Most of what I want to say about individual authors (and, incidentally, about groups, movements, tendencies, and so on) will be found in the separate commentaries, but I have been asked to pull together what is there said or implied at various points by a short introduction giving explicit attention to the poetic 'weather' of each of the last four decades. I know that in the space available this is to deal in half-truths and approximations, but the assumption is that a report of this kind may still be useful to some people, half a loaf being better than no bread.

Fortunately there is no need to describe again in detail the characteristic insipidities of the Georgian poets with their cult of respectability (after the absinthe and sin of the Nineties) and their pastoral week-end England of trout streams, cricket, parish churches, and tea (without desire) under the elms: their influence on later poets has been negligible. (If these remarks appear brutal, then oblivion has been too kind to the Georgians in enabling us to forget how limply they wrote and how fondly they were addicted to fakes and stereotypes of feeling.)[1] Equally 'the radical opposition', represented by *Wheels* (an anthology first issued in 1916), can be quickly passed over. Miss Sitwell, as

1. A more friendly view of the Georgians is expressed in *Georgian Poetry* (Penguin Poets D59), edited by James Reeves.

she then was, was the presiding genius of these irritated replies
to the tame volumes of *Georgian Poetry* edited by Edward Marsh.
Although Wilfred Owen and other good poets contributed to
Wheels, and many of the pieces printed there have a certain
technical liveliness, on the whole the content of the poems is un-
interesting. If anyone is ever tempted to forget the debt we owe
to T. S. Eliot and other poets of the 'Revolutionary' generation
(from a natural impatience with the scurrilities and absurdities
of Pound's *Cantos* or the unction of *The Confidential Clerk* and
The Elder Statesman), to be recalled to his senses he has only to
remember what passed for poetry under Georgian auspices in
the English Association's disgraceful and much reprinted antho-
logy *Poems of To-day*. Without a Yankee invasion – and the
poetic revolution was the direct result of the invasion – this sort
of silliness might have gone on much longer.

Imagism needs to be introduced in a new paragraph. In time
the Imagist movement mainly lies outside the period covered by
this collection, but its demand for hardness, clarity, and pre-
cision in writing, its insistence on fidelity to appearances, and its
rejection of what was called irrelevant subjective emotion, had
later demonstrable effects. The movement was certainly more
American than English – Ezra Pound spoke of 'Amygism' be-
cause of Amy Lowell's enthusiasm – but it had English sup-
porters and adherents. T. E. Hulme, for example, who was
killed in the First World War, by his ideas exercised an impor-
tant influence on Pound and Eliot, and Hulme's 'complete
poetical works' – he was primarily a philosophical essayist –
can be found in an appendix to his posthumous volume, *Specula-
tions*: they consist of five Imagist fragments. Imagism can be
traced directly in Eliot's 'Preludes' and in such pieces as 'Morn-
ing at the Window', and more indirectly in the kind of descrip-
tive writing done by Pound in his 'Chinese' poems, by D. H.
Lawrence in his animal and flower pieces, and by Richard Ald-
ington in such a narrative as *A Dream in the Luxembourg*. The
Imagist aims of precision and clarity of outline have also to be
held in mind when we remember Pound's plea for the imita-
tion of Gautier's *Émaux et Camées*: this plea fathered Eliot's

'Sweeney' poems in quatrains and Pound's own famous sequence *Mauberley*. Further, the rejection of conventional verse forms by many poets in the twenties owed something, I think, to the Imagist repudiation of flabby writing by the Georgians. Other reasons, of course, predisposed poets to the adoption of *vers libre* – the mere desire for novelty, the imitation of Whitman, the study of Jacobean dramatic blank verse, awareness of what French poets had already done to the alexandrine in France. It was difficult, to say the least, for a poet of the poetic generation of the twenties – the qualification is important – to handle a conventional verse form such as the sonnet or the heroic couplet with any vitality during these years. After their long misuse these patterns had to be rested before they could be employed to advantage again in the thirties and later.

One way of looking at poetic periods is to notice what contemporary interests and knowledge penetrate the best verse written at the time, and what moods are permissible in treating of these matters. From this point of view T. S. Eliot must be saluted, however bookish and esoteric his early poetry may seem (up to and including *The Waste Land*), for his extension of the field of subject-matter available for poetic treatment and for the flexibility of tone that he showed to be possible in handling it. Christianity, the modern industrial city, and the background of European history are found a place in his poetry, as MacNeice has remarked, and wit, irony, and satire are weapons at his command. To argue that this widening of subject-matter and command of rapid changes of tone and tempo are in Eliot's favour is not to deny that comparatively simple nature-poems or love-poems could still be written successfully; but it is to suggest that good nature-poetry or love-poetry should reveal contemporaneity in some difference from earlier work in the same kind. In his choice of themes Edmund Blunden is a traditional poet, but especially by his use of rhythm and by word-selection he creates a subtle impression that he is aware of the artificiality of what he is doing, and this impression is a witness to the responsibility of his verse.

If we speak of the twenties as being concerned in poetry with culture and the maintenance of tradition, we have to forget the puerility of much of the verse published in the *London Mercury*, the absurdity of the *avant-garde* chopped prose of Bloomsbury and Paris, and the dullness of the innumerable slim volumes of garnered fancies issued by publishers out of habit or in the whimsical hope of cornering a future best-seller novelist. We have to put aside, that is to say, a quantitative assessment in favour of a qualitative one. Qualitatively the poetic twenties may be said to have undertaken the defence of culture and tradition because T. S. Eliot, their arch-poet, did so. That defence meant an acquaintance with the English and European past, not only literary, but religious and social. It meant, too, much critical activity in the attempt to understand and value the tradition. Eliot's critical work in prose accompanies his poetry with equal steps, and many critics have discovered the same preoccupations in both – the concern with 'metaphysical', wit, the rejection of the Miltonic sublime, etc. A poet educated to his finger-tips will tend to be allusive. He may give, as Mr Eliot clearly did, a magnificent example of intelligent dedication to poetry, but the danger of this Atlas-load of the past to be carried by the contemporary poet, if he is really to size up his own time, is, of course, the danger of smothering and losing the poetry, of its becoming clogged with erudition and complexity. At this moment (1921) Eliot saw no way out of the dilemma. He wrote:

> We can only say that it appears likely that poets in our civilization, as it exists at present, must be *difficult*. Our civilization comprehends great variety and complexity, and this variety and complexity, playing upon a refined sensibility, must produce various and complex results. The poet must become more and more comprehensive, more allusive, more indirect, in order to force, to dislocate if necessary, language into his meaning.[1]

This is not a statement that commands an immediate and unhesitating assent. Even in the most sophisticated ages there will

1. Some of these 'dislocations': Joyce's polyglot word-coinages, the Stein stutter (to use Wyndham Lewis's phrase), the *lingua franca* of *Transition*.

be poets without the least desire to grapple with the problems of their civilization synoptically, and there is nothing like general agreement that this is indeed what they ought to be doing, or that they cannot be reckoned serious artists if they choose to turn their backs on the task. Again, it is quite proper to ask if a complex age does need a complex poetry – Matthew Arnold thought that the complexity of his own times required an exemplary plainness on the part of the poet. The truth would seem to be that there is no necessary relation between the sophistication of an age and the degree of sophistication to be expected in its poetry. These are rumbling doubts and questions, but the word 'dislocate' brings us up sharply.[1] It shows us that if Eliot could pose as a supporter of tradition (in a sense that has already been sufficiently indicated), he was simultaneously a revolutionary firebrand. Macaulay's schoolboy now knows that 'a poem should not mean but be' – a quarter-truth from Symbolist aesthetic that had too much currency in defence of incoherence in the neo-romantic forties. Eliot's most revolutionary innovation in poetic method was his partial replacement of logical and narrative continuity by 'dislocated discourse', that is to say, by a type of poetic structure which mainly depends – the analogy is with musical form – for its unity of meaning on a reader's ability to keep track of recurrent motifs (phrases and images) in all their separations and disguises. Dislocated discourse makes for economical compression in writing but hard reading. It affords opportunity for some very striking poetic effects in the juxtaposition of what is disparate in style or scene, but it also forces us to ask ourselves how far we can really go along with Eliot's view of his own poetry as a 'traditional' development of the poetic inheritance. I see this particular poetic innovation as a Franco-American foreign body which English poetic anatomy has encapsulated and is in process of extruding – it is implicitly rejected by the best poetic practice of the thirties and fifties, and it is difficult not to believe that Dylan Thomas would have recognized much earlier the danger of building rich structures of rhythm and phrase without allowance for the necessary

1. Characteristically, it is a literary echo from the French.

pipes and plumbing of reasonable meaning if we had not all been
so pusillanimous – out of proper gratitude to Eliot as a poetic
liberator and from a natural dislike for Blimpish academicism –
about rejecting these 'dislocations'. I do not wish to exaggerate.
If *The Waste Land* is a triumph, it is one partly because of the
genius of its author in finding a technique for suggesting so
many things simultaneously and for operating on so many
planes of meaning. It is a most extraordinary poem, and perhaps
it has become so hackneyed to some of us that we fail to see how
truly extraordinary it is. Perhaps it was the only kind of
'masterpiece' possible in 1922, but after the lapse of forty years
I am not at all sure of the satisfactoriness of the kind. From the
vantage-point of 1961 Pound's influence on Eliot cannot be re-
garded with simple approval. How much of the difficulty of *The
Waste Land* is due to his reported excisions? I cannot help feel-
ing, too, that 'Gerontion' makes gross demands on our toler-
ance by the unintelligibility of its transitions, and that we prob-
ably owe this to Pound. I am not quite ready yet to agree with
Mr Graham Hough in repudiating all forms of dislocated dis-
course as an aberration, but I feel that the 'new' type of poetic
structure, which is used with mature subtlety and discretion in
Ash Wednesday and *Four Quartets*, produces an unhealthy self-
consciousness in poets and pedantry in critics. *The Waste Land*
strikes one as too clever and too full of tricks, serious enough
but serious even in what is almost a scholastic way – a poem-
coral for *Scrutiny* reviewers to cut their milk-teeth on, a poem
to end poems. From it one takes away felicitous bits and pieces,
'a heap of broken images' in an undesirable sense.

In 1932, ten years after the publication of *The Waste Land*,
Dr F. R. Leavis brought out his *New Bearings in English Poetry*,
an important book if we wish to discover the orthodox 'ad-
vanced' view of contemporary poetry held by an adult, purely
critical intelligence at the beginning of the thirties. *New Bear-
ings in English Poetry* contains three long essays devoted to
Gerard Manley Hopkins (whose poems were first published in
1918), Ezra Pound, and T. S. Eliot. The Pound of *Mauberley*

was rightly preferred to the Pound of the *Cantos* – the Ezra
Pound, that is, concerned like the Eliot of *The Waste Land* with
the necessary health and actual sickness of our contemporary
culture. To Eliot this was a matter of the community's loss of
vitality and of a sense of purpose as a result of a decay in reli-
gious beliefs. Pound expressed more simply his hatred of drab-
ness and levelling-down in a commercial and industrial society.
Over a century ago Alexis de Tocqueville spoke of the apo-
theosis of the mediocre in a democratic community and both
Pound and Eliot show more than a normal distrust of demo-
cratic tendencies in politics because they approach the social
problem too exclusively from the side of the maintenance of
cultural standards. W. B. Yeats, it will be remembered, saw
'mere anarchy ... loosed upon the world' in the squeezing out of
aristocrat and peasant by the time-ridden, gadget-employing
middle class. But to none of these poets is man primarily a poli-
tical animal with his natural habitat the hustings or the conspira-
torial backroom of a shabby café in a dock area. It would be an
exaggeration to say that any of the new poets of the thirties did
hold this view, but such an exaggeration would underline cor-
rectly enough a basic difference between the poetry of the
twenties and thirties.

In the last chapter of Dr Leavis's book, two poets were briefly
discussed and had their verses singled out for praise as growing-
points in any plausible future of poetry. The first of these poets
was William Empson; the second, whom Dr Leavis seemed to
prefer, was Ronald Bottrall. Bottrall was so distinguished, it
must be supposed, because his verse showed Eliot's pre-
occupation with cultural standards, because it was educated and
allusive. But by 1932 the time had gone by for a valuable de-
velopment in poetry in imitation of T. S. Eliot. Political and
economic forces at work in the world were compelling new
poets whose eyes strayed from their books to see the cultural
problem as one aspect of the general problem of the remaking of
our society. *Transitional Poem* (1929) by Cecil Day Lewis had
the usual *Waste Land* apparatus of notes containing references
to Dante, Spinoza, Wyndham Lewis, etc., but Auden's *Poems*

(1930), Spender's *Poems* (1932), and Day Lewis's *The Magnetic Mountain* (1933) revealed the new social attitude in various ways and upset Dr Leavis's predictions about the lines on which poetry was likely to develop. *The Magnetic Mountain* is too much a tract for the times at a journalistic level to be anything but a poetic failure as a whole, but a rather simple-minded fervour for a new world of political and economic justice is less evident in Auden and is more poetically conceived and felt by Spender – Auden from the beginning diluted his Marx with Freud, and in *The Destructive Element*, a book of prose criticism, Spender argued that a Marx–Freud marriage should be fruitful. The present point, however, is that all three poets – and others associated with them – would have accepted Michael Roberts's statement in his anthology *New Signatures* (1932), a statement obviously put together to counter Eliot's claim (already quoted) that poetry *must* be difficult in the complexities of the modern world.

> The solution of some too insistent problems may make it possible to write 'popular' poetry again ... because the poet will find that he can best express his newly-found attitude in terms of a symbolism which happens to be of exceptionally wide validity ... The poems in this book represent a clear reaction against esoteric poetry in which it is necessary for the reader to catch each recondite allusion.[1]

The most creative mind, the most original poetic force in the new movement of the thirties was W. H. Auden. Dr Johnson tells us that after Addison's *Spectator* papers on *Paradise Lost* most readers thought it 'necessary to be pleased' with Milton. Similarly in the thirties most young writers thought it necessary to be pleased with Auden, and a certain amount of social reference even in the personal lyric was the literary equivalent for a Party Card. The crudities of this view can be laughed at now, and, in the hands of poetasters, the results of it were often

---

1. Louis MacNeice in *Modern Poetry* (1938) was the first, I think, to set this quotation against the earlier one from Eliot's essay on *The Metaphysical Poets* (1921).

laughable then, but it is much harder to say that this insistence on social reference was a bad thing. The political aspect of the social attitude can be exaggerated. Auden spoke of a poet being 'a bit of a reporter' (not simply a *political* reporter). Geoffrey Grigson in the preface to his *New Verse* anthology (1939) revealed his method of assessing contemporary poems:

> I always judge poetry, first, by its relation to current speech, the language in which one is angry about Spain or in which one is pleasant or unpleasant to one's wife. I judge every poem written now, by poets under forty, by the degree to which it takes notice, for ends not purely individual, of the universe of objects and events.

The phrase about Spain may seem significant, but in reality it is not much more than a hurried genuflection to topicality. Louis MacNeice, too, has something to say in 1938 about the qualities necessary for the ideal poet.

> My own prejudice ... is in favour of poets whose worlds are not too esoteric. I would have a poet able-bodied, fond of talking, a reader of the newspapers, capable of pity and laughter, informed in economics, appreciative of women, involved in personal relationships, actively interested in politics, susceptible to physical impressions.

MacNeice obviously wants the poet to keep his eyes open – 'social reference' did not go beyond this in many poets of the thirties – and I suspect that 'informed in economics' and 'actively interested in politics' are more *Zeitgeist* than MacNeice.

New Verse, the most important verse-magazine of the thirties, founded by Grigson in 1933, had no left-wing axes to grind and was often attacked by left-wing enthusiasts for its political irresponsibility, but a glance through a few old numbers will show more quickly than pages of comment what is meant by 'social reference'. Subject-matter is sometimes directly political, most frequently in Stephen Spender, but the social approach to 'experience' by poets is evident in a more general way in their attitude to the problem of communication. Auden and

Spender are occasionally difficult in their early work (not always excusably), but one is aware of a concern for reaching a public, a care for intelligibility that prevents the more private extravagances found in the twenties. Behind the creation of light verse[1] (cf. Auden's ballads and the 'Letter to Lord Byron') and the reinstatement of traditional syntax and traditional forms and metres (the sonnet, the heroic couplet, *terza rima*, the sestina), as behind the move to employ new media (the sound strip of documentary films, the radio feature-programme) and the attempt to establish poetic drama, there lay an urge to proselytize. The poets wished to make contact with as wide an audience as possible, and they had designs on their public, they wished to teach it something. The 'social' poets had a reasonable hope that what they had to say would be understood, because their viewpoints, and the imagery used to illuminate them, were drawn from a direct analysis of the contemporary world. Louis MacNeice's way of putting this cannot be bettered:

> These new poets, in fact, were boiling down Eliot's 'variety and complexity' and finding that it left them with certain comparatively clear-cut issues. Instead, therefore, of attempting an impressionist survey of the contemporary world – a world which impinges on one but which one cannot deal with – they were deliberately simplifying it, distorting it perhaps (as the man of action also has to distort it) into a world where one gambles upon practical ideals, a world in which one takes sides.... This does not mean, however, that their world is a crude world of black and white, of sheep and goats.[2]

As a poetic personality MacNeice may be described as *l'homme moyen sensuel*. Not much of his verse is political in any

1. Auden's light verse expresses the normal Auden personality in a lighter mood; Eliot's light verse is a conscious unbending – the poet is going to play with the children, and he is aware that he has to get down to their level. This weakness – I believe it to be one – is analogous to that of Eliot's attempts at working-class colloquialisms. Cf. the pub cronies in *The Waste Land*, the unemployed in *The Rock*.

2. *Modern Poetry*, pp. 15, 25.

sense, but the above quotation and the earlier description of the
ideal poet (p. 26) give us an inkling of what his verse owes to the
social attitude of the thirties, and what it might have been with-
out that attitude and without Auden's direct influence. The
difference between MacNeice's volume of juvenilia, *Blind Fire-
works* (with its intelligent frivolousness and rather thin gaiety),
and *Poems* (1935) shows the kind of intellectual stiffening pro-
vided for him by 'social reference'. The case of Cecil Day Lewis
is more doubtful. It has been said that he is really a Georgian in
temper and natural interests, and that his latest (and best) work
shows this bent clearly enough, but I think that in his non-
political poetry he writes better than most of the Georgians, and
I am inclined to attribute this to the existence of the special
poetic character of the thirties.

We may sum up what has been said in the last few paragraphs
about the social poetry of the thirties by a quotation from
Stephen Spender. At that time, he writes:

> ... there was a group of poets who achieved a very wide
> reputation as a 'school' of modern poetry. They were not
> in a deliberate sense a literary movement ... [but] they had
> certain ideas in common. They consciously attempted to
> be modern, choosing in their poems imagery selected from
> machinery, slums, and the social conditions which sur-
> rounded them ... Their poetry emphasized the community,
> and, overwhelmed as it was by the sense of a communal
> disease, it searched for a communal cure in psychology and
> leftist politics ... To a great extent, their poetry, though
> leftist, expresses the problem of the liberal divided between
> his individual development and his social conscience.[1]

To turn to the forties and attempt to find a poetic character
for them is first to observe that even in the previous decade
there had been a reaction against poetry as 'social reporting' in
favour of poetry as 'individual development' or 'self-unravel-
ling'. This reaction is most noticeable in the work of Dylan
Thomas and George Barker. If the social poets wished to marry

1. *Poetry Since 1939*, p. 28.

Marx and Freud, Dylan Thomas may be said to have married
the Old Testament and Freud, and his Freud is seen through
D.·H. Lawrence. George Barker is of particular interest here,
because, possessing less self-assurance than Thomas, he hovered
so uneasily between the two kinds of writing in the thirties, to
the detriment, it must be said, of much of his verse. In 1939 a
group of young writers called themselves the New Apocalypse
and made the reaction overt. 'Their model for the writing of
poetry was Dylan Thomas,' Julian Symons has remarked, 'and
for many of their theories of art, as they have frequently ac-
knowledged, they are indebted to the ideas of Herbert Read.'
They rejected what they described as the self-conscious and in-
tellectualized manner of Auden and his associates, preferring to
become intoxicated with words, to create myths and to indulge
in Gothic effects. The New Apocalypse included few good
poets, and its importance is mainly to point to changes taking
place in the cultural weather. The Apocalyptics disliked the
machine, flirted with anarchism, and would have agreed with
the 'individualist' e. e. cummings who wrote

> dead every enormous piece
> of nonsense which itself must call
> a state submicroscopic is –
> compared with pitying terrible
> some alive individual.

The changes which were taking place in the cultural weather –
they were to become more obvious during the war years and the
years immediately following the war – were, like the changes
heralding the social poetry of the thirties, not a mere literary
fashion, but a reflection of forces in the actual world and of the
feelings of men and women about them. Militarism, bureaucracy,
Russian foreign policy, the melted eyeballs of the Japanese at
Hiroshima, weariness of slogans and propaganda lies, with a
hundred other matters great and small, conspired to produce an
atmosphere in which all political optimism and idealism seemed
childish. E. M. Forster's novels were read with wide apprecia-
tion because Forster found bed-rock only in charity in personal

relationships. Graham Greene was enjoyed, and he had written of a journey to Africa:

> There are others who prefer to look a stage ahead, for whom Intourist provides cheap tickets into a plausible future, but my journey represented a distrust of any future based on what we are.

There was an increased understanding and valuation of T. S. Eliot – the Eliot of *Four Quartets* – and a number of the younger poets found meaning and consolation in Christianity, were convinced like Newman of some 'aboriginal calamity' when they looked out on 'the disappointments of life, the defeat of good, the success of evil, physical pain, mental anguish, the prevalence and intensity of sin ... a vision to dizzy and appal'. The names of Anne Ridler, Kathleen Raine, Norman Nicholson, and David Gascoyne come to mind. There was a neo-romanticism in poetry which bound together writers of widely different temperament and technical adequacy – Vernon Watkins, Sidney Keyes, John Heath-Stubbs, Laurie Lee.

Geoffrey Grigson wrote harshly of neo-romanticism at the time in an essay published in *Polemic*:

> The 'romance' we are drifting back to is a romance without reason: it is altogether self-indulgent and liquescent. An Inky Cap mushroom grows up white and firm and then flops down into a mess of ink – which is our new romance ...

He may well have been right in thinking that we had no responsible body of opinion to make itself felt about what was 'true and untrue, possible and impossible, probable and improbable' in literature. The neo-romantic poets signally lacked the sense of limit provided in the thirties by the concern with communication. Too many of them, whatever the excuses that one tries to find for them in the nature of their times, cultivated their hysteria and built themselves ivory towers. Sometimes one was reminded of the eighteen-nineties, when, as Chesterton once said, Fabian drain-pipes had a nicer smell than the pan-pipes of the poets.

The verse of the more extreme neo-romantics was either dark, prolix, and unnecessarily involved – this was the commoner fault – or a lisping 'silly sooth'. Examples had better be suppressed. While all this 'poesy' was being produced and praised in the forties Dylan Thomas was independently travelling a long way from the riddling darkness of his earlier poems in the direction of greater discipline over his considerable gifts, and in the direction of a continuous, rather than a spasmodic, attempt at narrative meaning. Here his weak imitators were unable to follow him.

It is interesting when we consider the cultural weather of the forties to see what happened to the poetry of the social poets, Auden, Spender, and MacNeice. We find Auden moving – to borrow a phrase from Arthur Koestler – from the commissar to the yogi end of the spectrum: attempting in *For the Time Being* to understand the meaning of the Incarnation, expressing in *The Age of Anxiety* his sense of crisis and of an abandoned world. We find Spender in *Life and the Poet* unsaying what he had said in his *Forward from Liberalism*, and in his 'Spiritual Explorations' exploring the humanist position. We find MacNeice in 'The Kingdom' asserting the worth of the individual in a way that reminds us strongly of E. M. Forster's ideas. Something more is said about these developments in the commentary, but the reader can get a rapid picture of the magnitude of the change by comparing a 'political' chorus from *The Dog Beneath the Skin* with Herod's speech in *For the Time Being* or Malin's final soliloquy in *The Age of Anxiety*. Some of the poets of the thirties adopted a religious attitude in rejecting the adequacy of a social interpretation of reality: others went no further than Stephen Spender, who wrote in *Life and the Poet*:

> The ultimate aim of politics is not politics, but the activities which can be practised within the political framework of the State. ... A society with no values outside politics is a machine carrying its human cargo, with no purpose in its institutions reflecting their cares, eternal aspirations, loneliness, need for love.

This scrupulosity about the nature of the artist's social responsibility was distorted by the Apocalyptics and neo-romantics until apparently it seemed to them that the only valid way of protesting against regimentation and of asserting their individuality was to write verse that was private (as a padded cell is private), vague, and rhapsodical. By the end of the forties a new broom was very badly needed to sweep out the phosphorescent corners of decay.

The differences between the poetic characters of the forties and fifties can be conveniently approached by setting Dylan Thomas's 'Fern Hill' against Philip Larkin's 'I Remember, I Remember'. The comparison is not altogether fair – 'Fern Hill' is late Thomas and illustrates a coherence rare in his early poetry and not too frequent even in his late work ('The Ballad of the Long-Legged Bait' from *Deaths and Entrances* is the putative sire of more neo-romantic pseudo-poems), whereas Larkin's 'I Remember, I Remember', although successful in what it sets out to do, is not one of his seriously ambitious pieces. Yet to read the poems together is instructive for the light shed on two poetic attitudes. Thomas's poem may be described in Robert Conquest's words as an uncritical evocation of 'the *naïvetés* and nostalgias of childhood' – a rhythmically powerful and verbally glittering representation of the Rousseauistic–Wordsworthian commonplace that heaven and hyper-aesthesia of the senses lie about us in our infancy. 'I Remember, I Remember', with Hood's line for its title to signpost the sort of road we are on, is a highly self-conscious performance: in it this commonplace, along with other autobiographical clichés about childhood and adolescence, is guyed in terms that require some degree of literary awareness on the reader's part. How far the poem is personal in any sense is left an open question. Both Auden ('Blinding mythologies of flowers and fruits ... spoken to by an old hat ...') and D. H. Lawrence ('The boys all biceps and the girls all chest ... their farm where I could be / "Really myself" ...') receive pinpricks, and the general intention is apparently to deflate the idea that childhood is necessarily a momentous stage of our being and to raise an eyebrow at the simple acquiescence of the public in this and analogous notions. The deceptively casual ironic manner, the unemphatic naturalness of diction, the wakeful and half-humorous sense of social context (which is even more evident in Donald Davie's 'The Garden Party'), the implication that romantic feelings usually contain an element of wishful exaggeration – these are as much to be expected in a fifties poem by one of the *New Lines* poets (and it should be understood at once that the poetic character of the fifties derives from the practice of these poets and their sympathizers) as they would be wildly improbable in a forties poem by a neo-romantic writer.

'In the 1940s,' wrote Robert Conquest in his introduction to *New Lines* (1956), 'the mistake was made of giving the Id, a sound player on the percussion side under a strict conductor, too much of a say in the doings of the orchestra as a whole'; and he identifies the strict conductor later when he adds, 'The most glaring fault awaiting correction when the new period opened was the omission of the necessary intellectual component from poetry.' This is quite in line with Geoffrey Grigson's criticism of mushrooming neo-romanticism and is undeniably true: if the average level of poetic writing was higher in the late fifties than ten years earlier, the improvement was certainly due to an insistence on the role of the intelligence in the poetic process – an insistence that made incoherence and extravagance slightly disreputable, put the myth-makers to sullen retreat, and encouraged respect for poems that were shaped and syntactically wholesome. But what first impresses anyone who studies the poetry of the fifties is less the emphasis on intelligence, welcome as this is, than the fact that the poetic revolution has a mainly literary motivation. The social poets of the thirties wrote differently from T. S. Eliot because they thought that they had something important to say which would not be understood if they dressed it in his 'complexity'. It was their need to communicate a 'message' that was responsible for a change in poetic manner. Even the Apocalyptics and neo-romantics of the forties were driven to their form of private expression at least as much by their weariness of wartime propaganda and the threat to individuality that they discovered in the bloated appearance of the militaristic state as by their direct dislike of 'social reporting' in poetry. By contrast the poetry of the fifties develops a character chiefly, though not exclusively, by its resistance to a literary idea, namely, that poets should regard their task

> ... simply as one of making an arrangement of images of sex and violence tapped straight from the unconscious (a sort of upper-middle-brow equivalent of the horror comic) ...

From this resistance spring the demand for intelligibility, the renunciation of 'disgusting hyperboles' and suspicion of highly figurative language, the approval shown for perspicuity and economy of effect.[1]

The formulation of the neo-romantic recipe for a poem is again Mr Conquest's. It is roughly true to say that his *New Lines* did for the poets of the fifties what the *New Country* of Michael Roberts did for Auden and other poets in the nineteen-thirties: it created a recognizable public image of the new poetry. Two years before the appearance of *New Lines* a writer in the *Spectator* had dubbed the new poets 'The Movement' – the name had a wide currency for a few years and is still used for its convenience; and it was, I think, a year earlier still, in 1953, that the reading public began to have an inkling that neo-romantic attitudes in poetry were seriously dissented from. The occasion was the death of Dylan Thomas in New York in November 1953, and the distaste of the 'Movement' poets for the fulsome and sometimes semi-hysterical tributes paid to 'the one un-doubting Thomas' first made ordinary readers aware that a new poetic generation had emerged who strictly rationed their ad-

1. Donald Davie as the chief theoretician and writer of the most elegant prose among the *New Lines* poets explores the poetic values of 'chaste' diction and syntactical nicety in two books of criticism: *Purity of Diction in English Verse* (1952) and *Articulate Energy* (1957). The keen interest in critical ideas by many of the new poets reflects the fact that many of them teach or have taught English literature in English or American universities.

miration for Thomas's poetic achievement and thought his in-
fluence on other poets for the most part disastrous. There was a
certain irony in this appearance of Dylan Thomas as the horned
and tailed arch-enemy. If he made the new poets impatient,
Edith Sitwell made them angry. The astonishing vogue that her
later work had at the end of the forties is beginning to be for-
gotten now, but it needs to be brought out that the reaction
against neo-romantic poetry was an antagonistic response not
only to the clotted darkness of the imitators of the early Thomas,
but also to the work of those poets who, taking a hint from
Edith Sitwell, opened their Blakes and splashed about in puddles
of myth, delighting in portentousness and prismatic effects.

By 1956 the battle against neo-romanticism was more than
half-won, but the position at the beginning of the decade had
been rather different. There was something almost desperate in
1950 about John Wain's recommendation of Robert Graves and
William Empson as poetic models in the effort to get intelli-
gence back into poetry, but the selection of these two poets was
less odd than it appears at first sight, and in commenting on it
we should be able to explain why the poetic revolution of the
fifties had such a literary character.[1] Mr Wain's reason for select-
ing Graves and Empson was that these writers were independent
of ideological commitments as T. S. Eliot and Auden, who
might otherwise have been proposed as models, were not. In his
introduction to *New Lines* Mr Conquest for similar reasons
approves of George Orwell and his 'principle of real, rather than
ideological, honesty', claiming in nearly the same breath that the
significant poetry of the fifties is distinguished from earlier
modern poetry by 'submitting to no great systems of theoretical
constructs', and so runs parallel to the empirical tradition of
post-war philosophy in Britain. Here Mr Conquest is speaking
and speculating for himself, but obviously Eliot and Auden were

1. The choice was not really happy as Mr Wain would be the first to
admit – neo-romantics also invoked the name of Robert Graves, and the
many leathery little imitations of Empson by poetic neophytes proved to
be quite as unpalatable and unsustaining as the sad confectionery produced
by the imitators of Edith Sitwell and Dylan Thomas.

not felt to be helpful mentors by the new poets. Eliot was gravely respected as a 'founding father' of the republic of modern poetry, Auden's 'large and rational talent' was admired, but neither of these poets distrusted general ideas or shied away from political or religious commitment as most of the *New Lines* poets implicitly or explicitly seem to have done. Donald Davie thinks the political stance of the thirties 'impressive and absurd'; Thom Gunn expresses his 'lack of concern with religion' as a member of the 'National Service' generation; Kingsley Amis has gone on record as saying (in 1955) that 'Nobody wants any more poems on the grander themes for a few years.' In Mr Amis's fine poem 'Against Romanticism'

> ... the brain raging with prophecy,
> Raging to discard real time and place,
> Raging to build a better time and place ...

is condemned for its romanticism, and these lines can surely be taken as glancing disparagingly at the poetic world of *Four Quartets* ('Raging to discard real time and place ...') and at the political utopianism of the social poetry of the thirties ('Raging to build a better time and place ...'). Neo-romanticism was without much finesse, but here two intellectually superior kinds of poetry are identified as betraying subtler forms of the romantic wish to evade everyday reality. The new poetry, then, had to steer between the rocks of political and religious commitment on the one hand and the gulping quicksands of neo-romantic extravagance and inflation of feeling on the other. To both crude and subtle romantics Amis prefers 'A traveller who walks a temperate zone', and Davie emphasizes the same preference when he writes

> A neutral tone is nowadays preferred ...

> Appear concerned only to make it scan!
> How dare we now be anything but numb?

This attitude might be labelled neo-Augustan, but the epithet is not a useful one to apply to the poetry of *New Lines* as a whole

- if only for the reason that Philip Larkin's poems are not in the least neo-Augustan in feeling or technique (he is a romantic in the sense that Camus is a romantic novelist, with intelligence and irony used to diminish the ego and make absurdity bearable). His *The Less Deceived* (1955) is still the best collection of verse produced by any of the *New Lines* poets. The definition that most nearly embraces the typical poetry of the fifties might well be 'poetry of the unenthusiastic imagination'. (To the philosophical empiricist of the present Hegel's philosophical system is, I suppose, a sort of Romantic poem, not much to be preferred to P. J. Bailey's *Festus*.) The characteristic virtues of a *New Lines* poem by Robert Conquest, Elizabeth Jennings, or John Holloway – to forget for the moment the stronger or more individual talents of Larkin, Davie, and Thom Gunn – are clarity and elegance: something is said positively in well-turned phrases, the movement is sedately brisk, the air is hygienic. If some 'Movement' poems are unadventurous and inclined to be dull, at least they are not blowsy, raucous, or dishevelled. The new poetry observes decorum. The new poets always take care to see that their dress is fully adjusted before appearing in print.

The assertion that the characteristic poetry of the fifties is too limited, circumspect, and arid would be made by surviving neo-romantics and other poets who uncomfortably feel themselves awarded second-class citizenship by being shut out of the *New Lines* fold. It would be the complaint, for example, of the writers who appeared in *Mavericks* (1956), an anthology produced in opposition to *New Lines* and edited by Dannie Abse and Howard Sergeant. 'The general level of *Mavericks* is certainly lower than that of *New Lines*', as Anthony Thwaite has said, but the fact of opposition allows me to note in passing that not all the good poetry of the fifties was written by 'Movement' poets – Auden, Roy Fuller, Norman Nicholson, Thomas Kinsella, Charles Tomlinson, Norman MacCaig, Jon Silkin, and Ted Hughes are names to dismiss such a misconception – and that these complaints of sterility and unadventurousness have nowhere been voiced more brutally than by the *New Lines* poets themselves. Donald Davie suspects Larkin and Amis of a willed 'provincialism' of attitude, a sort of castration of their possible poetic selves by a refusal to learn from the poetry of other ages and countries. Larkin and Amis probably think that Davie has begun to prefer literature to life. I am not sure where Wain would stand in this matter, but he shares Davie's objection to Larkin's Betjemania. (A taste for Betjeman's poems, which I must admit that I share, is regarded as a rather sinister sign of provincialism.) Meanwhile Charles Tomlinson, whose work Davie admires but failed to have included in *New Lines*, describes Larkin and other *New Lines* poets as 'middle-brow entertainers' and thinks that post-war poetry in England has been dismally unenterprising. The obvious 'flip' retort has been made that Mr Tomlinson is too narrowly an 'aesthetic' poet preoccupied with the discovery of a moral climate in landscape without figures. To the ordinary reader of poetry these differences may appear insignificant, but what they tell us in 1960 is that the *New Lines* poets were never more than negatively united by what they disliked, and that there is nothing to prevent centrifugal forces spinning them further and further from a common centre now that the bug-eyed monster of the neo-romantic poem has been scotched. It is probably too soon to say where the differences that have developed among the fifties poets may lead, but my own opinion is that the rift between 'provincialism' and 'literary cosmopolitanism' is a real one because it is based on temperamental differences. Poets entertain the critical views that enable them to go on writing poems, but of course they like to think that their ideas may have a wide, or even a universal, application.

K. A.

December 1961

W. B. YEATS

W. B. Yeats was born at Sandymount in Ireland in 1865 and educated at schools in Hammersmith and Dublin. He studied art for three years before turning to literature, and his first volume of poems was The Wanderings of Oisin (*1889*). *With Lady Gregory and others he helped to establish the Irish National Theatre in 1899. From 1922 to 1928 he was a Senator of the Irish Free State, and in 1923 he was awarded the Nobel Prize for Literature. He died at Cap Martin in the south of France in January 1939 and was buried in the cemetery at Roquebrune. He had been busy correcting his last poems to within forty-eight hours of his death – there is an account of these last days in* Letters on Poetry from W. B. Yeats to Dorothy Wellesley (*1940*). *His body was brought back to Ireland for reburial at Drumcliffe near Sligo in September 1948, this task being – Yeats would have appreciated it – the first expedition of the Irish Navy outside territorial waters.*

Yeats is the greatest English poet since Wordsworth (for whose poetry he had a very limited respect). In a short note it is impossible to mention even the main events of his life, or to give anything like a list of his publications. These can be found in the many biographies and critical studies, among the most useful of which are The Poetry of W. B. Yeats (*1941*) *by Louis MacNeice,* The Development of Yeats (*1942*) *by V. K. Narayan Menon,* J. M. Hone's W. B. Yeats 1865–1939 (*1942*), Yeats: the Man and the Masks (*1949*) *by R. Ellman,* W. B. Yeats (*1949*) *by A. N. Jeffares, and* The Lonely Tower (*1950*) *by T. R. Henn. There is a* Bibliography of the Writings of W. B. Yeats (*1951*) *by Allan Wade, who has also edited the* Letters of W. B. Yeats (*1954*), *but the short bibliography in G. S. Fraser's British Council pamphlet ('Writers and Their Work' series, No. 50) will be full enough for most readers. J. E. Unterecker's* A Reader's Guide to W. B. Yeats (*1959*) *is useful.*

The following books by Yeats may be recorded: Collected Poems

(*1950*), Collected Plays (*1952*), Autobiographies (*1926*), A Vision (*1937*), On the Boiler (*1939*), Mythologies (*1959*), Essays and Introductions (*1961*). *The last prints, for the first time, a 'general introduction' to his works written by the poet in 1937. A Vision is important for the study of Yeats's ideas – it should be regarded, as Anthony Thwaite says, as 'a poetic source-book rather than a scientific work'.* Collected Poems (*1950*) *supersedes earlier collections and contains the magnificent* Last Poems (*1939*), *which were published posthumously. Readers of modern poetry will be interested in Yeats's eccentric introduction to the* Oxford Book of Modern Verse, 1892–1935 (*1936*) *and in Auden's verses on the death of Yeats, which are to be found in* Another Time (*1940*).

'*I had learned to think in the midst of the last phase of Pre-Raphaelitism,*' *Yeats tells us. His poetic development is from romantic themes carried by hypnotic rhythms and a Yellow Book diction – 'Innisfree' is dated 1893 – to the treatment of any and every theme in active, wideawake rhythms and a diction perpetually refreshed by contact with common speech. He did not come to love the actual, if by the actual we mean the modern scientific, commercial, middle-class world, but he came to face it and to oppose to it the ideal of an improbable aristocracy. The change in the poetry of Yeats is gradual and continuous, but it is first strikingly evident in the poems published in* The Green Helmet (*1912*). *His romantic passion for Maude Gonne and what it came to mean in reflection, the Easter Rebellion of 1916 – these are two elements behind the transformation of the dreamy younger man into the arrogant, candid, ironic great poet of the 1920s and 1930s.*

'*How small a fragment of our own nature can be brought to perfect expression, nor that even but with great toil, in a much divided civilization,*' *says Yeats in the* Autobiographies. *This insight defines not only his own problem but the problem facing most contemporary poets, and the measure of his greatness as a writer is his success in stating the difficulty and the integrity with which he worked for its solution.*

*The earliest of his poems printed here is '*A Song*', which comes from* The Wild Swans at Coole (*1919*). *Like '*Long-Legged Fly*'* *from* Last Poems (*1939*), *it illustrates the superb use made of the refrain by Yeats.* 'A Prayer for My Daughter' *from* Michael Robartes and the Dancer (*1921*) *is included as an example of his mastery of stubborn material – the reflections are given lyrical intensity by Yeats's passionate, near-tragic view of life and by his use of reference and symbol.* 'Leda and the Swan' *is from* The Tower (*1928*) *and* 'Byzantium' *from* The Winding Stair (*1933*). *The last poem should be read in conjunction with* 'Sailing to Byzantium' (The Tower). 'Sailing to Byzantium' *contrasts the ephemerality of man with the permanence of art, represented there by the golden bird –* 'I have read somewhere that in the Emperor's palace at Byzantium was a tree made of gold and silver, and artificial birds that sang.' *For a discussion of the genesis and meaning of* 'Byzantium' *see A. N. Jeffares in the* Review of English Studies (*Vol. 22, 1946: No. 85*) *and for critical comment on both poems see William Empson in* A Review of English Literature (*Vol. 1, 1960: No. 3*).

'The Circus Animals' Desertion' *from* Last Poems *is an autobiographical poem about not being able to write a poem (cf. Coleridge's* 'Dejection'). *Yeats rehearses the themes of his earlier work and relates his myths and symbols to his own life and needs, but he knows that*

> Players and painted stage took all my love
> And not those things that they were emblems of.

A Prayer for My Daughter

Once more the storm is howling, and half hid
Under this cradle-hood and coverlid
My child sleeps on. There is no obstacle
But Gregory's wood and one bare hill
Whereby the haystack and roof-levelling wind,
Bred on the Atlantic, can be stayed;
And for an hour I have walked and prayed
Because of the great gloom that is in my mind.

I have walked and prayed for this young child an hour
And heard the sea-wind scream upon the tower,
And under the arches of the bridge, and scream
In the elms above the flooded stream;
Imagining in excited reverie
That the future years had come,
Dancing to a frenzied drum,
Out of the murderous innocence of the sea.

May she be granted beauty and yet not
Beauty to make a stranger's eye distraught,
Or hers before a looking-glass, for such,
Being made beautiful overmuch,
Consider beauty a sufficient end,
Lose natural kindness and maybe
The heart-revealing intimacy
That chooses right, and never find a friend.

Helen being chosen found life flat and dull
And later had much trouble from a fool,
While that great Queen, that rose out of the spray,
Being fatherless could have her way
Yet chose a bandy-leggèd smith for man.
It's certain that fine women eat
A crazy salad with their meat
Whereby the Horn of Plenty is undone.

In courtesy I'd have her chiefly learned;
Hearts are not had as a gift but hearts are earned
By those that are not entirely beautiful;
Yet many, that have played the fool
For beauty's very self, has charm made wise,
And many a poor man that has roved,
Loved and thought himself beloved,
From a glad kindness cannot take his eyes.

May she become a flourishing hidden tree
That all her thoughts may like the linnet be,
And have no business but dispensing round
Their magnanimities of sound,
Nor but in merriment begin a chase,
Nor but in merriment a quarrel.
O may she live like some green laurel
Rooted in one dear perpetual place.

My mind, because the minds that I have loved,
The sort of beauty that I have approved,
Prosper but little, has dried up of late,
Yet knows that to be choked with hate
May well be of all evil chances chief.
If there's no hatred in a mind
Assault and battery of the wind
Can never tear the linnet from the leaf.

An intellectual hatred is the worst,
So let her think opinions are accursed.
Have I not seen the loveliest woman born
Out of the mouth of Plenty's horn,
Because of her opinionated mind
Barter that horn and every good
By quiet natures understood
For an old bellows full of angry wind?

Considering that, all hatred driven hence,
The soul recovers radical innocence
And learns at last that it is self-delighting,
Self-appeasing, self-affrighting,
And that its own sweet will is Heaven's will;
She can, though every face should scowl
And every windy quarter howl
Or every bellows burst, be happy still.

And may her bridegroom bring her to a house
Where all's accustomed, ceremonious;
For arrogance and hatred are the wares
Peddled in the thoroughfares.
How but in custom and in ceremony
Are innocence and beauty born?
Ceremony's a name for the rich horn,
And custom for the spreading laurel tree.

A Song

I thought no more was needed
Youth to prolong
Than dumb-bell and foil
To keep the body young.
O who could have foretold
That the heart grows old?

Though I have many words,
What woman's satisfied,
I am no longer faint
Because at her side?
O who could have foretold
That the heart grows old?

I have not lost desire
But the heart that I had;
I thought 'twould burn my body
Laid on the death-bed,
For who could have foretold
That the heart grows old?

Leda and the Swan

A sudden blow: the great wings beating still
Above the staggering girl, her thighs caressed
By the dark webs, her nape caught in his bill,
He holds her helpless breast upon his breast.

How can those terrified vague fingers push
The feathered glory from her loosening thighs?
And how can body, laid in that white rush,
But feel the strange heart beating where it lies?

A shudder in the loins engenders there
The broken wall, the burning roof and tower
And Agamemnon dead.
                                  Being so caught up,
So mastered by the brute blood of the air,
Did she put on his knowledge with his power
Before the indifferent beak could let her drop?

Byzantium

The unpurged images of day recede;
The Emperor's drunken soldiery are abed;
Night resonance recedes, night-walkers' song
After great cathedral gong;
A starlit or a moonlit dome disdains
All that man is,
All mere complexities,
The fury and the mire of human veins.

Before me floats an image, man or shade,
Shade more than man, more image than a shade;
For Hades' bobbin bound in mummy-cloth
May unwind the winding path;

A mouth that has no moisture and no breath
Breathless mouths may summon;
I hail the superhuman;
I call it death-in-life and life-in-death.

Miracle, bird or golden handiwork,
More miracle than bird or handiwork,
Planted on the star-lit golden bough,
Can like the cocks of Hades crow,
Or, by the moon embittered, scorn aloud
In glory of changeless metal
Common bird or petal
And all complexities of mire or blood.

At midnight on the Emperor's pavement flit
Flames that no faggot feeds, nor steel has lit,
Nor storm disturbs, flames begotten of flame,
Where blood-begotten spirits come
And all complexities of fury leave,
Dying into a dance,
An agony of trance,
An agony of flame that cannot singe a sleeve.

Astraddle on the dolphin's mire and blood,
Spirit after spirit! The smithies break the flood,
The golden smithies of the Emperor!
Marbles of the dancing floor
Break bitter furies of complexity,
Those images that yet
Fresh images beget,
That dolphin-torn, that gong-tormented sea.

Long-Legged Fly

That civilization may not sink,
Its great battle lost,
Quiet the dog, tether the pony
To a distant post;
Our master Caesar is in the tent
Where the maps are spread,
His eyes fixed upon nothing,
A hand under his head.
Like a long-legged fly upon the stream
His mind moves upon silence.

That the topless towers be burnt
And men recall that face,
Move most gently if move you must
In this lonely place.
She thinks, part woman, three parts a child,
That nobody looks; her feet
Practise a tinker shuffle
Picked up on a street.
Like a long-legged fly upon the stream
Her mind moves upon silence.

That girls at puberty may find
The first Adam in their thought,
Shut the door of the Pope's chapel,
Keep those children out.
There on that scaffolding reclines
Michael Angelo.
With no more sound than the mice make
His hand moves to and fro.
Like a long-legged fly upon the stream
His mind moves upon silence.

The Circus Animals' Desertion

I

I sought a theme and sought for it in vain,
I sought it daily for six weeks or so.
Maybe at last, being but a broken man,
I must be satisfied with my heart, although
Winter and summer till old age began
My circus animals were all on show,
Those stilted boys, that burnished chariot,
Lion and woman and the Lord knows what.

II

What can I but enumerate old themes?
First that sea-rider Oisin led by the nose
Through three enchanted islands, allegorical dreams,
Vain gaiety, vain battle, vain repose,
Themes of the embittered heart, or so it seems,
That might adorn old songs or courtly shows;
But what cared I that set him on to ride,
I, starved for the bosom of his faery bride?

And then a counter-truth filled out its play,
The Countess Cathleen was the name I gave it;
She, pity-crazed, had given her soul away,
But masterful Heaven had intervened to save it.
I thought my dear must her own soul destroy,
So did fanaticism and hate enslave it,
And this brought forth a dream and soon enough
This dream itself had all my thought and love.

And when the Fool and Blind Man stole the bread
Cuchulain fought the ungovernable sea;
Heart-mysteries there, and yet when all is said
It was the dream itself enchanted me:

Character isolated by a deed
To engross the present and dominate memory.
Players and painted stage took all my love,
And not those things that they were emblems of.

III

Those masterful images because complete
Grew in pure mind, but out of what began?
A mound of refuse or the sweepings of a street,
Old kettles, old bottles, and a broken can,
Old iron, old bones, old rags, that raving slut
Who keeps the till. Now that my ladder's gone,
I must lie down where all the ladders start,
In the foul rag-and-bone shop of the heart.

LAURENCE BINYON

*Laurence Binyon was born in Lancaster in 1869 – he was a cousin
of Stephen Phillips – and educated at St Paul's School and Trinity
College, Oxford. He entered the service of the British Museum in
1893 and soon found himself in the Department of Prints and
Drawings. From 1913 to 1932 he was in charge of the sub-
department of Oriental Prints and Drawings, and he was Keeper
of the whole department 1932–3. In the following year he was Pro-
fessor of Poetry at Harvard University. He died in 1943.*

*Binyon was an authority on oriental art and a writer of books on
fine art, of plays, poems, and critical studies of literature. His Col-
lected Poems were issued in 1931, to be followed by The North
Star and Other Poems (1941) and the posthumous The Burning
of the Leaves (1944). The poem I have used is from this last
volume – a 'blitz' poem in the same restricted sense as parts of
Eliot's 'Little Gidding'.*

Binyon seems to me a good example of an academic poet. He

does not, that is to say, extend the area of contemporary sensibility or innovate technically, but he maintains with dignity the standards he inherits. It is possible that he will be remembered longest for his excellent translation of Dante's Divina Commedia *into English terza rima (The Inferno 1933, The Purgatorio 1938, The Paradiso 1943).*

The Burning of the Leaves

Now is the time for the burning of the leaves.
They go to the fire; the nostril pricks with smoke
Wandering slowly into the weeping mist.
Brittle and blotched, ragged and rotten sheaves!
A flame seizes the smouldering ruin, and bites
On stubborn stalks that crackle as they resist.

The last hollyhock's fallen tower is dust:
All the spices of June are a bitter reek,
All the extravagant riches spent and mean.
All burns! the reddest rose is a ghost.
Sparks whirl up, to expire in the mist: the wild
Fingers of fire are making corruption clean.

Now is the time for stripping the spirit bare,
Time for the burning of days ended and done,
Idle solace of things that have gone before,
Rootless hope and fruitless desire are there:
Let them go to the fire with never a look behind.
That world that was ours is a world that is ours no more.

They will come again, the leaf and the flower, to arise
From squalor of rottenness into the old splendour,
And magical scents to a wondering memory bring;
The same glory, to shine upon different eyes.
Earth cares for her own ruins, naught for ours.
Nothing is certain, only the certain spring.

WALTER DE LA MARE

Walter de la Mare was born of Huguenot stock in Kent in 1873 and educated at St Paul's Cathedral Choir School. He spent eighteen years in business before devoting himself entirely to literature. His first book, Songs of Childhood *(1902), was published under a pseudonym, and his first prose work,* Henry Brocken, *under his own name in 1904. His* Memoirs of a Midget *(1921) was awarded the James Tait Black Prize. He was an anthologist of genius – see, for example,* Early One Morning *(1935), which exploits absorbingly his preoccupation with childhood, and* Love *(1943) – and a short-story writer whose powers of creating an atmosphere, particularly the atmosphere of the uncanny, were exceptional. Graham Greene has written illuminatingly on the short stories in* A Tribute *(mentioned below). His best-known tales of the supernatural are probably 'All Hallows' and 'Seaton's Aunt', both of which are excellent. Among his publications of poetry may be mentioned* Collected Poems *(1942),* Collected Rhymes and Verses *(1944),* The Burning Glass *(1945),* The Traveller *(1946),* Winged Chariot *(1951), and* O Lovely England *(1953). He died in 1956.*

There is a study of his work by Forrest Reid published in 1922, and in 1948 a volume entitled A Tribute to Walter de la Mare on his 75th Birthday *was brought out. This symposium is a useful introduction to his work as a whole. Mr Eliot's poem in it characterizes the poetry of Walter de la Mare with precision:*

> *By whom, and by what means, was this designed?*
> *The whispered incantation which allows*
> *Free passage to the phantoms of the mind.*
>
> *By you; by those deceptive cadences*
> *Wherewith the common measure is refined;*
> *By conscious art practised with natural ease.*

*The British Council 'Writers and Their Work' series included an
essay on the poet by Kenneth Hopkins in 1953. Tea with Walter
de la Mare (1957) by Walter Russell Brain is also worth con-
sulting.*

The poems given here are from Collected Poems *with the excep-
tion of 'A Portrait' from* The Burning Glass. *The long extract
from 'Dreams' is at once a theory of composition and a kind of
poetic apologia.*

The Children of Stare

Winter is fallen early
On the house of Stare;
Birds in reverberating flocks
Haunt its ancestral box;
Bright are the plenteous berries
In clusters in the air.

Still is the fountain's music,
The dark pool icy still,
Whereupon a small and sanguine sun
Floats in a mirror on,
Into a West of crimson,
From a South of daffodil.

'Tis strange to see young children
In such a wintry house;
Like rabbits' on the frozen snow
Their tell-tale footprints go;
Their laughter rings like timbrels
'Neath evening ominous:

Their small and heightened faces
Like wine-red winter buds;
Their frolic bodies gentle as
Flakes in the air that pass,

Frail as the twirling petal
From the briar of the woods.

Above them silence lours,
Still as an arctic sea;
Light fails; night falls; the wintry moon
Glitters; the crocus soon
Will open grey and distracted
On earth's austerity:

Thick mystery, wild peril,
Law like an iron rod: –
Yet sport they on in Spring's attire,
Each with his tiny fire
Blown to a core of ardour
By the awful breath of God.

From *Dreams*

Was it by cunning the curious fly
That preys in a sunbeam schooled her wings
To ride her in air all motionlessly,
Poised on their myriad winnowings?
Where conned the blackbird the song he sings?
Was Job the instructor of the ant?
Go bees for nectar to Hume and Kant?

Who bade the scallop devise her shell?
Who tutored the daisy at cool of eve
To tent her pollen in floreted cell?
What dominie taught the dove to grieve;
The mole to delve; the worm to weave?
Does not the rather their life-craft seem
A tranced obedience to a dream?

Thus tranced, too, body and mind, will sit
A winter's dawn to dark, alone,
Heedless of how the cold moments flit,
The worker in words, or wood, or stone:
So far his waking desires have flown
Into a realm where his sole delight
Is to bring the dreamed-of to mortal sight.

Dumb in its wax may the music sleep –
In a breath conceived – that, with ardent care,
Note by note, in a reverie deep,
Mozart penned, for the world to share.
Waken it, needle! And then declare
How, invoked by thy tiny tang,
Sound such strains as the Sirens sang!

Voyager dauntless on Newton's sea,
Year after year still brooding on
His algebraical formulae,
The genius of William Hamilton
Sought the square root of *minus* one;
In vain; till – all thought of it leagues away –
The problem flowered from a dream one day.

Our restless senses leap and say,
'How marvellous this! – How ugly that!'
And, at a breath, will slip away
The very thing they marvel at.
Time is the tyrant of their fate;
And frail the instant which must be
Our all of actuality.

If then to Solomon the Wise
Some curious priest stooped low and said,
'Thou, with thy lidded, sleep-sealed eyes,
This riddle solve from out thy bed:
Art thou – am I – by phantoms led?

Where is the real? In dream? Or wake?'
I know the answer the King might make!

And teeming Shakespeare: would he avow
The creatures of his heart and brain,
Whom, Prospero-like, he could endow
With all that mortal souls contain,
Mere copies that a fool can feign
Out of the tangible and seen? –
This the sole range of his demesne?

Ask not the Dreamer! See him run,
Listening a shrill and gentle neigh,
Foot into stirrup, he is up, he has won
Enchanted foothills far away.
Somewhere? Nowhere? Who need say?
So be it in secrecy of his mind
He some rare delectation find.

Ay, once I dreamed of an age-wide sea
Whereo'er three moons stood leper-bright;
And once – from agony set free –
I scanned within the womb of night,
A hollow inwoven orb of light,
Thrilling with beauty no tongue could tell,
And knew it for Life's citadel.

And – parable as strange – once, I
Was lured to a city whose every stone,
And harpy human hastening by
Were spawn and sport of fear alone –
By soulless horror enthralled, driven on:
Even the waters that, ebon-clear,
Coursed through its dark, raved only of *Fear!*

Enigmas these; but not the face,
Fashioned of sleep, which, still at gaze
Of daybreak eyes, I yet could trace,
Made lovelier in the sun's first rays;
Nor that wild voice which in amaze,
Wide-wok'n, I listened singing on –
All memory of the singer gone.

O Poesy, of wellspring clear,
Let no sad Science thee suborn,
Who art thyself its planisphere!
All knowledge is foredoomed, forlorn –
Of inmost truth and wisdom shorn –
Unless imagination brings
Its skies wherein to use its wings.

Two worlds have we: without; within;
But all that sense can mete and span,
Until it confirmation win
From heart and soul, is death to man.
Of grace divine his life began;
And – Eden empty proved – in deep
Communion with his spirit in sleep

The Lord Jehovah of a dream
Bade him, past all desire, conceive
What should his solitude redeem;
And, to his sunlit eyes, brought Eve.
Would that my day-wide mind could weave
Faint concept of the scene from whence
She awoke to Eden's innocence!

Starven with cares, like tares in wheat,
Wildered with knowledge, chilled with doubt,
The timeless self in vain must beat
Against its walls to hasten out
Whither the living waters fount;

And – evil and good no more at strife –
Seek love beneath the tree of life.

When then in memory I look back
To childhood's visioned hours, I see
What now my anxious soul doth lack
Is energy in peace to be
At one with nature's mystery:
And Conscience less my mind indicts
For idle days than dreamless nights.

Sunk Lyonesse

In sea-cold Lyonesse,
When the Sabbath eve shafts down
On the roofs, walls, belfries
Of the foundered town,
The Nereids pluck their lyres
Where the green translucency beats,
And with motionless eyes at gaze
Make minstrelsy in the streets.
And the ocean water stirs
In salt-worn casemate and porch.
Plies the blunt-snouted fish
With fire in his skull for torch.
And the ringing wires resound;
And the unearthly lovely weep,
In lament of the music they make
In the sullen courts of sleep:
Whose marble flowers bloom for aye:
And – lapped by the moon-guiled tide –
Mock their carver with heart of stone
Caged in his stone-ribbed side.

A Portrait

Old: yet unchanged; – still pottering in his thoughts;
Still eagerly enslaved by books and print;
Less plagued, perhaps, by rigid musts and oughts,
But no less frantic in vain argument;

Still happy as a child, with its small toys,
Over his inkpot and his bits and pieces, –
Life's arduous, fragile and ingenuous joys,
Whose charm failed never – nay, it even increases!

Ev'n happier in watch of bird or flower,
Rainbow in heaven, or bud on thorny spray,
A star-strewn nightfall, and that heart-break hour
Of sleep-drowsed senses between dawn and day;

Loving the light – laved eyes in those wild hues! –
And dryad twilight, and the thronging dark;
A Crusoe ravished by mere solitude –
And silence – edged with music's faintest *Hark!*

And any chance-seen face whose loveliness
Hovers, a mystery, between dream and real;
Things usual yet miraculous that bless
And overwell a heart that still can feel;

Haunted by questions no man answered yet;
Pining to leap from A clean on to Z;
Absorbed by problems which the wise forget;
Avid for fantasy – yet how staid a head!

Senses at daggers with his intellect;
Quick, stupid; vain, retiring; ardent, cold;
Faithful and fickle; rash and circumspect;
And never yet at rest in any fold;

Punctual at meals; a spendthrift, close as Scot;
Rebellious, tractable, childish – long gone grey!
Impatient, volatile, tongue wearying not –
Loose, too; which, yet, thank heaven, was taught to pray;

'Childish' indeed! – a waif on shingle shelf
Fronting the rippled sands, the sun, the sea;
And nought but his marooned precarious self
For questing consciousness and will-to-be;

A feeble venturer – in a world so wide!
So rich in action, daring, cunning, strife!
You'd think, poor soul, he had taken Sloth for bride, –
Unless the imagined is the breath of life;

Unless to speculate bring virgin gold,
And *Let's-pretend* can range the seven seas,
And dreams are not mere tales by idiot told,
And tongueless truth may hide in fantasies;

Unless the alone may their own company find,
And churchyards harbour phantoms 'mid their bones,
And even a daisy may suffice a mind
Whose bindweed can redeem a heap of stones;

Too frail a basket for so many eggs –
Loose-woven: Gosling? cygnet? Laugh or weep?
Or is the cup at richest in its dregs?
The actual realest on the verge of sleep?

One yet how often the prey of doubt and fear,
Of bleak despondence, stark anxiety;
Ardent for what is neither now nor here,
An Orpheus fainting for Eurydice;

Not yet inert, but with a tortured breast
At hint of that bleak gulf – his last farewell;
Pining for peace, assurance, pause and rest,
Yet slave to what he loves past words to tell;

A foolish, fond old man, his bed-time nigh,
Who still at western window stays to win
A transient respite from the latening sky,
And scarce can bear it when the Sun goes in.

EDWARD THOMAS

Edward Thomas was born in 1878 and educated at St Paul's School and Lincoln College, Oxford. He was always a writer, but he first wrote verse seriously – it is now known that there were some earlier attempts – at the suggestion of the American poet, Robert Frost, with whose work the poems of Thomas have many points of contact in subject, mood, and tone. He was then over thirty years old. Wilfred Gibson's 'The Golden Room' refers to the company of Georgian poets who met in July 1914 at ' the old Nailshop':

> *Our neighbours from The Gallows, Catherine*
> *And Lascelles Abercrombie; Rupert Brooke;*
> *Elinor and Robert Frost, living a while*
> *At Little Iddens, who'd brought over with them*
> *Helen and Edward Thomas ...*

He had married much earlier in 1899, and the story of his courtship and marriage is movingly told in Helen Thomas's As It Was *(1926) and* World Without End *(1931). He served in the Artists' Rifles in the First World War and was killed in action at Arras in 1917.*

> *Thomas lies*
> *'Neath Vimy Ridge, where he, among his fellows*
> *Died, just as life had touched his lips to song.*

There is a memorial to him at Froxfield, Hampshire.

    *Much of Thomas's published prose was bread-and-butter work –
topography and biography such as* The Heart of England *(1906),*
The South Country *(1909), and the studies of Borrow, Jefferies,
and Maeterlinck; but even in his most occasional writing – he was
for a time a critic and essayist for the* Daily Chronicle – *there is
something to reward a reader with patience. His poetry is to be
found in* Collected Poems *(1920), which has a preface by Walter
de la Mare. There is a critical study of Thomas's writings,* Edward
Thomas *(1956), by H. Coombes, which is better on the poetry than
the prose (although its author is inclined to apologize unnecessarily
for Thomas's melancholy).*

    *Edward Thomas can be classed as a Georgian only by accident.
He was, as Dr Leavis has remarked, 'a very original poet who de-
voted great technical subtlety to the expression of a distinctively
modern sensibility'. Noteworthy in the poems is an acuteness of
sensation faithfully and modestly transcribed in unobtrusive, hesi-
tating rhythms and a diction which does not draw attention to itself.
'Old Man' has been well discussed in Chapter II of* New Bearings
in English Poetry *(1932). 'No One So Much As You' is included
as a love-poem; its gentleness, honesty, and poignancy belong pecu-
liarly to Thomas.*

Old Man

> Old Man, or Lad's-love – in the name there's nothing
> To one that knows not Lad's-love, or Old Man,
> The hoar-green feathery herb, almost a tree,
> Growing with rosemary and lavender.
> Even to one that knows it well, the names
> Half decorate, half perplex, the thing it is:
> At least, what that is clings not to the names
> In spite of time. And yet I like the names.

The herb itself I like not, but for certain
I love it, as some day the child will love it
Who plucks a feather from the door-side bush
Whenever she goes in or out of the house.
Often she waits there, snipping the tips and shrivelling
The shreds at last on to the path, perhaps
Thinking, perhaps of nothing, till she sniffs
Her fingers and runs off. The bush is still
But half as tall as she, though it is as old;
So well she clips it. Not a word she says;
And I can only wonder how much hereafter
She will remember, with that bitter scent,
Of garden rows, and ancient damson trees
Topping a hedge, a bent path to a door,
A low thick bush beside the door, and me
Forbidding her to pick.
                              As for myself,
Where first I met the bitter scent is lost.
I, too, often shrivel the grey shreds,
Sniff them and think and sniff again and try
Once more to think what it is I am remembering,
Always in vain. I cannot like the scent,
Yet I would rather give up others more sweet,
With no meaning, than this bitter one.

I have mislaid the key. I sniff the spray
And think of nothing; I see and I hear nothing;
Yet seem, too, to be listening, lying in wait
For what I should, yet never can, remember:
No garden appears, no path, no hoar-green bush
Of Lad's-love, or Old Man, no child beside,
Neither father nor mother, nor any playmate;
Only an avenue, dark, nameless, without end.

No One So Much As You

No one so much as you
Loves this my clay,
Or would lament as you
Its dying day.

You know me through and through
Though I have not told,
And though with what you know
You are not bold.

None ever was so fair
As I thought you:
Not a word can I bear
Spoken against you.

All that I ever did
For you seemed coarse
Compared with what I hid
Nor put in force.

My eyes scarce dare meet you
Lest they should prove
I but respond to you
And do not love.

We look and understand,
We cannot speak
Except in trifles and
Words the most weak.

For I at most accept
Your love, regretting
That is all: I have kept
Only a fretting

That I could not return
All that you gave
And could not ever burn
With the love you have,

Till sometimes it did seem
Better it were
Never to see you more
Than linger here

With only gratitude
Instead of love –
A pine in solitude
Cradling a dove.

HAROLD MONRO

Harold Monro was born at Brussels in 1879 and lived there till the age of seven when his family moved to Wells in Somerset. He was educated at Radley and Caius College, Cambridge, and later spent some years in Ireland, Italy, and Switzerland. In Florence he met the novelist Maurice Hewlett, who encouraged him in his ideas of writing and promoting poetry. He founded the famous Poetry Book-shop (which was responsible for the collections of Georgian Poetry *edited by Edward Marsh) in 1913 and produced* The Chapbook *(1919–25), which succeeded earlier periodicals such as* The Poetry Review *and* Poetry and Drama. *His anthology* Twentieth Century Poetry *(1929), a not too successful attempt at being catholic in taste, nevertheless introduced many ordinary readers to the more interesting modern poets and rightly excluded the usual 'show-poems', as Monro calls them. He died in 1932 and the* Collected Poems *were edited by his wife, Alida Monro, in 1933. The book*

contains a biographical sketch by the Imagist poet F. S. Flint and a
critical note by T. S. Eliot.

Some of Harold Monro's work has the weaknesses of Georgian
poetry, but at his best he is saved from the mawkishness, clumsiness,
and/or namby-pambiness of the Masefields, Drinkwaters, Hodg-
sons, etc., by his thoughtfulness and 'awkward sincerity'. 'Living',
one of his strongest poems in my view, was a favourite with the poet
according to Mrs Monro.

Living

Slow bleak awakening from the morning dream
Brings me in contact with the sudden day.
I am alive – this I.
I let my fingers move along my body.
Realization warns them, and my nerves
Prepare their rapid messages and signals.
While Memory begins recording, coding,
Repeating; all the time Imagination
Mutters; You'll only die.

Here's a new day. O Pendulum move slowly!
My usual clothes are waiting on their peg.
I am alive – this I.
And in a moment Habit, like a crane,
Will bow its neck and dip its pulleyed cable,
Gathering me, my body, and our garment,
And swing me forth, oblivious of my question,
Into the daylight – why?

I think of all the others who awaken,
And wonder if they go to meet the morning
More valiantly than I;
Nor asking of this Day they will be living:
What have I done that I should be alive?

O, can I not forget that I am living?
How shall I reconcile the two conditions:
Living, and yet – to die?

Between the curtains the autumnal sunlight
With lean and yellow fingers points me out;
The clock moans: Why? Why? Why?
But suddenly, as if without a reason,
Heart, Brain and Body, and Imagination
All gather in tumultuous joy together,
Running like children down the path of morning
To fields where they can play without a quarrel:
A country I'd forgotten, but remember,
And welcome with a cry.

O cool glad pasture; living tree, tall corn,
Great cliff, or languid sloping sand, cold sea,
Waves; rivers curving: you, eternal flowers,
Give me content, while I can think of you:
Give me your living breath!
Back to your rampart, Death.

JAMES JOYCE

James Joyce was born in Dublin in 1882 and was educated at Clongowes Wood College, Belvedere College, and University College, Dublin. He was teaching languages at a Berlitz Institute in Trieste in 1904, and thenceforth lived in self-imposed exile from Ireland on the Continent, a sort of cultural 'wild goose'. In Paris, where he published his more important works, he was for many years a tutelary deity of the magazine Transition. *After the outbreak of the Second World War in 1939 he went to live in Switzerland, where he died in January 1941. For fuller details of his life reference may be made to* James Joyce: a definitive biography *(1941) by Herbert S. Gorman and the later* James Joyce *(1959) by Richard Ellman, but the important part of his life is in his books:* Dubliners *(1914)*, Portrait of the Artist as a Young Man *(1916)*, Ulysses *(1925), and* Finnegan's Wake *(1939). There is a study of the first of the two major works by Stuart Gilbert –* James Joyce's Ulysses *(1930) – and a useful analysis of the second,* A Skeleton Key to Finnegan's Wake *(1947) by J. Campbell and H. M. Robinson, from which the reader should graduate to J. S. Atherton's exciting and scholarly* The Books at the Wake *(1959). The best book for the Joyce beginner is* Introducing James Joyce *(1942), selections edited by T. S. Eliot. There is some acute criticism of Joyce in Eliot's* After Strange Gods *(1934) and Edmund Wilson's* The Wound and the Bow *(1941). The essay in the British Council 'Writers and Their Work' series is by J. I. M. Stewart.*

From the books of verse produced by Joyce, Chamber Music *and* Pomes Penyeach, *it is impossible to take the novelist very seriously as a poet, but 'The Ballad of Persse O'Reilly' is in a different class. It is written in the language of* Finnegan's Wake, *which is a kind of 'Babylonish dialect' – a phrase used by Dr Johnson in speaking of Milton's language in* Paradise Lost. *Mr Eliot has pointed out the parallel between the blind and musically gifted Milton and the blind and musically gifted Joyce. Joyce's blindness or near-blindness forced him away from the visual to the musical and emotional associations of words, and his linguistic erudition supplied another element for the construction of the language of* Finnegan's Wake. *I think it possible that this book, over which Joyce spent sixteen years, will exercise an increasing influence as it is more intelligently studied and better understood. Auden's* The Age of Anxiety *shows the power of Joyce's emotional rhetoric by direct imitation at several points – see 'The Seven Stages' passim and Rosetta's final soliloquy. At the same time the book is firmly embedded in the revolutionary 'tradition' of the 1920s, along with* The Waste Land *and* Pound's *Cantos: a sacred monster of a novel, a cumbersome white elephant.*

Finnegan's Wake – *'a compound of fable, symphony, and night-*

mare' (Campbell and Robinson) – is an allegory on many planes of 'the fall and resurrection of mankind'. The 'hero' is H. C. Earwicker, a Dublin tavern-keeper in Chapelizod, whose universal quality is indicated by the names Here Comes Everybody and Haveth Childers Everywhere. He is a candidate in a local election, but he loses his reputation as a result of some never quite defined impropriety in Phoenix Park and suffers from the guilt of it ever afterwards. In another context of meaning Phoenix Park is the Garden of Eden and the impropriety is Original Sin. Three down-and-outs, Peter Cloran, O'Mara, and Hosty, 'an ill-starred beachbusker', pick up the rumour of Earwicker's Fall, and Hosty lampoons him in the 'rann', 'The Ballad of Persse O'Reilly'. Note that perce-oreille=*earwig.*

The Ballad of Persse O'Reilly

Have you heard of one Humpty Dumpty
How he fell with a roll and a rumble
And curled up like Lord Olofa Crumple
By the butt of the Magazine Wall,
     (*Chorus*) Of the Magazine Wall,
          Hump, helmet and all?

He was one time our King of the Castle
Now he's kicked about like a rotten old parsnip.
And from Green street he'll be sent by order of His Worship
To the penal jail of Mountjoy
     (*Chorus*) To the jail of Mountjoy!
          Jail him and joy.

He was fafafather of all schemes for to bother us
Slow coaches and immaculate contraceptives for the populace,
Mare's milk for the sick, seven dry Sundays a week,
Openair love and religion's reform,
     (*Chorus*) And religious reform,
          Hideous in form.

Arrah, why, says you, couldn't he manage it?
I'll go bail, my fine dairyman darling,
Like the bumping bull of the Cassidys
All your butter is in your horns.
    (*Chorus*) His butter is in his horns.
            Butter his horns!

(*Repeat*) Hurrah there, Hosty, frosty Hosty, change that shirt
    on ye,
Rhyme the rann, the king of all ranns!

        Balbaccio, balbuccio!

We had chaw chaw chops, chairs, chewing gum, the chicken-
    pox and china chambers
Universally provided by this soffsoaping salesman.
Small wonder He'll Cheat E'erawan our local lads nicknamed
    him
When Chimpden first took the floor
    (*Chorus*) With his bucketshop store
            Down Bargainweg, Lower.

So snug he was in his hotel premises sumptuous
But soon we'll bonfire all his trash, tricks and trumpery
And 'tis short till sheriff Clancy'll be winding up his unlimited
    company
With the bailiff's bom at the door,
    (*Chorus*) Bimbam at the door.
            Then he'll bum no more.

Sweet bad luck on the waves washed to our island
The hooker of that hammerfast viking
And Gall's curse on the day when Eblana bay
Saw his black and tan man-o'-war.
    (*Chorus*) Saw his man-o'-war
            On the harbour bar.

Where from? roars Poolbeg. Cookingha'pence, he bawls
    Donnez-moi scampitle, wick an wipin'fampiny
Fingal Mac Oscar Onesine Bargearse Boniface
Thok's min gammelhole Norveegickers moniker
Og as ay are at gammelhore Norveegickers cod.
    (*Chorus*) A Norwegian camel old còd.
           He is, begod.

Litt it, Hosty, lift it, ye devil ye! up with the rann, the rhyming
    rann!

It was during some fresh water garden pumping
Or, according to the *Nursing Mirror*, while admiring the
    monkeys
That our heavyweight heathen Humpharey
Made bold a maid to woo
    (*Chorus*) Woohoo, what'll she doo!
           The general lost her maidenloo!

He ought to blush for himself, the old hayheaded philosopher,
For to go and shove himself that way on top of her.
Begob, he's the crux of the catalogue
Of our antediluvial zoo,
    (*Chorus*) Messrs Billing and Coo.
           Noah's larks, good as noo.

He was joulting by Wellinton's monument
Our rotorious hippopopotamuns
When some bugger let down the backtrap of the omnibus
And he caught his death of fusiliers,
    (*Chorus*) With his rent in his rears.
           Give him six years.

'Tis sore pity for his innocent poor children
But look out for his missus legitimate!
When that frew gets a grip of old Earwicker
Won't there be earwigs on the green?
    (*Chorus*) Big earwigs on the green,
             The largest ever you seen.

    Suffoclose! Shikespower! Seudodanto! Anonymoses!

Then we'll have a free trade Gaels' band and mass meeting
For to sod the brave son of Scandiknavery.
And we'll bury him down in Oxmanstown
Along with the devil and Danes,
    (*Chorus*) With the deaf and dumb Danes,
             And all their remains.

And not all the king's men nor his horses
Will resurrect his corpus
For there's no true spell in Connacht or hell
    (*bis*) That's able to raise a Cain.

WYNDHAM LEWIS

*Wyndham Lewis was born in the U.S.A. in 1884 and educated in
England at Rugby and the Slade School. He died in 1957. He was
a man of genius: a painter, novelist, sociologist, literary critic, and
several other things as well as a poet. What he wanted the public to
know about himself can be discovered by reading his autobiographies,*
Blasting and Bombardiering (*1937*) *and* Rude Assignment
(*1950*) – *the first is entertaining on the literary figures of the
twenties and thirties: Mr Eliot, for example, appears as 'a sleek,
tall, attractive transatlantic apparition with a sort of Gioconda
smile'.* Men Without Art (*1934*) *and* The Writer and the

Absolute (*1952*) *are volumes of literary criticism. Among Lewis's
novels may be mentioned* Tarr (*1918*), The Apes of God (*1930*),
The Self Condemned (*1954*), *and* The Human Age – *of which
the first book,* Childermass, *was published in 1928, and the second
and third books,* Monstre Gai *and* Malign Fiesta, *in 1955. E. W. F.
Tomlin's pamphlet (1955) in the British Council 'Writers and
Their Work' series is an excellent short introduction to Lewis, and
its bibliography refers to the longer studies by H. G. Porteus (1932),
Geoffrey Grigson (1951), and H. Kenner (1954). John Hollo-
way's essay in* The Charted Mirror (*1960*) *pleads forcibly for the
proper recognition of Lewis's achievement as a novelist.*

*Wyndham Lewis furnished me with the following notes on the
writing of* One-Way Song (*1*) *and on verse satire (2) in 1948:*

> (*1*) *Many people have inquired how it was that I, novelist,
> pamphleteer, sociologist, and so on, suddenly took it into my
> head to produce a volume of verse. The answer is very simple:
> I was in the first place, and for years, when young, a writer of
> verse. One fine day I took it into my head to write a novel. So
> the inquiry, if at all, should be framed the other way round.
> Also, however, I was a painter – one strangely 'advanced' for
> 1913; also I lived in Great Britain. It follows that I found
> it necessary to become a pamphleteer to defend my paintings
> against attack and a critic that I might expound the doctrines
> responsible for the difficulties that so bewildered and angered
> the public. Then I was a soldier and understood war un-
> doubtedly better than men who had not been that and years
> afterwards wrote pamphlet-books against new wars (but there
> are always new wars!). Many other things: books upon
> 'Time' and upon how men can best manage their rulers. But
> one fine day I did think I would again express myself in verse.
> Hence* One-Way Song.

> (*2*) *Verse-satire, in which class* One-Way Song, *I
> imagine, would be found, belongs to the comic muse. It is far
> more at home in France than in this country, where satire
> must always remain a scandal, and verse be regarded as an
> occasion for something 'rather lovely', rather than something*

*hideously true, or blisteringly witty. Certainly Mr Eliot in the
twenties was responsible for a great vogue for verse-satire. An
ideal formula of ironic, gently 'satiric', self-expression was
provided by that master for the undergraduate underworld,
tired and thirsty for poetic fame in a small way. The results of
Mr Eliot are not Mr Eliot himself: but satire with him has
been the painted smile of the clown. Habits of expression en-
suing from that mannerism are, as a fact, remote from the
central function of satire.*

    *In its essence the purpose of satire — whether verse or prose —
is aggression. (When whimsical, sentimental, or 'poetic' it is
a sort of bastard humour.) Satire has a great big glaring tar-
get. If successful, it blasts a great big hole in the centre.
Directness there must be and singleness of aim: it is all aim,
all trajectory. In that sense* One-Way Song *would only be
found to answer the description 'satiric verse' in certain sec-
tions. In those sections it is, I believe, at least authentic satire.*

If So the Man You Are, 14

The man I am to blow the bloody gaff
If I were given platforms? The riff-raff
May be handed all the trumpets that you will.
Not so the golden-tongued. The window-sill
Is all the pulpit they can hope to get,
Of a slum-garret, sung by Mistinguette,
Too high up to be heard, too poor to attract
Anyone to their so-called 'scurrilous' tract.
What wind an honest mind advances? Look
No wind of sickle and hammer, of bell and book,
No wind of any party, or blowing out
Of any mountain hemming us about
Of 'High Finance', or the foothills of same.
The man I am who does *not* play the game!
Of these incalculable ones I am
Not to be trusted with free-speech to damn,

To be given enough rope – just enough to hang.
To be hobbled in a dry field. As the bird sang
Who punctured poor Cock Robin, by some sparrow
Condemned to be shot at with toy bow and arrow.
You will now see how it stands with all of those
Who strong propensities for truth disclose.
It's no use buddy – you are for it boy
If not from head to foot a pure alloy!
If so the man you are that lets the cat
Out of the bag, you're a marked fellow and that's flat.

One-Way Song, XXIV

In any medium except that of verse
Forthwith I could enlighten you. Too terse,
And as it were compact, this form of art –
Which handles the finished product only – the hard
Master-material of selected sound.
The intellect has its workshops underground;
We cannot go back, out of this dance of words,
To become the teacher. Here we behave as birds –
The brain-that-sweats *offends*, it breaks our spell,
You do see that? we really must not *smell*
In this role: it is aristocratic but
Cudgel your brains in this case you must *not*.
So you will understand that argument,
Except in intent stylistic, or to invent
A certain pattern, is out of the question here.
I can only release, as elegant as deer,
A herd of wandering shapes, which *may* go straight,
But are just as likely to have grandly strayed,
Before we write finis out of sight and reach.
I cannot help this. It is noblesse oblige.

D. H. LAWRENCE

David Herbert Lawrence, the son of a coal-miner, was born at Eastwood in Nottinghamshire in 1885 and educated at Nottingham High School and University College, Nottingham. There is a large (and often tiresome) Lawrence literature, so that it is only necessary to note a few salient facts of his life: his qualifying as a school teacher – one of his best 'rhyming' poems is 'The Last Lesson of the Afternoon'; his marriage to Frieda in 1914; his travels in Italy, Australia, and New Mexico – see Twilight in Italy *(1916),* Sea and Sardinia *(1921),* Mornings in Mexico *(1927); and his death of tuberculosis near Nice in 1930. His reputation as a novelist was made with* The White Peacock *(1911) and* Sons and Lovers *(1913).* The Rainbow *(1915) was the subject of a police prosecution. Later novels of importance are* Women in Love *(1921),* Aaron's Rod *(1922),* Kangaroo *(1923), and* Lady Chatterley's Lover *(1928). The last appeared in a bowdlerized version in England in 1932 and in a full text, published by Penguin Books, in 1960 (after a trial at the Old Bailey which was in equal parts hilarious and instructive). Lawrence's* Collected Poems *were published in 1928, to be followed by* Last Poems *(1933), edited by Richard Aldington.* Collected Poems *(1957), in three volumes, supersedes these two books. Lawrence's* Letters, *edited by Aldous Huxley with a useful introduction, were issued in 1932, but this edition is shortly to be replaced by a fuller collection of letters edited by Harry T. Moore, who is also Lawrence's biographer. Kenneth Young is the author of the essay on Lawrence in the British Council 'Writers and Their Work' series. One of the best criticisms of Lawrence as a poet is to be found in* The Shaping Spirit: Studies in Modern English and American Poets *(1958) by A. Alvarez. It is a little too enthusiastic and does not allow sufficiently perhaps for the large number of poetic failures in the* Collected Poems, *but it seizes firmly on Lawrence's central poetic gift – the use of his intelligence to ensure a complete immediacy of feeling.*

'The Mosquito' is one of the less familiar pieces of 'Birds, Beasts, and Flowers', a section of his Collected Poems containing a high proportion of his best work. These pieces, Lawrence tells us, 'were begun in Tuscany, in the autumn of 1920, and finished in New Mexico in 1923, in my thirty-eighth year'. 'Bavarian Gentians' originally appeared in Last Poems. Both these poems are in free verse – I use that term not in the sense of a divagation from the norm of the blank verse line more extreme than that practised by the Jacobean dramatists (see Eliot's Introduction to Ezra Pound's Selected Poems), but in the other recognized sense of a cadenced form of writing, buttressed with repetitions, parallelisms, and occasional rhymes, derived at first hand from Whitman and beyond him from the translators of the metrical portions of the Bible. This has been defended as a highway of poetic development by Sir Herbert Read, but it seems to me to be a cul-de-sac: except in the hands of a Lawrence the writing is liable to be diffuse and to sprawl, and even in his hands, although it allows him an exceptional naked directness (Vers libre, said Lawrence, 'has no finish ... It is the instant; the quick'), too often the poems seem only gradually to warm into life. Too much attention has to be given to rhythm when form is so fluid; and this seems to correlate with a lack of verbal sparkle and excitement. The third poem, 'Innocent England', celebrates Lawrence's contempt and indignation at the suppression of his exhibition of paintings in London in 1928: the authorities feared for public morals because he painted pubic hair on his nudes.

Louis MacNeice in a journalistic, provocative 'Alphabet of Literary Prejudices' remarks under the heading 'Dark God':

As D. H. Lawrence was well slapped down in the twenties by Mr Wyndham Lewis there is no need now to take another slap at one who, in spite of his unfortunate effect on adolescents, was a great writer and a godsend. Lawrence had imagination without common sense – and got away with it – but in most people this divorce will degrade imagination itself.

I should add that I consider 'The Mosquito' an excellent poem. The other two pieces achieve what they set out to do. A useful

Selected Poems *was edited by W. E. Williams for Penguin Books in 1950.*

The Mosquito

When did you start your tricks,
Monsieur?

What do you stand on such high legs for?
Why this length of shredded shank,
You exaltation?

Is it so that you shall lift your centre of gravity upwards
And weigh no more than air as you alight upon me,
Stand upon me weightless, you phantom?

I heard a woman call you the Winged Victory
In sluggish Venice.
You turn your head towards your tail, and smile.

How can you put so much devilry
Into that translucent phantom shred
Of a frail corpus?

Queer, with your thin wings and your streaming legs,
How you sail like a heron, or a dull clot of air,
A nothingness.

Yet what an aura surrounds you;
Your evil little aura, prowling, and casting a numbness on my
    mind.

That is your trick, your bit of filthy magic:
Invisibility, and the anaesthetic power
To deaden my attention in your direction.

But I know your game now, streaky sorcerer.

Queer, how you stalk and prowl the air
In circles and evasions, enveloping me,
Ghoul on wings
Winged Victory.

Settle, and stand on long thin shanks
Eyeing me sideways, and cunningly conscious that I am aware,
You speck.

I hate the way you lurch off sideways into air
Having read my thoughts against you.

Come then, let us play at unawares,
And see who wins in this sly game of bluff.
Man or mosquito.

You don't know that I exist, and I don't know that you exist.
Now then!

It is your trump,
It is your hateful little trump,
You pointed fiend,
Which shakes my sudden blood to hatred of you:
It is your small, high, hateful bugle in my ear.

Why do you do it?
Surely it is bad policy.

They say you can't help it.

If that is so, then I believe a little in Providence protecting the
      innocent.
But it sounds so amazingly like a slogan,
A yell of triumph as you snatch my scalp.

Blood, red blood
Super-magical
Forbidden liquor.

I behold you stand
For a second enspasmed in oblivion,
Obscenely ecstasied
Sucking live blood,
My blood.

Such silence, such suspended transport,
Such gorging,
Such obscenity of trespass.

You stagger
As well as you may.
Only your accursed hairy frailty,
Your own imponderable weightlessness
Saves you, wafts you away on the very draught my anger makes
    in its snatching.

Away with a paean of derision,
You winged blood-drop.

Can I not overtake you?
Are you one too many for me,
Winged Victory?
Am I not mosquito enough to out-mosquito you?

Queer, what a big stain my sucked blood makes
Beside the infinitesimal faint smear of you!
Queer, what a dim dark smudge you have disappeared into!

Bavarian Gentians

Not every man has gentians in his house
in Soft September, at slow, Sad Michaelmas.

Bavarian gentians, big and dark, only dark
darkening the day-time torch-like with the smoking blueness of
       Pluto's gloom,
ribbed and torch-like, with their blaze of darkness spread blue
down flattening into points, flattened under the sweep of white
       day
torch-flower of the blue-smoking darkness, Pluto's dark-blue
       daze,
black lamps from the halls of Dis, burning dark blue,
giving off darkness, blue darkness, as Demeter's pale lamps give
       off light,
lead me then, lead me the way.

Reach me a gentian, give me a torch
let me guide myself with the blue, forked torch of this flower
down the darker and darker stairs, where blue is darkened on
       blueness,
even where Persephone goes, just now, from the frosted
       September
to the sightless realm where darkness is awake upon the dark
and Persephone herself is but a voice
or a darkness invisible enfolded in the deeper dark
of the arms Plutonic, and pierced with the passion of dense
       gloom,
among the splendour of torches of darkness, shedding darkness
       on the lost bride and her groom.

Innocent England

Oh what a pity, Oh! don't you agree
that figs aren't found in the land of the free!

Fig-trees don't grow in my native land;
there's never a fig-tree near at hand

when you want one; so I did without;
and that is what the row's about.

Virginal, pure policemen came
and hid their faces for very shame,

while they carried the shameless things away
to gaol, to be hid from the light of day.

And Mr Mead, that old, old lily
said: 'Gross! coarse! hideous!' – and I, like a silly

thought he meant the faces of the police-court officials,
and how right he was, and I signed my initials

to confirm what he said: but alas, he meant
my pictures, and on the proceedings went.

The upshot was, my pictures must burn
that English artists might finally learn

when they painted a nude, to put a *cache sexe* on,
a cache sexe, a cache sexe, or else begone!

A fig-leaf; or, if you cannot find it
a wreath of mist, with nothing behind it.

A wreath of mist is the usual thing
in the north, to hide where the turtles sing.

Though they never sing, they never sing,
don't you dare to suggest such a thing

or Mr Mead will be after you.
– But what a pity I never knew

A wreath of English mist would do
as a cache sexe! I'd have put a whole fog.

But once and forever barks the old dog,
so my pictures are in prison, instead of in the Zoo.

ANDREW YOUNG

Andrew Young was born in Elgin in 1885 and educated at Edinburgh University, which conferred an honorary doctorate on him in 1951. He came south in 1920 to live at Hove and was Vicar of Stonegate, Sussex, from 1941 until 1959. He now lives in retirement at Arundel. He is a Canon of Chichester Cathedral and is well known as an authority on wild flowers.

Although he published a Collected Poems *as long ago as 1936, it is only since the war that he has had much recognition as a poet, and most of the honours that have come his way are even more recent: the Edinburgh doctorate of 1951 (mentioned above), the Queen's Medal for Poetry (1952) and the Duff Cooper Memorial Prize (1960).* Collected Poems *(1950) adds the poems from* Speak to the Earth *(1939) and* The Green Man *(1947) to those contained in the earlier collected edition and has itself been followed by* Out of the World and Back *(1958). Canon Young's other*

works include Nicodemus (*1937*), A Prospect of Flowers (*1945*),
Into Hades (*1952*), *and* A Prospect of Britain (*1956*).

   'A Prospect of Death' is originally from Speak to the Earth.
*Young has been called 'an English Robert Frost', but in spite of
some points of likeness this is excessive praise. Better to remark of
his work with Edwin Muir that it is metaphysical in turn, has a
mastery of detail, and is 'never trivial and never commonplace'.*

A Prospect of Death

If it should come to this,
You cannot wake me with a kiss,
Think I but sleep too late
Or once again keep a cold angry state.

So now you have been told;
I or my breakfast may grow cold,
But you must only say
'Why does he miss the best part of the day?'

Even then you may be wrong;
Through woods torn by a blackbird's song
My thoughts will often roam
While graver business makes me stay at home.

There will be time enough
To go back to the earth I love
Some other day that week,
Perhaps to find what all my life I seek.

So do not dream of danger;
Forgive my lateness or my anger;
You have so much forgiven,
Forgive me this or that, or Hell or Heaven.

CHARLES WILLIAMS

Charles Williams was born in London in 1886 and educated at St Albans Grammar School and University College, London. He was a member of the staff of the London branch of the Oxford University Press for thirty-six years, and it was while he worked there that he wrote his novels, criticism, and poetry. He lectured at the City of London Literary Institute, and during the Second World War made a reputation at Oxford as a lecturer and private tutor. He died in May 1945.

His novels may be described fairly as supernatural thrillers and include two which have been widely read: War in Heaven *and* All Hallows Eve. *Better known still, at least by literary students, are* The English Poetic Mind *(1932) and* The Figure of Beatrice *(1943). Another influential prose book by Charles Williams is* The Descent of the Dove *(1939), which has the sub-title 'A Short History of the Holy Spirit in the Church'. Some of his poetry was published as early as 1912, but his present reputation and influence rest on* Taliessin Through Logres *(1938) and* The Region of the Summer Stars *(1944).* The Image of the City *(1959), a collection of essays edited by Anne Ridler, includes papers on Shakespeare, Hopkins, Lawrence, and others, as well as Williams's own notes on the Arthurian legend.*

*Arthurian Torso *(1948), containing the prose fragment 'The Figure of Arthur' by Charles Williams and an ingenious commentary by C. S. Lewis on Williams's Arthurian poems, is necessary reading for anyone hoping to grasp the ideas behind and the meaning of the two mature poetic works listed above. 'The Calling of Arthur' is reprinted from* Taliessin Through Logres. *In this poem Merlin calls Arthur to his inheritance, the throne which has to be seized from Cradlemas, King of London, 'the last feeble, fragile, and sinister representative of Roman civilization' with his emerald monocle, gilded mask, and pretended pity for his miserable subjects. It is an early and comparatively straightforward poem in* *the Arthurian sequence – this is my reason for selecting it – and in the view of Mr C. S. Lewis one of the best as word-music. 'There are poems in which Williams has produced word music equalled by only two or three in this century and surpassed by none. "The Calling of Arthur" responds metrically to every movement of the emotion ...' While I agree that this poem is in rhythm and melody one of the best in the two Arthurian volumes, the first part of this statement seems to me to be quite groundless. I also consider Mr Lewis's general estimate of the importance of Charles Williams as a poet wildly off the mark.*

It would be wrong to leave such a remark without some explanation. Like other writers, Mr Lewis has in my opinion been hypnotized by his memories of the man, and by his conviction of the importance and wisdom of the things Williams had to say, into imagining that they are said (and happily) in the poems. The truth is that these things are barely half-said: all Mr Lewis's ingenuity is needed to disentangle even the story, and the full 'philosophical' meaning is still further to seek. Again, it seems to me that the honesty of the writer does not prevent him at times from being metrically clumsy and in expression uncouth and, more rarely, bathetic. In sum, I think the poems are a literary oddity of great interest, and I include one of them because the influence of Williams's personality and ideas – including poetic ideas – on Eliot, Auden, and younger writers such as Anne Ridler is admitted. I think the effect of his poetry – simply as poetry – has been and will be negligible.

A more favourable view of Charles Williams as a poet is taken in John Heath-Stubbs's pamphlet for the British Council 'Writers and Their Work' series (1955), which also contains a bibliography by Linden Huddlestone. The reader may also be interested in 'The Art of the Enemy', Essays in Criticism *(January 1957), a sharp attack by Robert Conquest on the ideas and values expressed in the Arthurian poems.*

The Calling of Arthur

Arthur was young; Merlin met him on the road.
    Wolfish, the wizard stared, coming from the wild,
    black with hair, bleak with hunger, defiled
from a bed in the dung of cattle, inhuman his eyes.

Bold stood Arthur; the snow beat; Merlin spoke:
    Now am I Camelot; now am I to be builded.
    King Cradlemas sits by Thames; a mask o'ergilded
covers his wrinkled face, all but one eye.

Cold and small he settles his rump in the cushions.
    Through the emerald of Nero one short-sighted eye
    peers at the pedlars of wealth that stand plausibly by.
The bleak mask is gilded with a maiden's motionless smile.

The high aged voice squeals with callous comfort.
    He sits on the bank of Thames, a sea-snail's shell
    fragile, fragilely carved, cast out by the swell
on to the mud; his spirit withers and dies.

He withers; he peers at the tide; he squeals.
    He warms himself by the fire and eats his food
    through a maiden's motionless mouth; in his mood
he polishes his emerald, misty with tears for the poor.

The waste of snow covers the waste of thorn;
    on the waste of hovels snow falls from a dreary sky;
    mallet and scythe are silent; the children die.
King Cradlemas fears that the winter is hard for the poor.

Draw now the tide, spring morn, swing now the depth;
    under the snow that falls over brick and prickle,
    the people ebb; draw up the hammer and sickle.
The banner of Bors is abroad; where is the king?

Bors is up; his wife Elayne behind him
    mends the farms, gets food from Gaul; the south
    is up with hammer and sickle, and holds Thames mouth.
Lancelot hastens, coming with wagons and ships.

The sea-snail lies by Thames; O wave of Pendragon,
    roll it, swallow it; pull the mask o'ergilded
    from the one-eyed face that blinks at the comfort builded
in London's ruins; I am Camelot; Arthur, raise me.

Arthur ran; the people marched; in the snow
    King Cradlemas died in his litter; a screaming few
    fled; Merlin came; Camelot grew.
In Logres the King's friend landed, Lancelot of Gaul.

SIEGFRIED SASSOON

Siegfried Sassoon was born in 1886 and educated at Marlborough and Clare College, Cambridge. He served with the Sussex Yeomanry and the Royal Welch Fusiliers in France and Palestine during the First World War and won the M.C. He was in hospital at Craiglockhart with Wilfred Owen, who wrote of him enthusiastically 'as a man; as a friend and a poet':

> *Know that since mid September, when you still regarded me as a tiresome little knocker on your door, I hold you as Keats + Christ + Elijah + my Colonel + my father-confessor + Amenophis IV in profile.*

The hospital magazine, The Hydra, printed verse by both poets. Another picture of Sassoon during the war can be found in Robert Graves's Goodbye to All That (1929). This was the year in which Sassoon's The Memoirs of a Fox-hunting Man was awarded both the Hawthornden Prize and the James Tait Black

Memorial Prize. The Complete Memoirs of George Sherston, *which incorporates* The Memoirs of a Fox-hunting Man, *was published in 1937. It is a semi-autobiographical narrative and should be read in connexion with* Siegfried's Journey (*1945*). *Sassoon's* Collected Poems *appeared in 1946. A later collection is* Sequences (*1956*). *Mr Sassoon received a C.B.E. in 1951 and was awarded the Royal Gold Medal for Poetry in 1957.*

I have represented the poet here by pieces written during the First and Second World Wars ('The Death-Bed' and 'The Child at the Window'). Originally I chose 'Repression of War Experience' to stand for the early work, but Mr Sassoon considers it already a period-piece as a 'war-protest' poem and suggested 'The Death-Bed' in its place as 'a better bit of verse'. He remarks modestly of his own poetry that it 'belongs to the pre-Eliot period in technique and expression'.

The Death-Bed

He drowsed and was aware of silence heaped
Round him, unshaken as the steadfast walls;
Aqueous like floatings rays of amber light,
Soaring and quivering in the wings of sleep.
Silence and safety; and his mortal shore
Lipped by the inward, moonless waves of death.

Someone was holding water to his mouth.
He swallowed, unresisting; moaned and dropped
Through crimson gloom to darkness; and forgot
The opiate throb and ache that was his wound.
　　Water – calm, sliding green above the weir.
　　Water – a sky-lit alley for his boat,
　　Bird-voiced, and bordered with reflected flowers
　　And shaken hues of summer; drifting down,
　　He dipped contented oars, and sighed, and slept.

Night, with a gust of wind, was in the ward,
Blowing the curtain to a glimmering curve.
Night. He was blind; he could not see the stars
Glinting among the wraiths of wandering cloud;
Queer blots of colour, purple, scarlet, green,
Flickered and faded in his drowning eyes.

Rain – he could hear it rustling through the dark;
Fragrance and passionless music woven as one;
Warm rain on drooping roses; pattering showers
That soak the woods; not the harsh rain that sweeps
Behind the thunder, but a trickling peace,
Gently and slowly washing life away.

. . .

He stirred, shifting his body; then the pain
Leapt like a prowling beast, and gripped and tore
His groping dreams with grinding claws and fangs.
   But someone was beside him; soon he lay
   Shuddering because that evil thing had passed.
   And death, who'd stepped toward him, paused and stared.

Light many lamps and gather round his bed.
Lend him your eyes, warm blood, and will to live.
Speak to him; rouse him; you may save him yet.
He's young; he hated War; how should he die
When cruel old campaigners win safe through?

But death replied: 'I choose him.' So he went,
And there was silence in the summer night;
Silence and safety; and the veils of sleep.
Then, far away, the thudding of the guns.

The Child at the Window

Remember this, when childhood's far away;
The sunlight of a showery first spring day;
You from your house-top window laughing down,
And I, returned with whip-cracks from a ride,
On the great lawn below you, playing the clown.
Time blots our gladness out. Let this with love abide ...

The brave March day; and you, not four years old,
Up in your nursery world – all heaven for me.
Remember this – the happiness I hold –
In far off springs I shall not live to see;
The world one map of wastening war unrolled,
And you, unconscious of it, setting my spirit free.

For you must learn, beyond bewildering years,
How little things beloved and held are best.
The windows of the world are blurred with tears,
And troubles come like cloud-banks from the west.
Remember this, some afternoon in spring,
When your own child looks down and makes your sad heart
    sing.

EDWIN MUIR

*Edwin Muir was born at Deerness in the Orkneys in 1887 and
educated at Kirkwall Burgh School until the age of fourteen. After
this he became a clerk in commercial and shipbuilding firms in Glas-
gow. In 1919 he married Willa Anderson and settled in London
as a free-lance journalist. In 1921 he went with his wife to Prague
and the next seven years were spent 'nomadically' on the Continent.*

(*It was during this period that he became known as a poet, critic, and translator. His translations of Kafka, which were produced in collaboration with his wife, introduced that writer to English audiences.*) *There was a return to nomadism between 1942 and 1949 when Muir was serving the British Council in Edinburgh, Prague, and Rome. Subsequently he became Warden of Newbattle Abbey College in Scotland. He died in 1958. He tells his own story in* An Autobiography (*1954*), *which replaces the earlier* The Story and the Fable (*1940*) *and should be read by serious readers of the poems.*

Six collections of verse, the earliest dated 1925, are included representatively or wholly in Collected Poems 1921–51 (*1952*), *which was edited by J. C. Hall for the poet. In 1956* One Foot in Eden *was the spring choice of the Poetry Book Society, which Muir had assisted as a selector on its foundation in 1954. A new* Collected Poems 1921–58 *appeared posthumously in 1960. It was being prepared for publication by the poet in 1958 – an author's note records that twenty-seven poems omitted by Mr Hall from the earlier collected edition are included 'because they express certain things which I wished to say at the time and have not said in the same way again' – and was completed after his death by Willa Muir and J. C. Hall. They include among 'Poems not previously Collected' a number of unpublished poems, some of which are incomplete and unrevised. Muir's work in prose, apart from his translations and autobiography, includes two notable books:* The Structure of the Novel (*1928*), *which was a sound pioneering piece of literary criticism, and* Essays on Literature and Society (*1949*). *There are some appreciative pages on Muir as a poet in Anthony Thwaite's* Contemporary English Poetry (*1959*), *but the best introduction to Muir's work as a whole is certainly J. C. Hall's essay (1956) in the British Council 'Writers and Their Work' series.*

'The Wayside Station', a fine descriptive piece, is reprinted from The Narrow Place (*1943*) *and 'The Combat', which is more typical of Muir's art of metaphysical parable, from* The Labyrinth (*1949*). *If space and money had allowed, I should also have liked to include 'The Horses' from* One Foot in Eden (*1956*). *Edwin Muir's earlier poetry was often involved and thin in texture – I find*

Variations on a Time Theme (*1934*) *nearly unreadable – but since* Journeys and Places (*1937*) *the pressure of experience behind the gnomic and visionary elements seems to have increased, and his later poems are more memorable than the poems in his earlier books. If I do not feel that his poetic stature is quite as high as Mr Hall and other good critics might claim, I am convinced of the individuality of Muir's poetic gift. But it worries me that the poems so rarely 'explode' into meaning – for me Muir remains an extremely honest and often rewarding but not very exciting poet.*

The Wayside Station

Here at the wayside station, as many a morning,
I watch the smoke torn from the fumy engine
Crawling across the field in serpent sorrow.
Flat in the east, held down by stolid clouds,
The struggling day is born and shines already
On its warm hearth far off. Yet something here
Glimmers along the ground to show the seagulls
White on the furrows' black unturning waves.

But now the light has broadened.
I watch the farmstead on the little hill,
That seems to mutter: 'Here is day again'
Unwillingly. Now the sad cattle wake
In every byre and stall,
The ploughboy stirs in the loft, the farmer groans
And feels the day like a familiar ache
Deep in his body, though the house is dark.
The lovers part
Now in the bedroom where the pillows gleam
Great and mysterious as deep hills of snow,
An inaccessible land. The wood stands waiting
While the bright snare slips coil by coil around it,
Dark silver on every branch. The lonely stream

That rode through darkness leaps the gap of light,
Its voice grown loud, and starts its winding journey
Through the day and time and war and history.

The Combat

It was not meant for human eyes,
That combat on the shabby patch
Of clods and mangled grass that lies
Somewhere beneath the secret skies
For eye of toad or adder to catch.

And having seen it I accuse
The crested animal in his pride,
Arrayed in all those royal hues
Which hide the claws he well can use
To tear the heart out of the side.

Body of leopard, eagle's head
And whetted beak, and lion's mane,
And frost-grey hedge of feathers spread
Behind – he seemed of all things bred.
I shall not see his like again.

As for his enemy, there came in
A soft round beast as brown as clay;
All rent and patched his wretched skin;
A battered bag he might have been,
Some old used thing to throw away.

Yet he awaited face to face
The furious beast and the swift attack.
Soon over and done. That was no place
Or time for chivalry or for grace.
The fury had him on his back.

And two soft paws like hands flew out
To right and left while the trees stood by.
One would have said beyond a doubt
This was the very end of the bout,
But that the creature would not die.

For ere the death-blow he was gone,
Writhed, whirled, huddled into his den,
Safe somehow there. The fight was done,
And he had lost who had all but won.
But oh his deadly fury then.

A while the place lay bare, forlorn,
Drowsing as in relief from pain.
The cricket chirped, the grating thorn
Stirred, and a little sound was born.
The champions took their posts again.

And all began. The stealthy paw
Slashed out and in. Could nothing save
These rags and tatters from the claw?
Nothing. And yet I never saw
A beast so helpless and so brave.

And now, while the trees stand watching, still
The unequal battle rages there,
And the killing beast that cannot kill
Swells and swells in his fury till
You well might think it was despair.

T. S. ELIOT

Thomas Stearns Eliot was born of New England stock in St Louis, Missouri, in 1888, and educated at Harvard, Merton College, Oxford, and the Sorbonne. He settled in England in 1915 and became a naturalized British subject in 1927. After schoolmastering at Highgate – John Betjeman was a pupil – he was employed in the foreign department of Lloyds Bank in the City. In 1922 he founded The Criterion, *the best English literary review of its time, and soon after was appointed a Director of the publishing house of Faber and Faber, a post he held until his death. The unequal* T. S. Eliot: a symposium (Editions Poetry London, 1948) *contains two contributions of great biographical interest: Wyndham Lewis on the 'Early London Environment' and F. V. Morley's 'T. S. Eliot as a Publisher'. The Order of Merit was bestowed on him in 1948, and his enormous influence on contemporary writing was also recognized by the award of the Nobel Prize for Literature. His other literary honours are too many to mention in full: he held an honorary doctorate of many English and American universities, was an Honorary Fellow of Magdalene College, Cambridge, and was Clark Lecturer at Cambridge (1926) and Charles Eliot Norton Visiting Professor at Harvard (1932–3). There is a bibliography of his writings by D. Gallup (Yale, 1947), but the ordinary reader or student will find enough in the useful check-list of published writings contained in* Focus Three: T. S. Eliot – a study of his writings by various hands (1947) *and in the bibliography attached to M. C. Bradbrook's pamphlet on* T. S. Eliot *in the British Council 'Writers and Their Work' series in 1950.*

T. S. Eliot's first volume of verse was Prufrock (1917). The Waste Land, *target for the arrows of the conventionally orthodox for many years, followed in 1922.* Collected Poems 1909–1935 (1936) *contains these and* Ash Wednesday, *as well as shorter poems written before 1935.* Four Quartets – *the first part, 'Burnt*

Norton', *appeared in* Collected Poems, *the other parts separately –*
was published in 1944. Other poetic works are the five verse plays,
Murder in the Cathedral (*1935*), The Family Reunion (*1939*),
The Cocktail Party (*1950*), The Confidential Clerk (*1954*), *and*
The Elder Statesman (*1959*), *and a book of verses for children,*
Old Possum's Book of Practical Cats (*1939*).

The best of the plays is still The Family Reunion. *The* Cock-
tail Party *has a good scene in Act II (the interview between Har-*
court-Reilly and Edward and Lavinia), Bonamy Dobrée *has found*
it possible to praise The Confidential Clerk, *but I have never heard*
a good word said for The Elder Statesman. *What is difficult to*
swallow in the post-war plays is a portentousness in the religious
element that reminds me of embarrassing scenes in the novels of
Charles Williams – 'Go in peace. And work out your salvation with
diligence' is Eliot, but it could easily be taken for one of those unlikely
farewells in War in Heaven. *It is rash to attempt to characterize*
Eliot's poetry in a few lines, but at this distance from the 'revo-
lution' the wisecrack that he has written 'the finest French poetry in
the English language' does underline a feeling that his poems illus-
trate the English poetic tradition but never quite belong to it in the
way that the poems of Yeats, Auden, and Graves – with their often
blithe disregard for what Philip Larkin calls the 'myth-kitty' –
obviously do. Characteristics of the Eliot poetic note are such facts
as that he unbends awkwardly, finds enthusiasm distasteful, inter-
poses a brahminical distance between himself and his subject-matter.
Even when the feeling is remarkably pure and strong as in Ash
Wednesday VI *and* Little Gidding II *he remains almost too*
measured and unruffled – the effects are always worked for and con-
trived, never (as so often with Yeats) simply and inevitably found.
But virtues are defined by limitations and the importance for later
poets of the example of Eliot's poetic seriousness and intelligent
dedication can hardly be over-estimated. He is quite possibly 'the
greatest poetic influence in the world today' (Spender) precisely in
this sense, although it is generally agreed that the direct influence of
his poems on later poetic practice in England has been slight. Readers
will find a further brief discussion of Eliot's poetry in the intro-
duction to this anthology.

Apart from being in all probability 'the greatest poetic influence in the world today', T. S. Eliot is a literary critic of major importance, standing in relation to the present age much as Matthew Arnold (whom he sometimes, naturally enough, treats less than justly) did to the Victorian Age. As a critic he has modified the manner in which a whole generation regards 'the English poetic mind', and many of the shifts of emphasis in taste for which he has been responsible now seem with minor corrections natural and inevitable to students. The first critical essays and reviews were collected in The Sacred Wood *(1920), but the reader will now turn to* Selected Essays *(1932) for the critical work up to that date, and to later books such as* The Use of Poetry and the Use of Criticism *(1933),* After Strange Gods *(1934),* What is a Classic? *(1945), and* On Poetry and Poets *(1957).* The Idea of a Christian Society *(1939) and* Notes towards the Definition of Culture *(1948), social criticism from a religious and cultural standpoint, should also be mentioned here.* Poetry and Drama *(1951) and* The Three Voices of Poetry *(1953) help us to understand the plays. M. C. Bradbrook has written brightly on Eliot' literary criticism in* Focus Three.

Certain critical writings on Eliot's work have already been mentioned. Attention should be drawn to F. O. Matthiessen's The Achievement of T. S. Eliot *(1935, revised edition 1947); to R. Preston's* Four Quartets Rehearsed *(1946); to L. Unger's* T. S. Eliot: a Selected Critique *(1948), which collects extracts from various critical studies and includes a check-list of books and articles on Eliot up to 1948; to H. Gardner's* The Art of T. S. Eliot *(1949); and to G. Williamson's* A Reader's Guide to T. S. Eliot *(1955).*

In 1948 I wrote that my choice of poems from Eliot's work to represent him in this anthology was limited by the fact that Four Quartets *was not then available for reproduction and that in the place of the second movement from* Little Gidding, *which I badly wanted to print, I was including extracts from* Murder in the Cathedral *and* The Family Reunion. *In 1960 I am able to add* Little Gidding II *to my selection. What I wrote about it in 1948 still seems apt.*

This movement, which begins with the lyric 'Ash on an Old Man's Sleeve' and develops into the superb rhetoric of the Dantesque interview with the 'familiar compound ghost', is Mr Eliot's finest sustained passage of poetic writing, intense, grave, disciplined, and moving. It is, I think, unequalled by any other modern English poet except Yeats.

As with Yeats and Auden I feel dissatisfied with my selection of poems even now – the work of all three poets is too various for adequate representation even in the comparatively large amount of space allotted to them.

Sweeney Erect

> *And the trees about me,*
> *Let them be dry and leafless; let the rocks*
> *Groan with continual surges; and behind me,*
> *Make all a desolation. Look, look, wenches!*

Paint me a cavernous waste shore
    Cast in the unstilled Cyclades,
Paint me the bold anfractuous rocks
    Faced by the snarled and yelping seas.

Display me Aeolus above
    Reviewing the insurgent gales
Which tangle Ariadne's hair
    And swell with haste the perjured sails.

Morning stirs the feet and hands
    (Nausicaa and Polypheme).
Gesture of orang-outang
    Rises from the sheets in steam.

This withered root of knots of hair
    Slitted below and gashed with eyes,
This oval O cropped out with teeth:
    The sickle motion from the thighs

Jackknifes upward at the knees
    Then straightens out from heel to hip
Pushing the framework of the bed
    And clawing at the pillow slip.

Sweeney addressed full length to shave
    Broadbottomed, pink from nape to base,
Knows the female temperament
    And wipes the suds around his face.

(The lengthened shadow of a man
    Is history, said Emerson
Who had not seen the silhouette
    Of Sweeney straddled in the sun.)

Tests the razor on his leg
    Waiting until the shriek subsides.
The epileptic on the bed
    Curves backward, clutching at her sides.

The ladies of the corridor
    Find themselves involved, disgraced,
Call witness to their principles
    And deprecate the lack of taste

Observing that hysteria
    Might easily be misunderstood;
Mrs Turner intimates
    It does the house no sort of good.

But Doris, towelled from the bath,
    Enters padding on broad feet,
Bringing sal volatile
    And a glass of brandy neat.

From *The Waste Land*

A Game of Chess

The Chair she sat in, like a burnished throne,
Glowed on the marble, where the glass
Held up by standards wrought with fruited vines
From which a golden Cupidon peeped out
(Another hid his eyes behind his wing)
Doubled the flames of sevenbranched candelabra
Reflecting light upon the table as
The glitter of her jewels rose to meet it,
From satin cases poured in rich profusion;
In vials of ivory and coloured glass
Unstoppered, lurked her strange synthetic perfumes,
Unguent, powered, or liquid – troubled, confused
And drowned the sense in odours; stirred by the air
That freshened from the window, these ascended
In fattening the prolonged candle-flames,
Flung their smoke into the laquearia,
Stirring the pattern on the coffered ceiling.
Huge sea-wood fed with copper
Burned green and orange, framed by the coloured stone,
In which sad light a carvèd dolphin swam.
Above the antique mantel was displayed
As though a window gave upon the sylvan scene
The change of Philomel, by the barbarous king
So rudely forced; yet there the nightingale
Filled all the desert with inviolable voice
And still she cried, and still the world pursues,
'Jug Jug' to dirty ears.
And other withered stumps of time
Were told upon the walls; staring forms
Leaned out, leaning, hushing the room enclosed.
Footsteps shuffled on the stair.
Under the firelight, under the brush, her hair
Spread out in fiery points
Glowed into words, then would be savagely still.

'My nerves are bad to-night. Yes, bad. Stay with me.
'Speak to me. Why do you never speak, Speak.
    'What are you thinking of? What thinking? What?
'I never know what you are thinking. Think.'

I think we are in rats' alley
Where the dead men lost their bones.

'What is that noise?'
              The wind under the door.
'What is that noise now? What is the wind doing?'
              Nothing again nothing.
                    'Do
'You know nothing? Do you see nothing? Do you remember
'Nothing?'

    I remember
Those are pearls that were his eyes.
'Are you alive, or not? Is there nothing in your head?'

                                     But

O O O O that Shakespeherian Rag —
It's so elegant
So intelligent
'What shall I do now? What shall I do?'
'I shall rush out as I am, and walk the street
'With my hair down, so. What shall we do to-morrow?
'What shall we ever do?'
              The hot water at ten.
And if it rains, a closed car at four.
And we shall play a game of chess,
Pressing lidless eyes and waiting for a knock upon the door.

When Lil's husband got demobbed, I said —
I didn't mince my words, I said to her myself,
HURRY UP PLEASE ITS TIME

Now Albert's coming back, make yourself a bit smart.
He'll want to know what you done with that money he gave you
To get yourself some teeth. He did, I was there.
You have them all out, Lil, and get a nice set,
He said, I swear, I can't bear to look at you.
And no more can't I, I said, and think of poor Albert,
He's been in the army four years, he wants a good time.
And if you don't give it him, there's others will, I said.
Oh is there, she said. Something o' that, I said.
Then I'll know who to thank, she said, and give me a straight
    look.
HURRY UP PLEASE ITS TIME
If you don't like it you can get on with it, I said.
Others can pick and choose if you can't.
But if Albert makes off, it won't be for lack of telling.
You ought to be ashamed, I said, to look so antique.
(And her only thirty-one).
I can't help it, she said, pulling a long face,
It's them pills I took, to bring it off, she said.
(She's had five already, and nearly died of young George.)
The chemist said it would be all right, but I've never been the
    same.
You *are* a proper fool, I said.
Well, if Albert won't leave you alone, there it is, I said,
What you get married for if you don't want children?
HURRY UP PLEASE ITS TIME
Well, that Sunday Albert was home, they had a hot gammon,
And they asked me in to dinner, to get the beauty of it hot—
HURRY UP PLEASE ITS TIME
HURRY UP PLEASE ITS TIME
Goonight Bill. Goonight Lou. Goonight May. Goonight.
Ta ta. Goonight. Goonight.
Good night, ladies, good night, sweet ladies, good night, good
    night.

From *Ash Wednesday*

Although I do not hope to turn again
Although I do not hope
Although I do not hope to turn

Wavering between the profit and the loss
In this brief transit where the dreams cross
The dreamcrossed twilight between birth and dying
(Bless me father) though I do not wish to wish these things
From the wide window towards the granite shore
The white sails still fly seaward, seaward flying
Unbroken wings

And the lost heart stiffens and rejoices
In the lost lilac and the lost sea voices
And the weak spirit quickens to rebel
For the bent golden-rod and the lost sea smell
Quickens to recover
The cry of quail and the whirling plover
And the blind eye creates
The empty forms between the ivory gates
And smell renews the salt savour of the sandy earth

This is the time of tension between dying and birth
The place of solitude where three dreams cross
Between blue rocks
But when the voices shaken from the yew-tree drift away
Let the other yew be shaken and reply.

Blessèd sister, holy mother, spirit of the fountain, spirit of the
    garden,
Suffer us not to mock ourselves with falsehood
Teach us to care and not to care
Teach us to sit still

Even among these rocks,
Our peace in His will
And even among these rocks
Sister, mother
And spirit of the river, spirit of the sea,
Suffer me not to be separated

And let my cry come unto Thee.

From *Murder in the Cathedral*

Thomas soliloquizes

Now is my way clear, now is the meaning plain:
Temptation shall not come in this kind again.
The last temptation is the greatest treason:
To do the right deed for the wrong reason.
The natural vigour in the venial sin
Is the way in which our lives begin.
Thirty years ago, I searched all the ways
That lead to pleasure, advancement and praise.
Delight in sense, in learning and in thought,
Music and philosophy, curiosity,
The purple bullfinch in the lilac tree,
The tiltyard skill, the strategy of chess,
Love in the garden, singing to the instrument,
Were all things equally desirable.
Ambition comes when early force is spent
And when we find no longer all things possible.
Ambition comes behind and unobservable.
Sin grows with doing good. When I imposed the King's law
In England, and waged war with him against Toulouse,
I beat the barons at their own game. I
Could then despise the men who thought me most contemptible,
The raw nobility, whose manners matched their finger nails.
While I ate out of the King's dish

To become servant of God was never my wish.
Servant of God has chance of greater sin
And sorrow, than the man who serves a king.
For those who serve the greater cause may make the cause serve
    them,
Still doing right: and striving with political men
May make that cause political, not by what they do
But by what they are. I know
What yet remains to show you of my history
Will seem to most of you at best futility,
Senseless self-slaughter of a lunatic,
Arrogant passion of a fanatic.
I know that history at all time draws
The strangest consequence from remotest cause.
But for every evil, every sacrilege,
Crime, wrong, oppression and the axe's edge,
Indifference, exploitation, you, and you,
And you, must all be punished. So must you.
I shall no longer act or suffer, to the sword's end.
Now my good Angel, whom God appoints
To be my guardian, hover over the swords' points.

From *The Family Reunion*

Chorus

In an old house there is always listening, and more is heard than
    is spoken.
And what is spoken remains in the room, waiting for the future
    to hear it.
And whatever happens began in the past, and presses hard on
    the future.
The agony in the curtained bedroom, whether of birth or of
    dying,
Gathers in to itself all the voices of the past, and projects them
    into the future.

The treble voices on the lawn
The mowing of hay in summer
The dogs and the old pony
The stumble and the wail of little pain
The chopping of wood in autumn
And the singing in the kitchen
And the steps at night in the corridor
The moment of sudden loathing
And the season of stifled sorrow
The whisper, the transparent deception
The keeping up of appearances
The making the best of a bad job
All twined and tangled together, all are recorded.
There is no avoiding these things
And we know nothing of exorcism
And whether in Argos or England
There are certain inflexible laws
Unalterable, in the nature of music.
There is nothing at all to be done about it,
There is nothing to do about anything,
And now it is nearly time for the news
We must listen to the weather report
And the international catastrophes.

From *Four Quartets*

Little Gidding II

Ash on an old man's sleeve
Is all the ash the burnt roses leave.
Dust in the air suspended
Marks the place where a story ended.
Dust inbreathed was a house –
The wall, the wainscot and the mouse.
The death of hope and despair,
      This is the death of air.

There are flood and drouth
Over the eyes and in the mouth,
Dead water and dead sand
Contending for the upper hand.
The parched eviscerate soil
Gapes at the vanity of toil,
Laughs without mirth.
    This is the death of earth.

Water and fire succeed
The town, the pasture and the weed.
Water and fire deride
The sacrifice that we denied.
Water and fire shall rot
The marred foundations we forgot,
Of sanctuary and choir.
    This is the death of water and fire.

In the uncertain hour before the morning
  Near the ending of interminable night
  At the recurrent end of the unending
After the dark dove with the flickering tongue
  Had passed below the horizon of his homing
  While the dead leaves still rattled on like tin
Over the asphalt where no other sound was
  Between three districts whence the smoke arose
  I met one walking, loitering and hurried
As if blown towards me like the metal leaves
  Before the urban dawn wind unresisting.
  And as I fixed upon the down-turned face
That pointed scrutiny with which we challenge
  The first-met stranger in the waning dusk
  I caught the sudden look of some dead master
Whom I had known, forgotten, half recalled
  Both one and many; in the brown baked features
  The eyes of a familiar compound ghost
Both intimate and unidentifiable.

So I assumed a double part, and cried
  And heard another's voice cry: 'What! are *you* here?'
Although we were not. I was still the same,
  Knowing myself yet being someone other –
  And he a face still forming; yet the words sufficed
To compel the recognition they preceded.
  And so, compliant to the common wind,
  Too strange to each other for misunderstanding,
In concord at this intersection time
  Of meeting nowhere, no before and after,
  We trod the pavement in a dead patrol.
I said: 'The wonder that I feel is easy,
  Yet ease is cause of wonder. Therefore speak:
  I may not comprehend, may not remember.'
And he: 'I am not eager to rehearse
  My thought and theory which you have forgotten.
  These things have served their purpose: let them be.
So with your own, and pray they be forgiven
  By others, as I pray you to forgive
  Both bad and good. Last season's fruit is eaten
And the fullfed beast shall kick the empty pail.
  For last year's words belong to last year's language
  And next year's words await another voice.
But, as the passage now presents no hindrance
  To the spirit unappeased and peregrine
  Between two worlds become much like each other,
So I find words I never thought to speak
  In streets I never thought I should revisit
  When I left my body on a distant shore.
Since our concern was speech, and speech impelled us
  To purify the dialect of the tribe
  And urge the mind to aftersight and foresight,
Let me disclose the gifts reserved for age
  To set a crown upon your lifetime's effort.
  First, the cold friction of expiring sense
Without enchantment, offering no promise
  But bitter tastelessness of shadow fruit

As body and soul begin to fall asunder.
Second, the conscious impotence of rage
    At human folly, and the laceration
    Of laughter at what ceases to amuse.
And last, the rending pain of re-enactment
    Of all that you have done, and been; the shame
    Of motives late revealed, and the awareness
Of things ill done and done to others' harm
    Which once you took for exercise of virtue.
    Then fools' approval stings, and honour stains.
From wrong to wrong the exasperated spirit
    Proceeds, unless restored by that refining fire
    Where you must move in measure, like a dancer.'
The day was breaking. In the disfigured street
    He left me, with a kind of valediction,
    And faded on the blowing of the horn.

ARTHUR WALEY

*Arthur Waley was born at Tunbridge Wells in 1889 and educated
at Rugby and King's College, Cambridge (of which he is an
Honorary Fellow). He was at one time Assistant Keeper of the
Department of Prints and Drawings at the British Museum, and
he worked in the Far Eastern section of the Ministry of Information
during the Second World War. He has perhaps a better claim than
Ezra Pound – see Mr Eliot's introduction to Pound's* Selected
Poems *– to be regarded as 'the inventor of Chinese poetry for our
time'. His publications cover more than forty years and include
translations of Chinese poetry, biographies of the Chinese poets Li
Po and Po Chü-i, and an introduction to the study of Chinese paint-
ing. He has also performed distinguished services for Japanese
literature with* The Nō Plays of Japan, The Tale of Genji, *etc.*

His most recent book is the interesting The Opium War Through Chinese Eyes (*1958*).

The reader is referred to 170 Chinese Poems (*1918*) *for a valuable introduction to Chinese poetry and a note on the method of translation adopted. From this note I extract the following:*

> *I have aimed at literal translation, not paraphrase. It may be perfectly legitimate for a poet to borrow foreign themes or material, but this should not be called translation.*
>
> *Above all, considering imagery to be the soul of poetry, I have avoided either adding images of my own or suppressing those of the original.*
>
> *Any literal translation of Chinese poetry is bound to be to some extent rhythmical, for the rhythm of the original obtrudes itself. Translating literally, without thinking of the metre of the version, one finds that about two lines out of three have a very definite swing similar to that of the Chinese lines. The remaining lines are just too short or too long, a circumstance very irritating to the reader, whose ear expects the rhythm to continue. I have therefore tried to produce rhythmic effects similar to those of the original ... I have not used rhyme ... What is generally known as 'blank verse' is the worst medium for translating Chinese poetry, because the essence of blank verse is that it varies the position of its pauses, whereas in Chinese the stop always comes at the end of the couplet.*

The poems given here are from Chinese Poems (*1946*), *a comprehensive selection from earlier volumes: both are by Po Chü-i, who lived* A.D. *772–846. There is a short biographical notice of the poet in* 170 Chinese Poems, *and Mr Waley's full biography of him,* The Life and Times of Po Chü-i, *appeared in 1949.*

The Chrysanthemums in the Eastern Garden

(Po Chü-i A.D. 812)

The days of my youth left me long ago;
And now in their turn dwindle my years of prime.
With what thoughts of sadness and loneliness
I walk again in this cold, deserted place!
In the midst of the garden long I stand alone;
The sunshine, faint; the wind and dew chill.
The autumn lettuce is tangled and turned to seed;
The fair trees are blighted and withered away.
All that is left are a few chrysanthemum-flowers
That have newly opened beneath the wattled fence.
I had brought wine and meant to fill my cup,
When the sight of these made me stay my hand.
            I remember, when I was young,
How quickly my mood changed from sad to gay.
If I saw wine, no matter at what season,
Before I drank it, my heart was already glad.
                        But now that age comes
A moment of joy is harder and harder to get.
And always I fear that when I am quite old
The strongest liquor will leave me comfortless.
Therefore I ask, you late chrysanthemum-flower,
At this sad season why do you bloom alone?
Though well I know that it was not for my sake,
Taught by you, for a while I will smooth my frown.

A Mad Poem addressed to my Nephews and Nieces

(*Po Chü-i* A.D. 835)

The World cheats those who cannot read;
I, happily, have mastered script and pen.
The World cheats those who hold no office;
I am blessed with high official rank.
Often the old have much sickness and pain;
With me, luckily, there is not much wrong.
People when they are old are often burdened with ties;
But *I* have finished with marriage and giving in marriage.
No changes happen to jar the quiet of my mind;
No business comes to impair the vigour of my limbs.
Hence it is that now for ten years
Body and soul have rested in hermit peace.
And all the more, in the last lingering years
What I shall need are very few things.
A single rug to warm me through the winter;
One meal to last me the whole day.
It does not matter that my house is rather small;
One cannot sleep in more than one room!
It does not matter that I have not many horses;
One cannot ride on two horses at once!
As fortunate as me among the people of the world
Possibly one would find seven out of ten.
As contented as me among a hundred men
Look as you may, you will not find one.
In the affairs of others even fools are wise;
In their own business even sages err.
To no one else would I dare to speak my heart.
So my wild words are addressed to my nephews and nieces.

ISAAC ROSENBERG

Isaac Rosenberg was born in Bristol in 1890. Seven years later his family moved to London where he attended an elementary school until he was fourteen. (He was one of eight children at home.) At this age he was apprenticed to an engraver and took evening classes in art at Birkbeck College. Although he began writing poetry as a boy, he wanted to make painting his career and in 1911 he was able to enter the Slade School. In 1912 he published Night and Day, *the first of three pamphlets of poems, but neither these nor his paintings brought him any material success. He went to South Africa in 1914 in the hope of curing a weakness in his lungs, but he returned to England in the following year, enlisted in the army, and was killed in action in April 1918. Gordon Bottomley edited his* Collected Poems *(1922) – this book contains a memoir by Laurence Binyon. The* Collected Works *(poetry, letters, prose pieces) were published in 1937. The editors were Gordon Bottomley and Denys Harding, and there is a foreword by Siegfried Sassoon.* Collected Poems *was reprinted in 1949.*

'God Made Blind' is one of Rosenberg's earlier pieces and is printed in preference to the better-known war poems such as the much-anthologized 'Break of Day in the Trenches'. It shows the effect of an enthusiastic reading of Donne. Rosenberg's poems display an ability to conceive an idea in poetic terms and render it rhythmically, but they are often spoilt for me by his appetite for the extravagant and his unpleasing poetic diction. Perhaps I do not make sufficient allowance for the difficulties that Rosenberg had to face at the time. 'He modelled words with fierce energy and aspiration,' says Sassoon; and again, 'his poetic visions are mostly in sombre colours and looming sculptural masses, molten and amply wrought'. Some critics have looked on him as a poet with promise of greatness – a view I cannot wholeheartedly share (though I have more sympathy with it than I once had); most critics are agreed that few of his actual poems are completely realized.

God Made Blind

It were a proud God-guiling, to allure
And flatter, by some cheat of ill, our Fate
To hold back the perfect crookedness its hate
Devised, and keep it poor,
And ignorant of our joy –
Masked in a giant wrong of cruel annoy,
That stands as some bleak hut to frost and night,
While hidden in bed is warmth and mad delight.

For all Love's heady valour and loved pain
Towers in our sinews that may not suppress
(Shut to God's eye) Love's springing eagerness,
And mind to advance his gain
Of gleeful secrecy
Through dolorous clay, which his eternity
Has pierced, in light that pushes out to meet
Eternity without us, heaven's heat.

And then, when Love's power hath increased so
That we must burst or grow to give it room,
And we can no more cheat our God with gloom,
We'll cheat Him with our joy.
For say! what can God do
To us, to Love, whom we have grown into?
Love! the poured rays of God's Eternity!
We are grown God – and shall His self-hate be?

HERBERT READ

*Herbert Read was born in Yorkshire in 1893, the son of a farmer,
and was studying at Leeds University when the First World War
began. He served as an infantry officer in France and Belgium and
was awarded the D.S.O. and M.C. After the war he held various
posts in the Civil Service, including a ten-year period in the Victoria
and Albert Museum, South Kensington, where he specialized in
ceramics and stained glass, before becoming Watson Gordon Pro-
fessor of Fine Art at Edinburgh University. From 1933 to 1939 he
was editor of* The Burlington Magazine, *and in 1937 he became a
director of the joint publishing firms of Kegan Paul and George
Routledge. He has been Clark Lecturer at Cambridge and Sydney
Jones Lecturer in Art at Liverpool University; and he holds an
Honorary D.Litt. of Leeds University. He is also an Hon. Fellow
of the Society of Industrial Artists. He was knighted in 1953.*

Herbert Read is a very prolific writer and apart from fiction
(The Green Child) *and autobiography* (Annals of Innocence and
Experience) *has written on aesthetics, literature, the history of art,
education, politics, and sociology. Some idea of his varied interests
and the intelligence he brings to bear on them can be obtained by
looking at* Herbert Read: an Introduction to his Work by
Various Hands, *edited by Henry Treece, or by turning the pages of
such collections of essays, lectures, and reviews as* The Politics of
the Unpolitical (1943) *or* A Coat of Many Colours (1945).
Among his best books on literature in my opinion are English
Prose Style (1928), Wordsworth (1930), Poetry and Anarchism
(1938), *and* The True Voice of Feeling (1953). *The last of these
makes clear his ideas about poetry. He is a pioneer in the field of
industrial art, and his* Meaning of Art (1931), Art Now (1933),
Art and Society (1936), *and* Education Through Art (1943)
*have done something to make the educable public less Philistine
about the visual arts.*

Collected Poems (1946, *second edition* 1953) *supersedes all*

previous volumes and has been followed by a new book of poems,
Moon's Farm (*1955*).

To a Conscript of 1940

Qui n'a pas une fois désespéré de l'honneur, ne sera jamais un héros.
Georges Bernanos

A soldier passed me in the freshly fallen snow,
His footsteps muffled, his face unearthly grey;
And my heart gave a sudden leap
As I gazed on a ghost of five-and-twenty years ago.

I shouted Halt! and my voice had the old accustom'd ring
And he obeyed it as it was obeyed
In the shrouded days when I too was one
Of an army of young men marching

Into the unknown. He turned towards me and I said:
'I am one of those who went before you
Five-and-twenty years ago: one of the many who never
    returned,
Of the many who returned and yet were dead.

We went where you are going, into the rain and the mud;
We fought as you will fight
With death and darkness and despair;
We gave what you will give – our brains and our blood.

We think we gave in vain. The world was not renewed.
There was hope in the homestead and anger in the streets,
But the old world was restored and we returned
To the dreary field and workshop, and the immemorial feud

Of rich and poor. Our victory was our defeat.
Power was retained where power had been misused
And youth was left to sweep away
The ashes that the fires had strewn beneath our feet.

But one thing we learned: there is no glory in the dead
Until the soldier wears a badge of tarnish'd braid;
There are heroes who have heard the rally and have seen
The glitter of a garland round their head.

Theirs is the hollow victory. They are deceived.
But you, my brother and my ghost, if you can go
Knowing that there is no reward, no certain use
In all your sacrifice, then honour is reprieved.

To fight without hope is to fight with grace,
The self reconstructed, the false heart repaired.'
Then I turned with a smile, and he answered my salute
As he stood against the fretted hedge, which was like white lace.

WILFRED OWEN

Wilfred Owen was born at Plas Wilmot, Oswestry, in 1893 and educated at the Birkenhead Institute and the University of London. He began writing verse in 1910 and was encouraged by the friendship of the French poet, Laurent Tailhade, whom he met when he went to Bordeaux after an illness to become a tutor. In 1915 he enlisted in the Artists' Rifles and was gazetted to the Manchester Regiment. After the Somme battles in 1917 he was invalided home and was sent to the Craiglockhart War Hospital, where he was happy, composing poetry, lecturing and making friends (see notice of Sassoon above). He returned to his regiment in 1918, and, after being awarded the M.C., was killed by machine-gun fire at the

*crossing of the Sambre Canal on 4 November 1918. His poems
were collected by Siegfried Sassoon and published in 1920. The
much fuller* The Poems of Wilfred Owen *(1933) was edited with
a memoir and notes by Edmund Blunden. A complete edition of
Owen's poems (including juvenilia) and an edition of the letters
are badly needed. Meanwhile we have to make do with D. S. R.
Welland's useful but too brief* Wilfred Owen: a Critical Study
(1960).

*Wilfred Owen was the most important of the 'war-poets' of the
First World War and his poetic endowment as revealed in his pub-
lished work allows us to think of him as potentially a great poet. He
certainly had the intelligence and the artistic integrity, and he was
able to experiment vitally in technical matters – he was, says Blun-
den, 'an unwearied worker in the laboratory of word, rhythm, and
music of language'. His discovery of the para-rhyme – and use of
it in the war-poems to create 'remoteness, darkness, emptiness,
shock' – was an invention of an important order, and its subsequent
too indiscriminate use by poets of the thirties should not blind us to
this fact. (But see Auden's* Poems 1930, *III, for an intelligent
employment of para-rhyme.) The peculiar power of Owen's poetry
seems to me to spring from the sudden maturity forced by war
experience on a naturally rich, Keatsian sensibility. 'My senses are
charred,' he wrote, 'I don't take the cigarette out of my mouth when
I write Deceased over their letters.' The final comment on his poems
ought to be his own. He had been planning a book of poems just be-
fore he was killed, and rough drafts of a Preface and Contents found
among his papers are given in Blunden's sensitive memoir. The fol-
lowing is from the Preface:*

> *This book is not about heroes. English Poetry is not yet fit
> to speak of them.*
> *Nor is it about deeds, or lands, nor anything about glory,
> honour, might, majesty, dominion, or power, except War.*
> *Above all I am not concerned with Poetry.*
> *My subject is War, and the pity of War.*
> *The Poetry is in the pity.*
> *Yet these elegies are to this generation in no sense consola-*

tory. They may be to the next. All a poet can do today is warn. That is why the true Poets must be truthful.

'*Strange Meeting*', *given here, is often spoken of as Wilfred Owen's masterpiece, but I find '*Insensibility*' the most satisfying of his poems.*

Exposure

Our brains ache, in the merciless iced east winds that knive us ...
Wearied we keep awake because the night is silent ...
Low, drooping flares confuse our memory of the salient ...
Worried by silence, sentries whisper, curious, nervous,
        But nothing happens.

Watching, we hear the mad gusts tugging on the wire,
Like twitching agonies of men among its brambles.
Northward, incessantly, the flickering gunnery rumbles,
Far off, like a dull rumour of some other war.
        What are we doing here?

The poignant misery of dawn begins to grow ...
We only know war lasts, rain soaks, and clouds sag stormy.
Dawn massing in the east her melancholy army
Attacks once more in ranks on shivering ranks of gray,
        But nothing happens.

Sudden successive flights of bullets streak the silence.
Less deadly than the air that shudders black with snow,
With sidelong flowing flakes that flock, pause, and renew,
We watch them wandering up and down the wind's nonchalance,
        But nothing happens.

Pale flakes with fingering stealth come feeling for our faces –
We cringe in holes, back on forgotten dreams, and stare, snow-
    dazed,
Deep into grassier ditches. So we drowse, sun-dozed,
Littered with blossoms trickling where the blackbird fusses.
           Is it that we are dying?

Slowly our ghosts drag home: glimpsing the sunk fires, glozed
With crusted dark-red jewels; crickets jingle there;
For hours the innocent mice rejoice: the house is theirs;
Shutters and doors, all closed: on us the doors are closed, –
           We turn back to our dying.

Since we believe not otherwise can kind fires burn;
Nor ever suns smile true on child, or field, or fruit.
For God's invincible spring our love is made afraid;
Therefore, not loath, we lie out here; therefore were born,
           For love of God seems dying.

Tonight, His frost will fasten on this mud and us,
Shrivelling many hands, puckering foreheads crisp.
The burying-party, picks and shovels in their shaking grasp,
Pause over half-known faces. All their eyes are ice,
           But nothing happens.

Insensibility

I

Happy are men who yet before they are killed
Can let their veins run cold.
Whom no compassion fleers
Or makes their feet
Sore on the alleys cobbled with their brothers.
The front line withers,

But they are troops who fade, not flowers
For poets' tearful fooling:
Men, gaps for filling:
Losses who might have fought
Longer; but no one bothers.

II

And some cease feeling
Even themselves or for themselves.
Dullness best solves
The tease and doubt of shelling,
And Chance's strange arithmetic
Comes simpler than the reckoning of their shilling.
They keep no check on armies' decimation.

III

Happy are these who lose imagination:
They have enough to carry with ammunition.
Their spirit drags no pack,
Their old wounds save with cold can not more ache.
Having seen all things red,
Their eyes are rid
Of the hurt of the colour of blood for ever.
And terror's first constriction over,
Their hearts remain small-drawn.
Their senses in some scorching cautery of battle
Now long since ironed,
Can laugh among the dying, unconcerned.

IV

Happy the soldier home, with not a notion
How somewhere, every dawn, some men attack,
And many sighs are drained.
Happy the lad whose mind was never trained:
His days are worth forgetting more than not.

He sings along the march
Which we march taciturn, because of dusk,
The long, forlorn, relentless trend
From larger day to huger night.

V

We wise, who with a thought besmirch
Blood over all our soul,
How should we see our task
But through his blunt and lashless eyes?
Alive, he is not vital overmuch;
Dying, not mortal overmuch;
Nor sad, nor proud,
Nor curious at all.
He cannot tell
Old men's placidity from his.

VI

But cursed are dullards whom no cannon stuns,
That they should be as stones;
Wretched are they, and mean
With paucity that never was simplicity.
By choice they made themselves immune
To pity and whatever moans in man
Before the last sea and the hapless stars;
Whatever mourns when many leave these shores;
Whatever shares
The eternal reciprocity of tears.

Strange Meeting

It seemed that out of battle I escaped
Down some profound dull tunnel, long since scooped
Through granites which titanic wars had groined.

Yet also there encumbered sleepers groaned,
Too fast in thought or death to be bestirred.
Then, as I probed them, one sprang up, and stared
With piteous recognition in fixed eyes,
Lifting distressful hands as if to bless.
And by his smile, I knew that sullen hall,
By his dead smile I knew we stood in Hell.
With a thousand pains that vision's face was grained;
Yet no blood reached there from the upper ground,
And no guns thumped, or down the flues made moan.
'Strange friend,' I said, 'here is no cause to mourn.'
'None,' said the other, 'save the undone years,
The hopelessness. Whatever hope is yours,
Was my life also; I went hunting wild
After the wildest beauty in the world,
Which lies not calm in eyes, or braided hair,
But mocks the steady running of the hour,
And if it grieves, grieves richlier than here.
For by my glee might many men have laughed,
And of my weeping something had been left,
Which must die now. I mean the truth untold,
The pity of war, the pity war distilled.
Now men will go content with what we spoiled.
Or, discontent, boil bloody, and be spilled.
They will be swift with swiftness of the tigress,
None will break ranks, though nations trek from progress.
Courage was mine, and I had mystery,
Wisdom was mine, and I had mastery;
To miss the march of this retreating world
Into vain citadels that are not walled.
Then, when much blood had clogged their chariot-wheels
I would go up and wash them from sweet wells,
Even with truths that lie too deep for taint.
I would have poured my spirit without stint
But not through wounds; not on the cess of war.
Foreheads of men have bled where no wounds were.
I am the enemy you killed, my friend.

I knew you in this dark; for so you frowned
Yesterday through me as you jabbed and killed.
I parried; but my hands were loath and cold.
Let us sleep now ...'

ALDOUS HUXLEY

Aldous Huxley was born in 1894, the third son of Leonard Huxley and grandson of the Victorian scientist. He was educated at Eton and Balliol College, Oxford – the process being interrupted by disease of the eyes – and then worked in London for some years as a journalist and dramatic critic. From that time onwards he devoted himself entirely to writing, living first on the Continent and then in California (where he moved in the thirties). He published nearly fifty books: novels, poems, plays, travel, biography, and philosophy. A standard collected edition is now being issued. He died in 1963.

Aldous Huxley was an extraordinarily well-read, amiable, intelligent and – up to a point – psychologically perceptive commentator on books, ideas, and people, but it is a question whether he ever wrote a good novel, and there is no question at all about his rank as a poet: he is not a poet, but a writer of verses – and the best of these are the lightest and most frivolous. The title-poem of Leda *(1920) is now painful to read. The two songs here given are from this volume and are good examples of nose-thumbing undergraduate wit. They are included because they seem to me to tell us something about one side of the twenties, and because they furnish a piquant, if ribald, comment on the Mr Huxley of* The Perennial Philosophy *(1946).*

Second Philosopher's Song

If, O my Lesbia, I should commit,
Not fornication, dear, but suicide,
My Thames-blown body (Pliny vouches it)
Would drift face upwards on the oily tide
With the other garbage, till it putrefied.

But you; if all your lovers' frozen hearts
Conspired to send you, desperate, to drown –
Your maiden modesty would float face down,
And men would weep upon your hinder parts.

'Tis the Lord's doing. Marvellous is the plan
By which this best of worlds is wisely planned.
One law he made for woman, one for man:
We bow the head and do not understand.

Fifth Philosopher's Song

A million million spermatozoa,
    All of them alive:
Out of their cataclysm but one poor Noah
    Dare hope to survive.

And among that billion minus one
    Might have chanced to be
Shakespeare, another Newton, a new Donne –
    But the One was Me.

Shame to have ousted your betters thus,
    Taking ark while the others remained outside!
Better for all of us, froward Homunculus,
    If you'd quietly died!

ROBERT GRAVES

Robert Graves was born in London in 1895 of mixed 'Irish-Scottish-Danish-German' parentage. He was educated at Charter-house and St John's College, Oxford. During the First World War he served with the Royal Welch Fusiliers in France and was offi-cially reported 'Died of Wounds' on his twenty-first birthday. He survived to read English at Oxford and to become (for one year) Professor of English Literature at Cairo on the recommendation of T. E. Lawrence. Goodbye to All That *(1929, new edition 1958) is an autobiographical account of this phase of his life: it is an excep-tionally truthful, interesting, and well-written book. Since that time Graves has lived by writing.*

During the thirties he worked in Majorca where (in association with Laura Riding) he ran the Seizin Press, publishing a number of books and the critical miscellany Epilogue. *He came back to England during the Spanish Civil War and lived in this country (except for short periods in France and America) until 1947 when he returned to settle in Majorca. This is his permanent home from which he makes occasional forays to lecture and broadcast in Eng-land and America. In February 1961 he was elected Professor of Poetry at Oxford in succession to W. H. Auden.*

Mr Graves is probably best known by the ordinary reading pub-lic for his 'historical' novels: I, Claudius *(1934), for which he was awarded the Hawthornden Prize and the James Tait Black Prize, and its sequel* Claudius the God *(1934);* Count Belisarius *(1938);* Wife to Mr Milton *(1943);* The Golden Fleece *(1944);* King Jesus *(1946);* Homer's Daughter *(1955); and* They Hanged My Saintly Billy *(1957). But he has also published a good deal of criticism, including the admirable* On English Poetry *(1922),* The Common Asphodel *(1949), a collection of essays, and* The Crowning Privilege *(1955, reprinted in Penguin Books 1959), which includes his Clark Lectures for 1954–5 at Cam-bridge.* The White Goddess *(1948, revised edition 1952), sub-*

*titled 'an historical grammar of poetic myth', will madden the con-
ventional for its 'mélange adultère de tout' and its unflinching in-
sight into the nature of poetic experience. Another product of this
group of interests is* Greek Myths *(1955, Penguin Books). Martin
Seymour-Smith's essay (1956) in the British Council ' Writers and
Their Work' series contains a brief discussion of* The White
Goddess.

*Mr Graves's other prose works are too many and too miscel-
laneous to enumerate and characterize – there is a useful check-list
to 1955 in Mr Seymour-Smith's pamphlet – but I must not omit
to mention* But It Still Goes On *(1930), which contains 'The
Shout' – one of the best short stories ever written;* The Reader Over
Your Shoulder *(1943), a handbook for writers of English prose (in
collaboration with Alan Hodge);* Seven Days in New Crete
(1949), a novel; and The Nazarene Gospel Restored *(1953, in
collaboration with Joshua Pedro), which Mr Eliot refused for
Faber's because it was not 'more drily written'.*

*The bibliography of the poems is sure to provide headaches for
future scholars.* Collected Poems *(1938) draws on nineteen earlier
volumes, but omits a great deal of good work – 'whatever I felt mis-
represented my poetic seriousness at the time when it was written.'
This collection has a foreword in which the poet describes his own
poetic development: 'I should say that my health as a poet lies in my
mistrust of the comfortable point-of-rest.'* Work in Hand *(1942),
with Alan Hodge and Norman Cameron, and* Poems 1938–45
(1945) lead on to Collected Poems *(1948), which was followed by*
Poems and Satires *(1951) and* Poems *(1953). The* Crowning
Privilege *(1955) and* Steps *(1958) also contain new poems. The
reigning* Collected Poems *is dated 1959. In the same year ap-
peared* The Anger of Achilles, *a translation of the* Iliad, *and
in 1960* The Penny Fiddle, *an admirable book of poems for
children.*

*The poetry of Robert Graves is in some ways the purest poetry
produced in our time, waving no flags, addressed to no congrega-
tions, designed neither to comfort nor to persuade. It is poetry with
roots in everyday experience, but it always has the quality of making
that experience new, pungent, and exciting. (In this respect it is*

rather like being in Mr Graves's company – the conversation is excellent and odd things happen.) Of the poems included in this anthology 'Welsh Incident' is the lightest. I choose it because it is very funny and written with great skill. (I wish I had had room for | Wellcome, to the Caves of Artá!' as another specimen of light verse: it is composed with immense virtuosity in the language of a Spanish leaflet for tourists.) 'Lollocks' is a small, perfectly acceptable example of myth-making. 'Never Such Love' and 'The Thieves' are love poems of a sort too truthful for the many to admire without misgiving. (To say that they stand with the later Yeats will not please Mr Graves, who is unaccountably silly about Yeats in his Clark Lectures.) 'Warning to Children' and 'To Evoke Posterity' seem to me to be among Graves's finest poems. A paragraph in the foreword to Poems and Satires *(1951) has a general interest and provides a gloss on the second of these poems.*

> *Personally, I have little regard for posterity ... Whatever view they may take of my work ... must necessarily be a mistaken one, because this is my age, not theirs, and even with my help they will never understand it. I write for my contemporaries.*

There is very little critical writing on Graves by his contemporaries, and even less that is worth reading. Mr Seymour-Smith's pamphlet has already been noted. J. M. Cohen's short Robert Graves *(1960) in the 'Writers and Critics' series is the first book to be devoted to the poetry.*

Warning to Children

Children, if you dare to think
Of the greatness, rareness, muchness,
Fewness of this precious only
Endless world in which you say
You live, you think of things like this:
Blocks of slate enclosing dappled
Red and green, enclosing tawny

Yellow nets, enclosing white
And black acres of dominoes,
Where a neat brown paper parcel
Tempts you to untie the string.
In the parcel a small island,
On the island a large tree,
On the tree a husky fruit.
Strip the husk and pare the rind off:
In the kernel you will see
Blocks of slate enclosed by dappled
Red and green, enclosed by tawny
Yellow nets, enclosed by white
And black acres of dominoes,
Where the same brown paper parcel –
Children, leave the string alone!
For who dares undo the parcel
Finds himself at once inside it,
On the island, in the fruit,
Blocks of slate about his head,
Finds himself enclosed by dappled
Green and red, enclosed by yellow
Tawny nets, enclosed by black
And white acres of dominoes,
With the same brown paper parcel
Still untied upon his knee.
And, if he then should dare to think
Of the fewness, muchness, rareness,
Greatness of this endless only
Precious world in which he says
He lives – he then unties the string.

Welsh Incident

'But that was nothing to what things came out
From the sea-caves of Criccieth yonder.'
'What were they? Mermaids? dragons? ghosts?'

'Nothing at all of any things like that.'
'What were they, then?'
                              'All sorts of queer things,
Things never seen or heard or written about,
Very strange, un-Welsh, utterly peculiar
Things. Oh, solid enough they seemed to touch,
Had anyone dared it. Marvellous creation,
All various shapes and sizes, and no sizes,
All new, each perfectly unlike his neighbour,
Though all came moving slowly out together.'
'Describe just one of them.'
                              'I am unable.'
'What were their colours?'
                              'Mostly nameless colours,
Colours you'd like to see; but one was puce
Or perhaps more like crimson, but not purplish.
Some had no colour.'
                              'Tell me, had they legs?'
'Not a leg or foot among them that I saw.'
'But did these things come out in any order?
What o'clock was it? What was the day of the week?
Who else was present? How was the weather?'
'I was coming to that. It was half-past three
On Easter Tuesday last. The sun was shining.
The Harlech Silver Band played *Marchog Jesu*
On thirty-seven shimmering instruments,
Collecting for Caernarvon's (Fever) Hospital Fund.
The populations of Pwllheli, Criccieth,
Portmadoc, Borth, Tremadoc, Penrhyndeudraeth,
Were all assembled. Criccieth's mayor addressed them
First in good Welsh and then in fluent English,
Twisting his fingers in his chain of office,
Welcoming the things. They came out on the sand,
Not keeping time to the band, moving seaward
Silently at a snail's pace. But at last
The most odd, indescribable thing of all
Which hardly one man there could see for wonder

Did something recognizably a something.'
'Well, what?'
         'It made a noise.'
                 'A frightening noise?'
'No, no.'
      'A musical noise? A noise of scuffling?'
'No, but a very loud, respectable noise –
Like groaning to oneself on Sunday morning
In Chapel, close before the second psalm.'
'What did the mayor do?'
                 'I was coming to that.'

Never Such Love

   Twined together and, as is customary,
   For words of rapture groping, they
   'Never such love,' swore, 'ever before was!'
   Contrast with all loves that had failed or staled
   Registered their own as love indeed.

   And was this not to blab idly
   The heart's fated inconstancy?
   Better in love to seal the love-sure lips,
   For truly love was before words were,
   And no word given, no word broken.

   When the name 'love' is uttered
   (Love, the near-honourable malady
   With which in greed and haste they
   Each other do infect and curse)
   Or, worse, is written down ...

Wise after the event, by love withered,
A 'never more!' most frantically
Sorrow and shame would proclaim
Such as, they'd swear, never before were:
True lovers even in this.

Lollocks

By sloth on sorrow fathered,
These dusty-featured Lollocks
Have their nativity in all disordered
Backs of cupboard drawers.

They play hide and seek
Among collars and novels
And empty medicine bottles,
And letters from abroad
That never will be answered.

Every sultry night
They plague little children,
Gurgling from the cistern,
Humming from the air,
Skewing up the bed-clothes,
Twitching the blind.

When the imbecile agèd
Are over-long in dying
And the nurse drowses,
Lollocks come skipping
Up the tattered stairs
And are nasty together
In the bed's shadow.

The signs of their presence
Are boils on the neck,
Dreams of vexation suddenly recalled
In the middle of the morning,
Languor after food.

Men cannot see them,
Men cannot hear them,
Do not believe in them –
But suffer the more,
Both in neck and belly.

Women can see them –
O those naughty wives
Who sit by the fireside
Munching bread and honey,
Watching them in mischief
From corners of their eyes,
Slily allowing them to lick
Honey-sticky fingers.

Sovereign against Lollocks,
Are hard broom and soft broom,
To well comb the hair,
To well brush the shoe,
And to pay every debt
As it falls due.

The Thieves

Lovers in the act dispense
With such meum-tuum sense
As might warningly reveal
What they must not pick or steal,
And their nostrum is to say:
'I and you are both away.'

After when they disentwine
You from me and yours from mine,
Neither can be certain who
Was that I whose mine was you.
To the act again they go
More completely not to know.

Theft is theft and raid is raid
Though reciprocally made.
Lovers, the conclusion is
Doubled sighs and jealousies
In a single heart that grieves
For lost honour among thieves.

To Evoke Posterity

To evoke posterity
Is to weep on your own grave,
Ventriloquizing for the unborn:
'Would you were present in flesh, hero,
What wreaths and junketings!'

And the punishment is known:
To be found fully ancestral,
To be cast in bronze for a city square,
To dribble green in times of rain
And stain the pedestal.

Spiders in the spread beard;
A life proverbial
On clergy lips a-cackle;
Eponymous institutes,
Their luckless architecture.

Two more dates of life and birth
For the hour of special study
From which all boys and girls of mettle
Twice a week play truant
And worn excuses try.

Alive, you have abhorred
The crowds on holiday
Jostling and whistling – yet would you air
Your death-mask, smoothly lidded,
Along the promenade?

EDMUND BLUNDEN

Edmund Blunden wrote to me in 1948:

I was born in 1896, educated at Christ's Hospital and published my first little books there, served with the Royal Sussex Regiment from 1915 to 1919' [he was awarded the M.C.] *and after a few terms at Oxford became a miscellaneous writer. In Japan, where I taught English Literature at Tokyo University from 1924 to 1927, I wrote* Undertones of War, *which may be my best production. From 1931 to 1944 I was Fellow of Merton College, Oxford, and sometime Sub-Warden. My last book of poems was* Shells by a Stream *(1944). I am at the moment in Japan again, appointed a member of the U.K. Liaison Mission; lecturing to many universities and schools.*

This modest and concise account omits the awards of the Hawthornden Prize in 1922 and of the Benson Medal of the Royal Society of Literature in 1930, and does not mention Mr Blunden's biographical studies of Leigh Hunt, Charles Lamb, John Taylor (the publisher of Keats), and Shelley. In 1948 Mr Blunden moved to Hongkong to become Professor of English at the univer-

sity. In February 1966 he was elected Professor of Poetry at Oxford in succession to Robert Graves. Poems 1914–1930 (1930), Poems 1930–1940 (1940), Shells by a Stream (1944), After the Bombing (1949), and Poems of Many Years (1957) span his poetic production, each of the two earlier collected editions containing the substance of several earlier volumes.

Mr Blunden has been lumped with the Georgians, but one has to observe how the attempt to 'compose' a pastoral world – sometimes even by echoes and imitations of Augustan pastoralists and by seeing landscapes not directly but through an artist's eyes – and the exquisite delicacy and formality of movement in many poems imply a criticism of a merely naïve direct approach to the writing of nature-poetry: and to notice how this separates him from the usual Georgian poet (see the poet's remarks on this matter in the Poetry Book Society Bulletin, No. 14). I particularly appreciate in Blunden the niceness of the observation – sometimes it is finical – and the subtle way human unease is hinted at in much verse which at first sight would appear to be purely descriptive. 'October Comes', with its haunting ominous lightness of rhythm and its near-archaisms in diction, illustrates some of these points well. This poem is from Shells by a Stream. 'The Pike' and the fine 'The Midnight Skaters' are from Poems 1914–1930.

The Pike

From shadows of rich oaks outpeer
The moss-green bastions of the weir,
Where the quick dipper forages
In elver-peopled crevices,
And a small runlet trickling down the sluice
Gossamer music tires not to unloose.

Else round the broad pool's hush
Nothing stirs,
Unless sometimes a straggling heifer crush
Through the thronged spinney where the pheasant whirs;

Or martins in a flash
Come with wild mirth to dip their magical wings,
While in the shallow some doomed bulrush swings
At whose hid root the diver vole's teeth gnash.

And nigh this toppling reed, still as the dead
        The great pike lies, the murderous patriarch
        Watching the waterpit sheer-shelving dark,
Where through the plash his lithe bright vassals thread.

        The rose-finned roach and bluish bream
        And staring ruffe steal up the stream
        Hard by their glutted tyrant, now
        Still as a sunken bough.

        He on the sandbank lies,
            Sunning himself long hours
        With stony gorgon eyes:
            Westward the hot sun lowers.

Sudden the gray pike changes, and quivering poises for
    slaughter;
        Intense terror wakens around him, the shoals scud
            awry, but there chances
        A chub unsuspecting; the prowling fins quicken, in
            fury he lances;
And the miller that opens the hatch stands amazed at the whirl
    in the water.

The Midnight Skaters

        The hop-poles stand in cones,
            The icy pond lurks under,
        The pole-tops steeple to the thrones
            Of stars, sound gulfs of wonder;

But not the tallest there, 'tis said,
Could fathom to this pond's black bed.

Then is not death at watch
    Within those secret waters?
What wants he but to catch
    Earth's heedless sons and daughters?
With but a crystal parapet
Between, he has his engines set.

Then on, blood shouts, on, on,
    Twirl, wheel and whip above him,
Dance on this ball-floor thin and wan,
    Use him as though you love him;
Court him, elude him, reel and pass,
And let him hate you through the glass.

October Comes

I heard the graybird bathing in the rill,
And fluttering his wings dry within thorn boughs
Which all embowered the rill; with tiny bill
The robin on red-berried spray bade rouse
        One whom I could not see, a field away;
        I heard the passing girl to her young man say,
'O look, there's a buttercup'; for Autumn brought them still.

Upon my hand the fly so small that sight
Hardly could shape him settled, quested, flew;
Above me crowns of cloud and thrones of light
Moved with the minutes, and the season's blue,
        Autumn's soft raiment, veiled some forms of dream
        Which I yet reverence; once more to my stream
The clear forget-me-not drew my eyes; the vole watched too.

He watched, and ate his chosen leaf; well-furred,
Well-fed he felt for water, winter, all.
Whoever else came by, midge, moth or bird,
The time was easy, nor did one leaf fall
    From willow or elm that hour, though millions
      glowed
    With such wild flame as evening shot abroad
To warn that even this calm was not perpetual.

SACHEVERELL SITWELL

*Sacheverell Sitwell, younger brother of Osbert and Edith Sitwell,
was born at Scarborough in 1897, and educated at Eton and Balliol
College, Oxford. He has published a biography of Liszt, studies of
Mozart and of baroque art — of these* Southern Baroque Art
*(1924) is often held to be the best — as well as much imaginative
miscellaneous prose typified by such a book as* Primitive Scenes and
Festivals *(1943). He has also written many volumes of poetry and
a piece of semi-autobiographical fiction,* All Summer in a Day
(1926). Among the collections of verse are Doctor Donne and
Gargantua *(1930),* Canons of Giant Art *(1933), and* Dance of
the Quick and the Dead *(1936). A useful volume of* Selected
Poems, *with a preface by Osbert Sitwell, was issued in 1948.*

*Selected Poems reveals the completeness of the poet's creation
of a lyrical 'aesthetic' world in which he is at home, and his per-
petual concern for the kind of craftsmanship needed to release his
imaginative vision.*

*The following two contrasted passages of description and reflec-
tion are taken from* Canons of Giant Art, *which is, I think, his best
collection of poetry.*

From *Upon an Image from Dante*

Clouds touched the church-towers
The streets were spray
A hundred feet in the air and all the world was waste
A hundred feet to sea and there was nothing living
Nothing but waves and the cauldron of the rocks:
So near the edge
In warm rooms and in the lamp-lit streets,
With a cab-horse trotting past the stuccoed houses
And the gale at the corner, that November night:
In the month of thunder, in the noise of timber
I was born in November by the stormy sea,
So near death to be born into the living,
Nearer than the rich man to the millions starving.

And the winter went, and many other winters,
And we walked by the sea's edge to Cornelian bay,
By a shore of wreckage, of the sundered timbers,
Finding dark jet and the wonders of the ammonite:
All there was of men was the smoke above their houses
Below the green baize cliff, up to the ruined castle,
Giving on the harbour, on the masted shipping.
So was all their coast, so Whitby and beyond,
A land of little harbours, little stilt-like houses
Standing in the tides;
Sometimes a doorway of the jawbones of a whale,
A netted anchor, or the figure from a ship,
Dredged from the seas, stood in a white-washed yard
For spoil from the shoals, from shimmer of the mackerel:
And the year went in wonders, the great spring-tide
Ebbed with the moon, in an electric morning
When air sparkled and flashed, when all the world was new;
That tide left the harbour dry; the keel-less ships
Leaned to one side, toppling on the sand;
It ebbed at another shore, far down the sea,

Laid bare for this, refulgent with new light
On rocks, not seen before, new islands in the plain
Glittering with pools, the little fronded seas
Where waved green weeds or dried their greener tresses
On mermaid rocks and crackled in their pods,
Instinct with iodine. The archipelago
Glistened, all shining, new-risen from the sea:
The salt airs out upon those frontiers
Were the breath of Creation till the spring-tide flowed
When the isles sank and vanished, and the leaning vessels
Righted their keels: the high tide, towering,
Took new sands and piled against the piers
Swollen in fury, as in a race of waters,
All, all for nothing, for one morning of the spring.

From *Agamemnon's Tomb*

The poor are fast forgotten,
They outnumber the living, but where are all their bones?
For every man alive there are a million dead,
Has their dust gone into earth that it is never seen?
There should be no air to breathe, with it so thick,
No space for wind to blow, nor rain to fall;
Earth should be a cloud of dust, a soil of bones,
With no room, even, for our skeletons;
It is wasted time to think of it, to count its grains,
When all are alike and there's no difference in them;
They wait in the dark corridors, in earth's black galleries,
But the doors never open; they are dead, dead, dead.
Ah! Seek not the difference in king or beggar:
The King has his gold with him, that will not buy,
It is better to have starved and to be used to it.
Is there no comfort down the long dead years,
No warmth in prison, no love left for dead bones;
Does no one come to kiss them? Answer, none, none, none.

Yet that was their longing, to be held and given,
To be handed to death while held in arms that loved them,
For his greater care, who saw that they were loved
And would take note of it and favour them in prison;
But, instead, he stood more near to them, his chill was in them,
And the living were warm, the last of love was warm;
Oh! One more ray of it, one beam before the winter,
Before they were unborn, beyond the blind, unborn,
More blind and puny, carried back into the dark,
But without rumour, with no fate to come,
Nothing but waiting, waiting long for nothing.

It was too late to weep, this was the last of time,
The light flickered, but tears would dim it more:
It was better to be calm and keep the taste of life;
But a sip or two of life, and then, forever, death.
Oh! The cold, the sinking cold, the falling from the edge
Where love was no help and could not hold one back,
Falling, falling, falling into blackest dark,
Falling while hands touched one, while the lips felt warm,
If one was loved, and was not left alone.

Now it was so little that a babe was more,
No more of self, a little feeble thing
That love could not help,
That none could love for what it was;
It looked, and love saw it, but it could not answer:
Life's mystery was finished, only death was clear,
It was sorry for the living, it was glad to die,
Death was its master, it belonged to death.

O kiss it no more, it is so cold and pale,
It is not of this world, it is no part of us;
Not the soul we loved, but something pitiful
The hands should not touch. Oh! Leave it where it lies;
Let the dead where they die; come out among the living;
Weep not over dead bones; your tears are wasted.

ROY CAMPBELL

Roy Campbell wrote in 1948:

> *I was born in October 1901, and brought up in the Union
> and Southern Rhodesia. I joined the 6th South African In-
> fantry when I was fifteen. I came to Europe in 1919 and have
> made three trips back home since then, two of them being on
> leave during this last war. I have lived most of my adult life
> in Spain, Portugal, and France – mostly in the horse-line. I
> fought in the Spanish War and this last war as a volunteer.
> I volunteered for the British Army on 3 September 1939, but,
> as I was over age and a South African subject, they wouldn't
> accept me till over a year afterwards. I did my Infantry train-
> ing with the Royal Welch Fusiliers and the South Wales
> Borderers at Brecon. I served in East and North Africa and
> ended up as a Sergeant in one of the East African Reception
> Units, a crack fighting unit which went to Burma. I was
> permanently disabled during training, with a broken hip joint,
> and discharged with a life pension after a year in hospital and
> convalescent camps. Being permanently crippled I had to take
> a sedentary job as a clerk. There is no more horse-breaking or
> bull-fighting for me. So I am now almost naturalized a Cock-
> ney of London Town.*

Later he settled in Portugal where he died in a car crash in the
spring of 1957.

Among his publications the following may be noticed: The
Flaming Terrapin (*1924*), The Wayzgoose (*1928*), Adamastor
(*1930*), The Georgiad (*1931*), Flowering Reeds (*1933*),
Mithraic Emblems (*1936*), Talking Bronco (*1940*), St John of
the Cross: Poems (*1952*), *a verse translation.* Broken Record
(*1934*) *is a book of reminiscences. His* Collected Poems *appeared
in two volumes in his lifetime (1949 and 1957), but a supplement-
ary volume of his translations has been issued posthumously.*

'*Poets in Africa*' *and* '*The Palm*' *are both to be found in* Sons of the Mistral (*1941*), *a good selection of Campbell's poems.* '*Poets in Africa*' *is an early poem of which the author says,* '*I very much regret the mood of self-pity in which it was written*', *but I include it as an example of his attractive (if sometimes absurd), aggressive verbal extravagance.* '*The Palm*', *a later piece, moves nicely on its trisyllabic feet.*

Roy Campbell has suffered in appreciation for his championship of Franco during the Spanish Civil War. I think it relevant, therefore, to cite Wyndham Lewis's comment on Campbell's views:

> *Of politics he has none, unless they are such as go with a great antipathy for the English 'gentleman' in all his clubmanesque varieties; a great attachment to the back-Veldt of his native South Africa; and a constant desire to identify himself with the roughest and simplest of his fellow-creatures in pub, farm, and bull-ring.*

Of course this has a disingenuous air coming from '*an old volcano of the Right*', *but the irrational and often unpleasant violence of Campbell's expressions of political opinion is a sort of testimony to a radical innocence.*

Poets in Africa

For grazing innocence a salad
Of lilies in the bud,
For those who dine on words a ballad,
For you and me a name of mud,
A rash of stars upon the sky,
A pox of flowers on the earth –
To such diseases of the eye
Habituated from our birth,

We had no time for make-believe
So early each began
To wear his liver on his sleeve,

To snarl, and be an angry man:
Far in the desert we have been
Where Nature, still to poets kind,
Admits no vegetable green
To soften the determined mind,

But with snarled gold and rumbled blue
Must disinfect the sight
Where once the tender maggots grew
Of faith and beauty and delight.
Each with a blister on his tongue,
Each with a crater in his tooth,
Our nerves are free: we have been stung
By the tarantulas of truth.

Each like a freezing salamander
Impervious and immune,
No snivelling sentiment shall pander
To our flirtations with the moon,
And though with gay batrachian chirrup
Her poets thrill the swampy reach,
Not with so glutinous a syrup
As moonlight shall we grease our speech.

Our cook, the Sun, in craggy kitchens
Amid the howling waste
Has fried the terrible sour lichens
So dainty to a poet's taste,
Which sovereign remedy is ours
Against the earth's infectious scars,
Its annual eczema of flowers
The pullulation of its stars –

Whose itch corrodes the soft medulla
Of kindlier brains than ours
Wherein, attuned to local colour,
Each cheap colonial virtue flowers,

Flits like a moth from bloom to blossom
Or to protective markings trusts,
In shady corners playing possum
To gratify its private lusts.

The fauna of this mental waste,
They cheer our lonely way
And round our doleful footsteps haste
To skip, to gambol, and to play;
The kite of Mercy sails above
With reeking claws and cry that clangs,
The old grey wolf of Brother-Love
Slinks in our track with yellow fangs.

True sons of Africa are we,
Though bastardized with culture,
Indigenous, and wild, and free
As wolf, as pioneer and vulture –
Yea, though for us the vision blearing
No membrane nictitates the light,
Though we are cursed with sense and hearing
And doubly cursed with second sight,

Still doomed that skyward screech to hear
That haunted us in youth,
We shall grow terrible through fear,
We shall grow venomous with truth,
And through these plains where thought meanders
Through sheepish brains in wormy life,
Our lives shall roll like fierce Scamanders
Their red alluvium of strife.

When in the moonlight, red and bloody,
The night has smeared the plain,
We rise from awful nights of study
With coal-red eyes and whirling brain –
Our minds like dark destructive engines

Prepare those catapults and slings
In whose preliminary vengeance
The thunder of the Future sings.

What though we have no walls or bastions
To shield our riddled hearts? —
Arrowed like convicts, twin Sebastians
Each in his uniform of darts,
When in his crimson garb outlandish
The martyr turns a porcupine
Who such fearful spikes can brandish,
Who in more fiendish war-paint shine?

The Palm

Blistered and dry was the desert I trod
When out of the sky with the step of a god,
Victory-vanned, with her feathers out-fanned,
The palm tree alighting my journey delayed
And spread me, inviting, her carpet of shade.
Vain were evasions, though urgent my quest,
And there as the guest of her lovely persuasions
To lie in the shade of her branches was best.
Like a fountain she played, spilling plume over plume in
A golden cascade for the winds to illumine,
Ascending in brilliance and falling in shade,
And spurning the ground with a tiptoe resilience,
Danced to the sound of the music she made.
Her voice intervened on my shadowed seclusion
Like the whispered intrusion of seraph or fiend,
In its tone was the hiss of the serpent's wise tongue
But soft as the kiss of a lover it stung —
'Unstrung is your lute? For despair are you silent?
Am I not an island in oceans as mute?
Around me the thorns of the desert take root;

Though I spring from the rock of a region accurst,
Yet fair is the daughter of hunger and thirst
Who sings like the water the valleys have nursed,
And rings her blue shadow as deep and as cool
As the heavens of azure that sleep on a pool.
And you, who so soon by the toil were undone,
Could you guess through what horrors my beauty had won
Ere I crested the noon as the bride of the sun?
The roots are my anchor struck fast in the hill,
The higher I hanker, the deeper they drill,
Through the red mortar their claws interlock
To ferret the water through warrens of rock.
Each inch of my glory was wrenched with a groan,
Corroded with fire from the base of my throne
And drawn like a wire from the heart of a stone:
Though I soar in the height with a shape of delight
Uplifting my stem like the string of a kite,
Yet still must each grade of my climbing be told,
And still from the summit my measure I hold,
Sounding the azure with plummet of gold,
Partaking the strain of the heavenward pride
That soars me away from the earth I deride,
Though my stem be a rein that would tether me down
And fasten a chain on the height of my crown,
Yet through its tense nerve do I measure my might,
The strain of its curb is the strength of my flight:
And when, by the hate of the hurricane blown,
It doubles its forces with fibres that groan,
Exulting I ride in the tower of my pride
To feel that the strength of the blast is my own ...
Rest under my branches, breathe deep of my balm
From the hushed avalanches of fragrance and calm,
For suave is the silence that poises the palm.
The wings of the egrets are silken and fine,
But hushed with the secrets of Eden are mine:
Your spirit that grieves like the wind in my leaves
Shall be robbed of its care by those whispering thieves

To study my patience and hear, the day long,
The soft foliations of sand into song –
For bitter and cold though it rasp to my root,
Each atom of gold is the chance of a fruit,
The sap is the music, the stem is the flute,
And the leaves are the wings of the seraph I shape
Who dances, who springs in a golden escape,
Out of the dust and the drought of the plain,
To sing with the silver hosannas of rain.'

MICHAEL ROBERTS

Michael Roberts was born at Bournemouth in 1902 and educated at King's College, London, and Trinity College, Cambridge. He was a schoolmaster in Newcastle upon Tyne (except for a break of three years in London) until he joined the B.B.C. European Service as General Intelligence Officer in 1941. His job was the collection of information from enemy-occupied countries. In 1943 he became editor of broadcasts for the clandestine press and contributed articles to underground papers in Belgium, France, Norway, etc. In 1945 he was appointed Principal of the College of St Mark and St John, Chelsea. He died in December 1948.

Michael Roberts was an active propagandist for the new poetry of the thirties. His anthologies New Signatures *(1932) and* New Country *(1933) introduced and explained that poetry when it still seemed queer and difficult, and his* Critique of Poetry *(1934) and* Faber Book of Modern Verse, *which has a long, interesting introduction, attempted respectively to find an aesthetic for the movement and to set it in a perspective of the best modern verse (not forgetting, of course, Hopkins). Roberts also published three books of verse, a study of T. E. Hulme, a monograph on scientific method entitled* Newton and the Origin of Colours, *and other volumes of*

criticism. His Collected Poems (*1958*) *contains some previously unpublished pieces and a memoir by his widow, Janet Roberts.*
  '*The Castle*' *is reprinted from* Orion Marches (*1939*).

The Castle

Words fall, words fail, like rocks, like falling stones;
Out of the towered clouds and the dark air,
Words fail, and a tree of blackness falls:
There is nothing at all to surrender or defend.

It was a grim castle, built in the bad years,
Built by an old man after years of failure,
Stuccoed with long complacency, and now
No more than an empty wineskin or a crushed fruit.

From the dark earth, the tree broke out, and men
Died with a frantic zeal, and spitting death:
Who knows what it was they died for?
Their bones are a fine dust, and their names forgotten.

Suburbs creep up the hill, and the trams are running,
Children find ghostly playmates in the ruins;
The sun glares on the emptiness, and vanished walls
Burn with a bitter death and unfulfilled perfection.

Stamp out the memory of old wars and lost causes:
Build a grave citadel of peace, or a tower of death:
The castle stands, inhuman, incorruptible,
Like a film before the eyes, or a mad vision.

WILLIAM PLOMER

*William Plomer was born at Pietersburg, N. Transvaal, in 1903
and educated at Rugby School. He has been a farmer in the Storm-
berg and a trader in Zululand, and he has also travelled widely,
having lived at various times in Greece and Japan. Between 1940
and 1945 he served at the Admiralty. A long list of books, including
novels, short stories, biography, and poetry, stands to his credit,
and he has edited the delectable* Kilvert's Diary *(1938–40) and a
short selection of Melville's poems (1943).* Double Lives *(1943)
is an autobiography of great subtlety and interest.*

Mr Plomer's poetic output consists of seven volumes: Notes for
Poems *(1928),* The Family Tree *(1929),* The Fivefold Screen
(1932), Visiting the Caves *(1936),* Selected Poems *(1940),* The
Dorking Thigh *(1945), and* A Shot in the Park *(1955). All
these are drawn on for his* Collected Poems *(1960). He has
claimed himself that his 'temperament and abilities are not those of
a whole-time poet', and his real poetic originality, although there
are some pleasant pieces in his 'serious' volumes, is to be found in
his light verse and ballad satires ('That light verse can be serious it
should not be necessary to insist …'). The satirical collections are*
The Dorking Thigh *and* A Shot in the Park. *In a prefatory note
to the earlier of these books, from which 'Father and Son: 1939' and
'A Ticket for the Reading Room' are taken, Mr Plomer writes:*

> *These satires are concerned with points in human experience
> at which the terrifying coincides with the absurd, the monstrous
> with the commonplace. Such points are perhaps commoner in
> our time than usual, for we have seen horror and absurdity on
> an enormous scale … The satires are intended to be read aloud,*
> con brio.

*They should also be read with Auden's satirical ballads in mind and
some of the early Betjeman pieces such as 'The Arrest of Oscar
Wilde at the Cadogan Hotel'. William Plomer is less in love with*

his victims than John Betjeman, and he is less of a moral psycho-
logist than the Auden of 'James Honeyman' and 'Miss Gee', but
his effects are more pointed. 'A Ticket for the Reading Room' ends
rather weakly, but I could not resist such a poetic reflection of the
seedy world of Graham Greene's pre-war novels.

Father and Son: 1939

A family portrait not too stale to record
Of a pleasant old buffer, nephew to a lord,
Who believed that the bank was mightier than the sword,
And that an umbrella might pacify barbarians abroad:
      Just like an old liberal
      Between the wars.

With an easy existence, and a cosy country place,
And with hardly a wrinkle, at sixty, in his face,
Growing old with old books, with old wine, and with grace,
Unaware that events move at a breakneck pace:
      Just like an old diehard
      Between the wars.

With innocuous tastes in common with his mate,
A love of his garden and his tidy snug estate,
Of dogs, music and children, and lying in bed late,
And no disposition to quarrel with his fate:
      Just like an old Englishman
      Between the wars.

With no religion or imagination, and a hazy lazy view
Of the great world where trouble kept cropping up anew,
With old clubmen for friends, who would seem stuffy to you,
Old faded prigs, but gentlemen (give them their due):
      Just like an old fossil
      Between the wars.

With a kindly old wife who subscribed for the oppressed,
With an O.B.E., and a coiffure like a last year's bird's nest,
Even more tolerant than anyone would have guessed,
Who hoped that in the long run all was for the best:
> Just like an old lady
> Between the wars.

With one child, a son, who in spite of his education
Showed only a modicum of common sense or cultivation,
Sometimes read the *Daily Worker* or the *New Statesman and
Nation.*
But neither, it must be admitted, with much concentration:
> Just like a young fribble
> Between the wars.

With a firm grasp of half-truths, with political short-sight,
With a belief we could disarm but at the same time fight,
And that only the Left Wing could ever be right,
And that Moscow, of all places, was the sole source of light:
> Just like a young hopeful
> Between the wars.

With a flash flat in Chelsea of a bogus elegance,
With surrealist pictures and books puffed by Gollancz,
With a degree of complacence which nothing could enhance,
And without one sole well-wisher to kick him in the pants:
> Just like a young smarty
> Between the wars.

With a precious mistress who thought she could paint
But could neither show respect nor exercise restraint,
Was a perfect goose-cap, and thought good manners quaint,
With affectation enough to try the patience of a saint:
> Just like a young cutie
> Between the wars.

With a succession of parties for sponges and bores,
With a traffic-jam outside (for they turned up in scores),
With first-rate sherry flowing into second-rate whores,
And third-rate conversation without one single pause:
> Just like a young couple
> Between the wars.

With week-ends in the country and holidays in France,
With promiscuous habits, time to sunbathe and dance,
And even to write books that were hardly worth a glance,
Earning neither reputation nor the publisher's advance:
> Just like a young writer
> Between the wars.

On a Sunday in September there were deck-chairs in the sun,
There was argument at lunch between the father and the son
(Smoke rose from Warsaw) for the beef was underdone
(Nothing points to heaven now but the anti-aircraft gun):
> With a hey nonny nonny
> And a hi-de-ho.

Oh, the twenties and the thirties were not otherwise designed
Than other times when blind men into ditches led the blind,
When the rich mouse ate the cheese and the poor mouse got the
> rind,
And man, the self-destroyer, was not lucid in his mind:
> With a hey nonny nonny
> And a hi-de-ho.

A Ticket for the Reading Room

> With a smile of secret triumph
>   Seedy old untidy scholar,
> Inkstains on his finger-nails,
>   Cobwebs on his Gladstone collar,

Down at heel and out at elbows
  Off he goes on gouty feet
(Where he goes his foxy smell goes),
  Off towards Great Russell Street.

Unaware of other people,
  Peace and war and politics,
Down the pavement see him totter
  Following his *idée fixe*.

Past the rowdy corner café
  Full of Cypriots and flies
Where the customers see daggers
  Looking from each other's eyes,

Past the sad but so-called Fun Fair
  Where a few immortal souls
Occupy their leisure hours
  Shooting little balls at holes,

Past the window full of booklets,
  Rubber goods and cures for piles,
Past the pub, the natty milk-bar
  Crowded with galactophiles,

Through the traffic, down the side-street
  Where an unfrocked parson thrives
('Palmist and Psychologist')
  Cutting short unwanted lives,

Through the shady residential
  Square in which a widow runs
A quiet gambling-hell, or 'bridge club',
  Fleecing other women's sons,

On he shuffles, quietly mumbling
   Figures, facts and formulae –
Bats are busy in the belfry,
   In the bonnet hums a bee.

At the Reading Room he settles
   Pince-nez on his bottle nose,
Reads and scribbles, reads and scribbles,
   Till the day draws to a close,

Then returns to oh, what squalor!
   Kippers, cake and dark brown tea,
Filthy sheets and filthier blankets,
   Sleep disturbed by mouse and flea.

What has the old man been doing?
   What's his game? Another book?
He is out to pour contempt on
   Esperanto, Vōlapük,

To fake a universal language
   Full of deft abbreviation
For the day when all mankind
   Join and form one happy nation.

In this the poor old chap resembles
   Prosperous idealists
Who talk as if men reached for concord
   With their clenched or grasping fists.

CECIL DAY LEWIS

Cecil Day Lewis, who with Auden and Spender was thought of as forming the original political-cum-poetical triumvirate of the thirties, was born in Ireland in 1904 and educated at Sherborne School and Wadham College, Oxford. He edited Oxford Poetry *with Auden in 1927, and, after leaving the university, became a schoolmaster in turn at Oxford, Helensburgh, and Cheltenham until 1935. He was employed at the Ministry of Information during the war. Since then he has been occupied with writing, lecturing, and broadcasting. He became Professor of Poetry at Oxford in 1951 (being Auden's immediate predecessor in this position).* The Buried Day (1960) *is an autobiographical account of the earlier part of his life. It is worth reading (although inferior in candour and insight to Stephen Spender's* World Within World) *and Poet Laureate in 1968.*

He is primarily a poet, but he has written novels, detective fiction (under the pseudonym of Nicholas Blake), and stories for children, as well as much criticism. His criticism includes A Hope for Poetry *(1934);* Poetry for You.(1945), *a book which has been popular in schools;* The Poetic Image (1947), *which is the published form of his Clark Lectures at Cambridge; and* Notable Images of Virtue *(1954). His 1951 Warton Lecture,* The Lyric Poetry of Thomas Hardy, *has a special interest for readers of his poems.*

Mr Day Lewis is a fluent poet and has a large published output in verse. Collected Poems 1929–36 (1948) *contains his work up to that time including both the pre-political poetry of* From Feathers to Iron (1931), *perhaps his best collection until* Word Over All (1943), *and the rather strident tub-thumping and pylon-praising of* The Magnetic Mountain (1933). *Later books include* Overtures to Death (1938), Word Over All (1943), Poems 1943–1947 (1948), *which is a volume of personal lyrics mixing the influences of Thomas Hardy and Edward Thomas, and* An Italian Visit (1953). Collected Poems (1954) *supersedes the 1948 collected edition and covers all the poetry from 1929 to 1953. The only volume since 1954 is* Pegasus and Other Poems *(1957).*

  Stephen Spender has observed that Day Lewis is a poet 'who is least sure of himself when he writes of his immediate feelings'. This statement can be accepted if such lyrics as 'Marriage of Two' and 'The Woman Alone' (from Poems 1943–1947*) can be taken as exceptions proving the rule. It is true that as a personal lyric poet he often fumbles and produces blurred or trite effects. His abilities as a translator or as a narrative poet – a good specimen is 'The Nabara' from* Overtures to Death *– can rarely be questioned in this way.* Poems 1943–1947 *contains an excellent example of translation in 'The Graveyard by the Sea', a version of Paul Valéry's* Le Cimetière Marin. *The parodies or imitations of Hardy, Yeats, Frost, Auden, and Dylan Thomas in* An Italian Visit *are further illustrations of a surprising poetic versatility. There is no real falling-off in quality in* Pegasus and Other Poems *– for many years now Day Lewis has been a remarkably consistent poetic performer. Anne Ridler notes of this last volume that it contains poems 'generated at a low poetic temperature', but this criticism can be applied to volumes published in the thirties and forties and connects with the 'professionalism' that the same critic comments on respectfully.*

  The four poems given here are arranged in chronological order. 'You That Love England', the first and weakest, is the only one from the strongly political phase. In brief it may be said that Day Lewis's failures are verbal, his successes rhythmical. This is a simplification, but the greater pleasure to be derived from his later volumes is more due, I think, to an increased power of making rhythmical patterns than to any change in subject-matter or deepening of sensibility.

You That Love England

You that love England, who have an ear for her music,
The slow movement of clouds in benediction,
Clear arias of light thrilling over her uplands,
Over the chords of summer sustained peacefully;
Ceaseless the leaves' counterpoint in a west wind lively,
Blossom and river rippling loveliest allegro,
And the storms of wood strings brass at year's finale:
Listen. Can you not hear the entrance of a new theme?

You who go out alone, on tandem, or on pillion,
Down arterial roads riding in April,
Or sad beside lakes where hill-slopes are reflected
Making fires of leaves, your high hopes fallen:
Cyclists and hikers in company, day excursionists,
Refugees from cursed towns and devastated areas;
Know you seek a new world, a saviour to establish
Long-lost kinship and restore the blood's fulfilment.

You who like peace, good sticks, happy in a small way
Watching birds or playing cricket with schoolboys,
Who pay for drinks all round, whom disaster chose not;
Yet passing derelict mills and barns roof-rent
Where despair has burnt itself out – hearts at a standstill,
Who suffer loss, aware of lowered vitality;
We can tell you a secret, offer a tonic; only
Submit to the visiting angel, the strange new healer.

You above all who have come to the far end, victims
Of a run-down machine, who can bear it no longer;
Whether in easy chairs chafing at impotence
Or against hunger, bullies and spies preserving
The nerve for action, the spark of indignation –
Need fight in the dark no more, you know your enemies.
You shall be leaders when zero hour is signalled,
Wielders of power and welders of a new world.

Passage from Childhood

His earliest memory, the mood
Fingered and frail as maidenhair,
Was this – a china cup somewhere
In a green, deep wood.
He lives to find again somewhere
That wood, that homely cup; to taste all
Its chill, imagined dews; to dare
The dangerous crystal.

Who can say what misfeatured elf
First led him into that lifelong
Passage of mirrors where, so young,
He saw himself
Balanced as Blondin, more headstrong
Than baby Hercules, rare as a one-
Cent British Guiana, above the wrong
And common run?

He knew the secrecy of squirrels,
The foolish doves' antiphony,
And what wrens fear. He was gun-shy,
Hating all quarrels.
Life was a hostile land to spy,
Full of questions he dared not ask
Lest the answer in mockery
Or worse unmask.

Quick to injustice, quick he grew
This hermit and contorted shell.
Self-pity like a thin rain fell,
Fouling the view:
Then tree-trunks seemed wet roots of hell,
Wren or catkin might turn vicious,
The dandelion clock could tell
Nothing auspicious.

No exile has ever looked so glum
With the pines fretful overhead,
Yet he felt at home in the gothic glade –
More than at home.
You will forgive him that he played
Bumble-puppy on the small mossed lawn
All by himself for hours, afraid
Of being born.

Lying awake one night, he saw
Eternity stretched like a howl of pain:
He was tiny and terrible, a new pin
On a glacier's floor.
Very few they are who have lain
With eternity and lived to tell it:
There's a secret process in his brain
And he cannot sell it.

Now, beyond reach of sense or reason,
His life walks in a glacial sleep
For ever, since he drank that cup
And found it poison.
He's one more ghost, engaged to keep
Eternity's long hours and mewed
Up in live flesh with no escape
From solitude.

The Poet

For me there is no dismay
Though ills enough impend.
I have learned to count each day
Minute by breathing minute –
Birds that lightly begin it,
Shadows muting its end –

As lovers count for luck
Their own heart-beats and believe
In the forest of time they pluck
Eternity's single leaf.

Tonight the moon's at the full.
Full moon's the time for murder.
But I look to the clouds that hide her –
The bay below me is dull,
An unreflecting glass –
And chafe for the clouds to pass,
And wish she suddenly might
Blaze down at me so I shiver
Into a twelve-branched river
Of visionary light.

For now imagination,
My royal, impulsive swan,
With raking flight – I can see her –
Comes down as it were upon
A lake in whirled snow-floss
And flurry of spray like a skier
Checking. Again I feel
The wounded waters heal.
Never before did she cross
My heart with such exaltation.

Oh, on this striding edge,
This hare-bell height of calm
Where intuitions swarm
Like nesting gulls and knowledge
Is free as the winds that blow,
A little while sustain me,
Love, till my answer is heard!
Oblivion roars below,
Death's cordon narrows: but vainly,
If I've slipped the carrier word.

Dying, any man may
Feel wisdom harmonious, fateful
At the tip of his dry tongue.
All I have felt or sung
Seems now but the moon's fitful
Sleep on a clouded bay,
Swan's maiden flight, or the climb
To a tremulous, hare-bell crest.
Love, tear the song from my breast!
Short, short is the time.

The Unwanted

On a day when the breath of roses
   Plumpened a swooning breeze
And all the silken combes of summer
   Opened wide their knees,
Between two sighs they planted one –
A willed one, a wanted one –
And he will be the sign, they said, of our felicities.

Eager the loins he sprang from,
   Happy the sheltering heart:
Seldom had the seed of man
   So charmed, so clear a start.
And he was born as frail a one,
As ailing, freakish, pale a one
As ever the wry planets knotted their beams to thwart.

Sun locked up for winter;
   Earth an empty rind:
Two strangers harshly flung together
   As by a flail of wind.
Oh was it not a furtive thing,
A loveless, damned, abortive thing –
This flurry of the groaning dust, and what it left behind!

Sure, from such warped beginnings
　　Nothing debonair
Can come? But neither shame nor panic,
　　Drugs nor sharp despair
Could uproot that untoward thing,
　　That all too fierce and froward thing:
Willy-nilly born it was, divinely formed and fair.

PETER QUENNELL

Peter Quennell was born in 1905 and educated at Berkhamsted and Balliol College, Oxford. His mother was the historian Marjorie Quennell. In 1930 Mr Quennell held the Chair of English Literature at the Government University of Tokyo. He has contributed widely to reviews and periodicals for many years and was editor of the Cornhill Magazine *from 1944 to 1951. He now edits* History To-day.

Mr Quennell has published a novel, The Phoenix Kind (*1931*), *and a collection of short stories,* Sympathy and Other Stories (*1933*), *both of which are distinguished by refinement of feeling. He is also the author of an interesting study,* Baudelaire and the Symbolists (*1929*), *and the editor of an anthology of Metaphysical poetry,* Aspects of Seventeenth Century Verse (*1933*). *These books of a generation ago are probably less known to the general public than his biographical studies of Byron (on whom he is an authority):* Byron – the Years of Fame (*1935*) *and* Byron in Italy (*1941*). *A more recent work on the poet is* Byron: A Self-Portrait (*1950*), *based on Byron's letters and diaries. Among the many other books Peter Quennell has written or edited room must be found for his* John Ruskin (*1949*), Hogarth's Progress (*1955*), *and three volumes of selections from Mayhew (1949, 1950, 1951).*

'The Flight into Egypt' *is from* Poems (*1926*), *a collection unduly neglected – probably because Mr Quennell has published no later poems. His writings, both in verse and prose, have a character-istic elegance, and the poem given here seems to me a very favourable example of the free verse of the twenties. It is earlier than Mr Eliot's* Journey of the Magi *(1927), by which at one time I imagined it to have been influenced.*

The Flight into Egypt

Within Heaven's circle I had not guessed at this,
I had not guessed at pleasure such as this,
So sharp a pleasure,
That, like a lamp burning in foggy night,
Makes its own orb and sphere of flowing gold
And tents itself in light.

Going before you, now how many days,
Thoughts, all turned back like birds against the wind,
Wheeled sullenly towards my Father's house,
Considered his blind presence and the gathered, bustling paean,
The affluence of his sweetness, his grace and unageing might.

My flesh glowed then in the shadow of a loose cloak
And my brightness troubled the ground with every pulse of the
        blood,
My wings lax on the air, my eyes open and grave,
With the vacant pride of hardly less than a god.

We passed thickets that quaked with hidden deer,
And wide shallows dividing before my feet,
Empty plains threaded, and between stiff aloes
I took the ass's bridle to climb into mountain pathways.

When cold bit you, through your peasant's mantle,
And my Father filled the air with meaningless stars,
I brought dung and dead white grass for fuel,
Blowing a fire with the breath of the holy word.

Your drudge, Joseph, slept; you would sit unmoving,
In marble quiet, or by the unbroken voice of a river,
Would sometimes bare your maiden breast to his mouth,
The suckling, to the conscious God balanced upon your knees.

Apart I considered the melodious names of my brothers,
As again in my Father's house, and the even spheres
Slowly, nightlong recalled the splendour of numbers;
I heard again the voluptuous measure of praise.

Sometimes pacing beneath clarity immeasurable
I saw my mind lie open and desert,
The wavering streams frozen up and each coppice quieted,
A whole valley in starlight with leaves and waters.

Coming at last to these farthest Syrian hills,
Attis or Adon, some ambushed lust looked out;
My skin grows pale and smooth, shrunken as silk,
Without the rough effulgence of a God.

And here no voice has spoken;
There is no shrine of any godhead here
No grove or hallowed fires,
And godhead seems asleep.

Only the vine has woven
Strange houses and blind rooms and palaces,
Into each hollow and crevice continually
Dropped yearlong irrecoverable flowers.

The sprawling vine has built us a close room,
Obedient Hymen fills the air with mist;
And to make dumb our theft
The white and moving sand that will not bear a print.

REX WARNER

Rex Warner, novelist and classical scholar, was born in 1905 and his boyhood was spent in Gloucestershire, where his father was a clergyman of the Church of England. He was educated at St George's, Harpenden, and Wadham College, Oxford, where he studied Classics and English. Since then he has taught these subjects at schools in England and Egypt. During the war he was a schoolmaster in the London area and from 1945 to 1947 he was Director of the British Institute at Athens. His Poems *were first published in 1937. They were re-issued in a revised edition as* Poems and Contradictions *(1945). During the late thirties and early forties Mr Warner enjoyed a vogue as a novelist with* The Wild Goose Chase *(1936),* The Professor *(1938),* The Aerodrome *(1941), and* Why Was I Killed? *(1943) – see the symposium on his novels and their relation to Kafka's work in* Focus One *(1945), edited by B. Rajan and A. Pearse – but it now seems likely that his reputation will rest chiefly on his Greek translations and other classical studies. Translations include the* Medea *(1944),* Hippolytus *(1950), and* Helen *(1951) of Euripides, the* Prometheus Bound *of Aeschylus (1947), Xenophon's* Anabasis *(1949), and* Thucydides *(1954). He has also published in recent years* Greeks and Trojans *(1951),* Views of Attica *(1951),* Eternal Greece *(1953, with Martin Hürlimann), and* The Young Caesar *and* The Greek Philosophers *in 1958.*

Rex Warner was friendly with Auden and Day Lewis at Oxford, and this association is commemorated by a banal couplet in The Magnetic Mountain:

> *Then I'll hit the trail for that promising land;*
> *May catch up with Wystan and Rex my friend ...*

and by the fourth ode of 'Six Odes' in Auden's The Orators.

Nile Fishermen

Naked men, fishing in Nile without a licence,
kneedeep in it, pulling gaunt at stretched ropes.
Round the next bend is the police boat and the officials
ready to make an arrest on the yellow sand.

The splendid bodies are stark to the swimming sand,
taut to the ruffled water, the flickering palms,
yet swelling and quivering as they tug at the trembling ropes.
Their faces are bent along the arms and still.

Sun is torn in coloured petals on the water,
the water shivering in the heat and the north wind;
and near and far billow out white swollen crescents,
the clipping wings of feluccas, seagull sails.

A plunge in the turbid water, a quick joke stirs
a flashing of teeth., an invocation of God.
Here is food to be fetched and living from labour.
The tight ropes strain and the glittering backs for the haul.

Round the bend comes the police boat. The men scatter.
The officials blow their whistles on the golden sand.
They overtake and arrest strong bodies of men
who follow with sullen faces, and leave their nets behind.

NORMAN CAMERON

Norman Cameron was born in India in 1905 and educated at
Fettes College and Oriel College, Oxford. After leaving the university he was for a while a superintendent of education in Nigeria before becoming an advertising copy-writer in London. In the thirties
he contributed frequently to Geoffrey Grigson's New Verse and to
Epilogue, the miscellany issued by Robert Graves and Laura
Riding. He was awarded the M.B.E. for work on propaganda to
German troops in Italy during the war, and he was with the British
Forces in Austria until early in 1947, when he returned to his work
in advertising. He died in 1953.

He brought out the following books of verse: The Winter House
(1935) and Work in Hand (1942) – the latter also containing
poems by Robert Graves and Alan Hodge. He also published Select
Verse Poems of Arthur Rimbaud (1942), an excellent volume of
translations. ('Naked Among the Trees' and 'The Invader' are
from his first and second books of verse respectively.) His Collected
Poems (1957) were published posthumously with an introduction by
Robert Graves.

Edwin Muir has described Cameron as 'a neat, semi-epigrammatic poet', but this is a tepid way of referring to his precision and
skill with words. The Winter House is a collection in which no
single poem appears to have been forced. His poems wear well, and
I suspect that they may be read when some fancied modern poets
with much bigger reputations are quite forgotten.

Naked Among the Trees

Formerly he had been a well-loved god,
Each visit from him a sweet episode,
Not like the outrageous Pentecostal rush
Or wilful Jahveh shrieking from a bush.

He bloomed in our bodies to the finger-tips
And rose like barley-sugar round the lips,
Then unawares was cleanly gone away,
With no relapse or aftertaint to pay.

We've forced the burgeoned lust he gave to us
Into a thousand manners of misuse,
Into the hot alarms, wishes and frets,
The drinking-bouts, the boasting and the bets.

And these have made his cult degenerate,
So that the booted Puritan magistrate
Did right to spur down on the devotees,
Catch them and whip them naked among the trees.

The Invader

Our shops and farms wide open lie;
Still the invader feels a lack:
Disquiet whets his gluttony
For what he may not carry back.

He prowls about in search of wealth
But has no skill to recognize
Our things of worth: we need no stealth
To mask them from his pauper eyes.

He calls for worship and amaze;
We give him yes-men in a row,
Reverberating that self-praise
He wearied of a while ago.

He casts around for some new whim,
Something preposterously more:
'Love me' he bids. We offer him
The slack embraces of a whore.

And when he spitefully makes shift
To share with us his pauperdom,
By forcing on us as a gift
The shoddy wares he brought from home,

And watches that we sell and buy
Amongst us his degrading trash,
He gets no gain at all. Though sly
With what he knows, the guns and cash,

What he knows not he may not touch:
Those very spoils for which he came
Are still elusive to his clutch –
They swerve and scorch him like a flame.

Invader-outcast of all lands,
He lives condemned to gorge and crave,
To foul his feast with his own hands:
At once the oppressor and the slave.

VERNON WATKINS

*Vernon Watkins was born in Wales of Welsh-speaking parents in
1906 and educated at Repton and Magdalene College, Cambridge.
After leaving the university he joined Lloyds Bank, and, except for
a spell of service with the R.A.F. during the Second World War,
has spent his whole life in or near Swansea. He is married and has
four children. He knew Dylan Thomas in his Swansea days and
their intimacy was kept up later by letters and visits.* Letters to
Vernon Watkins by Dylan Thomas *(1957) is a record of their
friendship. Although Vernon Watkins began writing verse at an
early age, he did not produce his first volume,* The Ballad of the
Mari Lwyd *(1941), until he was thirty-five years old. His second*

book, The Lamp and the Veil (*1945*), *consists of three long poems.
It was followed by* The Lady with the Unicorn (*1948*), *which
assembles the shorter pieces written after 1941. His most recent
collection,* The Death Bell (*1954*), *is divided into sections of poems
and ballads.* The Lady with the Unicorn *is his best volume in my
opinion. It is open to the reproaches that may be flung at most neo-
romantic writing, but it is less extravagant and obscure, less literary
and mythological – and where Mr Watkins is most mythological
he is least convincing – than many of the pieces in* The Death Bell.
*Some of the poems in this last collection give an impression of tired-
ness, and when Mr Watkins writes tiredly he is full of literary
echoes:*

> Leda remembers. The rush of wings cast wide.
> Sheer lightning, godhead, descending on the flood ...

and capable of such ineptitudes as:

> Here I
> Unsheathe a dagger to pierce the sun
> I have trapped the winds, lassooed the sea.

*Mr Watkins would almost certainly disagree with me about the
status of his mythological poems, and perhaps I should not say
more than that this type of poetry does not appeal to me. I think he
is too indulgent about obscurity (as if to say, 'Afflatus is all. Do not
tamper too much with what is given'), but I am very ready to admit
that he is one of the most accomplished writers of neo-romantic
verse and that he achieves some fine musical effects. 'The Peacocks'
and 'The Listening Days' from* The Lady with the Unicorn *and
'The Dead Shag' from* The Death Bell *are poems that please me –
they represent Watkins at his plainest and least ambitious.*

*The extract from 'The Broken Sea' was chosen in 1948 on the
basis of the poet's first two volumes only. I am fond of 'Cwmdonkin
railing and black-faced Inkerman Street', but, choosing again now,
I might select one of the three lyrics mentioned above, probably 'The
Peacocks'.*

From *The Broken Sea*

My lamp that was lit every night has burnt a hole in the shade.
A seawave plunges. Listen. Below me crashes the bay.
The rushing greedy water smothers the talk of the spade.
Now, on the sixth of November, I remember the tenth of May.

I was going to fly to your christening to give you a cup.
Here, like Andersen's tailor, I weave the invisible thread.
The burnt-out clock of St Mary's has come to a stop,
And the hand still points to the figure that beckons the house-
    stoned dead.

Child Shades of my ignorant darkness, I mourn that moment
    alive
Near the glow-lamped Eumenides' house, overlooking the ships
    in flight,
Where Pearl White focussed our childhood, near the foot of
    Cwmdonkin Drive,
To a figment of crime stampeding in the posters' wind-blown
    blight.

I regret the broken Past, its prompt and punctilious cares,
All the villainies of the fire-and-brimstone-visited town.
I miss the painter of limbo at the top of the fragrant stairs,
The extravagant hero of night, his iconoclastic frown.

Through the criminal thumb-prints of soot, in the swaddling-
    bands of a shroud,
I pace the familiar street, and the wall repeats my pace,
Alone in the blown-up city, lost in a bird-voiced crowd,
Murdered where shattering breakers at your pillow's head leave
    lace.

For death has burst upon you, yet your light-flooded eyes do
    not tremble
Where pictures for waking life stand in the spray's wild bead.
You are guarded, shrined in the torrent, fast-locked in the cave
    of the Sibyl,
In that terrifying delay of the waters' magical speed.

Asleep tonight in Paris, not knowing I walk your world,
You are deaf to the schoolyard's voices, where, escaped, the
    children meet,
The world of a child's one town, renascent, in rage unfurled
Between Cwmdonkin railing and black-faced Inkerman Street.

Waves, hooded, raging, thunder, hiding contagious guilt,
Tossing, high on the shale, the hard and scribbled stones.
An anchor's dirge is buried under the waters quilt.
Dazzling sunbeams have hidden the hook and the barnacled
    bones.

O indifferent grains of sand, O mother-of-pearl of the shell,
I hear the inconstant water, the blind, the wandering one.
The groan of Sophocles, and the groan of the leper's bell
Burst on annihilation: through your window breaks the sun.

I hear the breath of the storm. The engulfed, Gargantuan tide,
Heaped in hills by the moles, hurls to the mountain's head
The streets of sunrise. O windows burning on Townhill side,
O light of annunciation, unearthing the unknown dead!

JOHN BETJEMAN

John Betjeman — poet, topographer, church warden, and television personality — was born in 1906 and educated at Marlborough and Magdalen College, Oxford, where he was a contemporary of Auden and MacNeice but divided his time, it seems, between 'the leisured set in Canterbury Quad' and Pusey House. He has reviewed books widely and entertainingly and is at present book critic on the Daily Telegraph *and a free-lance writer, lecturer, and broadcaster. He is the author of various Shell Guides and co-editor (with John Piper, the painter) of Murray's series of Architectural Guides. He has also written the following works in prose:* Ghastly Good Taste (*1933*), An Oxford University Chest (*1938*), Antiquarian Prejudice (*1939*), *and* First and Last Loves (*1952*), *the last an agreeable volume of topographical essays.* Collins Guide to English Parish Churches (*1958*), *which he edited, has a masterly introduction.*

Mr Betjeman has published several volumes of verse: Mount Zion (*1932*), Continual Dew (*1937*), Old Lights for New Chancels (*1940*), New Bats in Old Belfries (*1945*), A Few Late Chrysanthemums (*1954*). *A volume of* Selected Poems, *chosen and introduced by John Sparrow, came out in 1948.* Collected Poems (*1958*), *compiled and introduced by the Earl of Birkenhead, has sold so many copies — one has to go back to Tennyson in the 1860s for a similar success — that schoolboys interviewed for entry into an English School at a modern university now automatically say 'Betjeman' when asked to name a modern poet (it was T. S. Eliot until 1959).* Summoned by Bells (*1960*), *an 'account of some moments in the sheltered life of a middle-class youth', is the first instalment of an autobiography in relaxed blank verse. It appeared in time for the Christmas trade and was at once saluted by Philip Larkin and reviled by John Wain, two of the best known 'Movement' poets of the fifties. I agree with Larkin.*

John Betjeman writes the nature poetry of the devastated Home

Counties and is the laureate of material ordinarily considered anti-poetic – 'I love suburbs and gas-lights and Pont Street and Gothic Revival churches and mineral railways, provincial towns and garden cities.' *This is the ordinary view of his work; it is at least half-true; and the poet has been glad enough to shelter behind it. Of this vein Sir John Summerson has written appreciatively:* 'Why are memories of gas-lit Congregational Chapels so moving? Why is there music in the preamble of Kelly's Directory? Why is the ugly and the second-rate so often charged with poetry when it gets old, worn, and forgotten? Answer these questions and you will know why Betjeman's poetry is poetry.' *Half-true, it is agreed, but* Collected Poems *also reveals a serious landscape artist in verse, who finds his landscapes far outside the Home Counties in Cornwall, Lincolnshire, and Ireland, and a lyric poet of simplicity and power in various poems remembering childhood or reflecting on death. Love, lust, fear, and compassion are among his themes in this part of his work, and in his hands innocence or naïveté develops a sharp cutting-edge.* 'Before the Anaesthetic' *is the poem, says Mr Sparrow,* 'in which he comes near, or as near as he has yet allowed himself, to laying bare his most intimate feelings'. *I am not sure that this is quite true, and there are certainly other lyrics of a similar kind with a more successful bite. The best criticism that has been published on Betjeman's poetry occurs in a review of* Collected Poems *by Philip Larkin* (Listen, *Spring 1959).* 'The strongest and most enduring thread that runs through the contradictions of impulse in this puzzling dazzling body of work is a quite unfeigned and uninflated fascination by human beings,' *he writes and adds that* 'neither the screens that he throws up of absurdity and satire, nor the amount of exploring that he does down alleys of minor interests, should prevent the recognition of his poetry's lasting quality as well as its novelty'. *A poet with Auden's admiration in one poetic generation and Larkin's in another may well rest content.*

'Death in Leamington' *is reprinted from* Mount Zion. *It represents the earlier, more facetious Betjeman and is relegated by Mr Sparrow – who calls it, very happily, the poet's* 'Innisfree' *– to the poet's juvenilia.* 'The Planster's Vision' *and* 'May-Day Song for North Oxford' *are from* New Bats in Old Belfries. *The first is* *satirical, even angry (and therefore not entirely successful – 'like silver pencils' is weak); the second is satirical-lyrical, as Polonius would have said, and enchanting. (It was abbreviated to the first two quatrains in* Selected Poems *(1948) but restored to its integrity ten years later.) 'The Cottage Hospital' is from* A Few Late Chrysan-themums. *It is one of the most successful serious poems, although those educated at 'progressive' schools or inhabiting garden suburbs may need to be protected from it.*

The Planster's Vision

Cut down that timber! Bells, too many and strong,
  Pouring their music through the branches bare,
  From moon-white church-towers down the windy air
Have pealed the centuries out with Evensong.
Remove those cottages, a huddled throng!
  Too many babies have been born in there,
  Too many coffins, bumping down the stair,
Carried the old their garden paths along.

I have a Vision of The Future, chum,
  The workers' flats in fields of soya beans
    Tower up like silver pencils, score on score:
And Surging Millions hear the Challenge come
  From microphones in communal canteens
    'No Right! No Wrong! All's perfect, evermore.'

May-Day Song for North Oxford

(Annie Laurie Tune)

Bellbroughton Road is bonny, and pinkly bursts the spray
Of prunus and forsythia across the public way,
For a full spring-tide of blossom seethed and departed hence,
Leaving land-locked pools of jonquils by sunny garden fence.

And a constant sound of flushing runneth from windows where
The toothbrush too is airing in this new North Oxford air;
From Summerfields to Lynam's, the thirsty tarmac dries,
And a Cherwell mist dissolveth on elm-discovering skies.

Oh! well-bound Wells and Bridges! Oh! earnest ethical search
For the wide high-table λογος of St C. S. Lewis's Church.
This diamond-eyed Spring morning my soul soars up the slope
Of a right good rough-cast buttress on the housewall of my
    hope.

And open-necked and freckled, where once there grazed the
    cows,
Emancipated children swing on old apple boughs,
And pastel-shaded book rooms bring New Ideas to birth
As the whitening hawthorn only hears the heart beat of the
    earth.

Death in Leamington

She died in the upstairs bedroom
    By the light of the ev'ning star
That shone through the plate glass window
    From over Leamington Spa.

Beside her the lonely crochet
    Lay patiently and unstirred,
But the fingers that would have work'd it
    Were dead as the spoken word.

And Nurse came in with the tea-things
    Breast high 'mid the stands and chairs —
But Nurse was alone with her own little soul,
    And the things were alone with theirs.

She bolted the big round window,
   She let the blinds unroll,
She set a match to the mantle,
   She covered the fire with coal.

And 'Tea!' she said in a tiny voice
   'Wake up! It's nearly *five*.'
Oh! Chintzy, chintzy cheeriness,
   Half dead and half alive!

Do you know that the stucco is peeling?
   Do you know that the heart will stop?
From those yellow Italianate arches
   Do you hear the plaster drop?

Nurse looked at the silent bedstead,
   At the gray, decaying face,
As the calm of a Leamington ev'ning
   Drifted into the place.

She moved the table of bottles
   Away from the bed to the wall,
And tiptoeing gently over the stairs
   Turned down the gas in the hall.

The Cottage Hospital

At the end of a long-walled garden
   in a red provincial town,
A brick path led to a mulberry
   scanty grass at its feet.
I lay under blackening branches
   where the mulberry leaves hung down
Sheltering ruby fruit globes
   from a Sunday-tea-time heat.

Apple and plum espaliers
   basked upon bricks of brown;
The air was swimming with insects,
   and children played in the street.

Out of this bright intentness
   into the mulberry shade
Musca domestica (housefly)
   swung from the August light
Slap into slithery rigging
   by the waiting spider made
Which spun the lithe elastic
   till the fly was shrouded tight.
Down came the hairy talons
   and horrible poison blade
And none of the garden noticed
   that fizzing, hopeless fight.

Say in what Cottage Hospital
   whose pale green walls resound
With the tap upon polished parquet
   of inflexible nurses' feet
Shall I myself be lying
   when they range the screens around?
And say shall I groan in dying,
   as I twist the sweaty sheet?
Or gasp for breath uncrying,
   as I feel my senses drown'd
While the air is swimming with insects
   and children play in the street?

WILLIAM EMPSON

William Empson was born in Yorkshire in 1906 and educated at Winchester and Magdalene College, Cambridge, where he distinguished himself in mathematics and literature. He has occupied Chairs of English Literature in Japan and China and is now Professor of English at Sheffield University. As a critic he is known by two stimulating books, Seven Types of Ambiguity (1930) *and* Some Versions of Pastoral (1935), *and one baffling one,* The Structure of Complex Words (1951). (*A new work of criticism,* Milton's God, *appeared in 1961.*) *He has also published two collections of verse,* Poems (1935) *and* The Gathering Storm (1940). Collected Poems (1955) *adds to the poems from the earlier volumes three short pieces written during the war and 'The Birth of Steel', a brief masque with additions by other hands for the visit of Queen Elizabeth II to Sheffield. The whole volume contains 119 pages (of which 27 pages are devoted to notes). The notes are sometimes helpful in interpreting poems often extraordinarily difficult because of intricacy of thought and an elliptical manner of expression.*

Mr Empson speaks good-humouredly of his 'clotted poetry', and the term is certainly not too strong for such a mind-breaker as 'Bacchus', which was on the stocks from 1933 to 1939. In his verse he seems to be almost exclusively concerned with working out problems of his own satisfaction, and the question of communication, which worried so many poets in the thirties, therefore remains a side-issue. The ideal reader of Empson would have to be trained in science and linguistics, and, because of personal references and allusions in the poems, also an intimate friend of the poet. Nothing could have been more surprising than the immense but short-lived popularity of Empson's poetry as a model for imitation in the early fifties. It was sparked off by an article by John Wain in the last number of Penguin New Writing (1950) *in which Robert Graves and*

Empson were recommended as prophylactics against neo-romantic infection. (Because of their 'viewiness' Auden and Eliot were not detached or cool enough for the new generation.) The result of the Empson cult was a crop of arid little villanelles and pieces in terza rima, *which may have amused but cannot have given much pleasure to the Master. It is sometimes held that Empson's best poems are all early – 'To an Old Lady', 'Arachne', and 'Legal Fiction', for example; but the more ambitious poems given below, though less easy to construe, are equally successful. The 'chatty' longer poem, 'Autumn on Nan-Yueh', is another Empson piece with which I am able to establish pleasurable relations.*

The three poems that I have chosen to represent Empson's achievement are all taken from The Gathering Storm. *(With room for a fourth I should have included 'To an Old Lady'.) I have chosen poems I understand, or think I understand, and therefore can admire. What I admire is the pertinacity with which a subject is teased out and the unsentimental statement of the teasing. There are some poems that I cannot understand at all. Mr G. S. Fraser's essay on Empson in* Vision and Rhetoric *(1959) is genuinely helpful to the new reader and is clearly on the right lines. It appreciates the distinguished qualities that really are to be found in Empson's work, but I think Mr Fraser goes too far when he speaks of him as a 'consistently good poet'. There are eight or nine good poems – slightly fewer than the number of good poems by Dylan Thomas; and I think it could be successfully argued that 'Bacchus' is as clearly a misapplication of a genuine poetic talent as, say, Thomas's 'Altar-wise by owl-light' sonnets.*

Aubade

Hours before dawn we were woken by the quake.
My house was on a cliff. The thing could take
Bookloads off shelves, break bottles in a row.
Then the long pause and then the bigger shake.
It seemed the best thing to be up and go.

And far too large for my feet to step by.
I hoped that various buildings were brought low.
The heart of standing is you cannot fly.

It seemed quite safe till she got up and dressed.
The guarded tourist makes the guide the test.
Then I said The Garden? Laughing she said No.
Taxi for her and for me healthy rest.
It seemed the best thing to be up and go.

The language problem but you have to try.
Some solid ground for lying could she show?
The heart of standing is you cannot fly.

None of these deaths were her point at all.
The thing was that being woken he would bawl
And finding her not in earshot he would know.
I tried saying Half an Hour to pay this call.
It seemed the best thing to be up and go.

I slept, and blank as that I would yet lie.
Till you have seen what a threat holds below,
The heart of standing is you cannot fly.

Tell me again about Europe and her pains,
Who's tortured by the drought, who by the rains.
Glut me with floods where only the swine can row
Who cuts his throat and let him count his gains.
It seemed the best thing to be up and go.

A bedshift flight to a Far Eastern sky.
Only the same war on a stronger toe.
The heart of standing is you cannot fly.

Tell me more quickly what I lost by this,
Or tell me with less drama what they miss
Who call no die a god for a good throw,
Who say after two aliens had one kiss
It seemed the best thing to be up and go.

But as to risings, I can tell you why.
It is on contradiction that they grow.
It seemed the best thing to be up and go.
Up was the heartening and the strong reply
The heart of standing is we cannot fly.

Reflection from Rochester

'But wretched Man is still in arms for Fear.'

'From fear to fear, successively betrayed' –
By making risks to give a cause for fear
(Feeling safe with causes, and from birth afraid),

By climbing higher not to look down, by mere
Destruction of the accustomed because strange
(Too complex a loved system, or too clear),

By needing change but not too great a change
And therefore a new fear – man has achieved
All the advantage of a wider range,

Successfully has the first fear deceived,
Thought the wheels run on sleepers. This is not
The law of nature it has been believed.

Increasing power (it has increased a lot)
Embarrasses 'attempted suicides',
Narrows their margin. Policies that got

'Virility from war' get much besides;
The mind, as well in mining as in gas
War's parallel, now less easily decides

On a good root-confusion to amass
Much safety from irrelevant despair.
Mere changes in numbers made the process crass.

We now turn blank eyes for a pattern there
Where first the race of armament was made;
Where a less involute compulsion played.
'For hunger or for love they bite and tear.'

Courage Means Running

Fearful 'had the root of the matter', bringing
Him things to fear, and he read well that ran;
Muchafraid went over the river singing

Though none knew what she sang. Usual for a man
Of Bunyan's courage to respect fear. It is the two
Most exquisite surfaces of knowledge can

Get clap (the other is the eye). Steadily you
Should clean your teeth, for your own weapon's near
Your own throat always. No purpose, view,

Or song but's weak if without the ballast of fear.
We fail to hang on those firm times that met
And knew a fear because when simply here

It does not suggest its transformation. Yet
To escape emotion (a common hope) and attain
Cold truth is essentially to get

Out by a rival emotion fear. We gain
Truth, to put it sanely, by gift of pleasure
And courage, but, since pleasure knits with pain,

Both presume fear. To take fear as the measure
May be a measure of self-respect. Indeed
As the operative clue in seeking treasure

Is normally trivial and the urgent creed
To balance enough possibles; as both bard
And hack must blur or peg lest you misread;

As to be hurt is petty, and to be hard
Stupidity; as the economists raise
Bafflement to a boast we all take as guard;

As the wise patience of England is a gaze
Over the drop, and 'high' policy means clinging;
There is not much else that we dare to praise.

CHRISTOPHER FRY

*Christopher Fry, whose father was an Anglican lay-preacher who
died when his son was three years old, was born at Bristol in 1907
and educated at Bedford Modern School. Since 1927 when he first
became an actor he has been — except for a brief interlude of school-
teaching — connected with the theatre as actor, producer, director,
and playwright. During the war he served with the Pioneer Corps.
Before the war he had written a musical comedy, devised pageants,
and published his first play* The Boy with a Cart (*1939*), *but his
real success came in the post-war years. His meteoric rise to the
astonishing reputation that he enjoyed with the theatre-going public
for such plays as* The Lady's Not for Burning (*1949*) *and* Venus

Observed (*1950*) *was probably owed to their occurrence in a particular place* (*grim, war-battered, peeling London with the fireweed waving on bomb-sites by the derelict N.F.S. tanks of static water*) *at a particular time* (*the Crippsian austerity era*). *Fry's flamboyant theatrical manner and his whimsical optimism-in-spite-of-all* ('*... something condones the world incorrigibly ...*') *chimed with the immediate tastes of a public hungry for a little colour and gaiety, streamers and blarney. The twists and swirls and quirks of Fry's rhetoric were a suitable accompaniment to the flounced, billowing skirts of the first post-war* '*New Look*' *in women's clothes, and his popularity could not survive a change in mental fashions. Christopher Fry's fame, which took him on to the cover of* Time *magazine, was as bright and brief as that of Stephen Phillips. His plays other than those already mentioned include* A Phoenix too Frequent (*1946*), The First Born (*1946*), A Sleep of Prisoners (*1951*), *and* The Dark is Light Enough (*1954*). *He has also adapted plays from the French and in 1952 he produced extra songs* (*words and music*) *for the film of* The Beggars' Opera. *The best of the plays are* A Phoenix too Frequent *and* The First Born, *in which the verbal inventiveness has not yet hardened into mannerism.*

Fry belongs to the theatre but his literary affiliations are with the spasmodic neo-romantic poets of the forties. The demands made by the stage kept him from their nonsense syntax, but he shares the neo-romantic passion for torrential metaphor and verbal fireworks. It is curious how often his tone comes close to that of Under Milk Wood. *Indeed Fry's ideas about the* '*terror and wonder*' *of experience –*

> *... a world as contradictory*
> *As a female, as cabbalistic as a male ...*

> *... How uneconomical*
> *The whole thing's been ...*

– *can be summed up quite neatly in Polly Garter's,* '*Oh, isn't life a terrible thing, thank God!*' *Derek Stanford produced his enthusiastic study,* Christopher Fry: An Appreciation, *in 1951, when the playwright's reputation was at its peak. He is also the author of the*

British Council pamphlet on Fry (1954) in the 'Writers and Their Work' series.

'Dynamene's Lament' is a speech from A Phoenix Too Frequent, a one-act comedy based on Petronius's tale of the Ephesian matron. This is Fry at his most acceptable.

Dynamene's Lament

From *A Phoenix Too Frequent*

>   ... For me
> The world is all with Charon, all, all,
> Even the metal and plume of the rose garden,
> And the forest where the sea fumes overhead
> In vegetable tides, and particularly
> The entrance to the warm baths in Arcite Street
> Where we first met; – all! – the sun itself
> Trails an evening hand in the sultry river
> Far away down by Acheron. I am lonely,
> Virilius. Where is the punctual eye
> And where is the cautious voice which made
> Balance-sheets sound like Homer and Homer sound
> Like balance-sheets? The precision of limbs, the amiable
> Laugh, the exact festivity? Gone from the world.
> You were the peroration of nature, Virilius.
> You explained everything to me, even the extremely
> Complicated gods. You wrote them down
> In seventy columns. Dear curling calligraphy!
> Gone from the world, once and for all. And I taught you
> In your perceptive moments to appreciate me.
> You said I was harmonious, Virilius,
> Moulded and harmonious, little matronal
> Ox-eye, your package. And then I would walk
> Up and down largely, as it were making my own
> Sunlight. What a mad blacksmith creation is
> Who blows his furnaces until the stars fly upward

And iron Time is hot and politicians glow
And bulbs and roots sizzle into hyacinth
And orchis, and the sand puts out the lion,
Roaring yellow, and oceans bud with porpoises,
Blenny, tunny and the almost unexisting
Blindfish; throats are cut, the masterpiece
Looms out of labour; nations and rebellions
Are spat out to hang on the wind – and all is gone
In one Virilius, wearing his office tunic,
Checking the pence column as he went.
Where's animation now? What is there that stays
To dance? The eye of the one-eyed world is out.

LOUIS MACNEICE

*Louis MacNeice was born at Belfast in 1907 of Irish parents – his
father being Bishop of Down, Connor, and Dromore – and educated
at Marlborough and Merton College, Oxford. He took a first in
Classical Mods. and Greats and was appointed a Lecturer in
Classics at Birmingham University in 1930. He went to Bedford
College, London, in 1936 as a Lecturer in Greek. In the same year
he visited Spain and (with Auden) Iceland – the second journey in
order to write Letters from Iceland. He visited America early in
1939 to lecture at various universities, and he was Lecturer in
Poetry at Cornell University in the first part of 1940. From 1941
to 1949 he was a member of the staff of the B.B.C., engaged in
writing and producing radio plays and features. In 1950 he was
Director of the British Institute at Athens. Belfast gave him an
Honorary D.Litt. in 1957. He died in 1963.*

In the thirties Louis MacNeice was a contributor to New Verse,
*and his name was closely linked with the names of Auden and
Spender. But even then he was more shy of politics than either of his
friends. 'If the writer is political at all,' he said, 'it is his special*

function to preserve his critical faculty. He must not see things (such as the Spanish War) purely in terms of black and white.' More can be discovered of his attitude to politics and of the course of his poetic development in his sound, unpretentious primer, Modern Poetry *(1938).*

MacNeice published what he calls 'a book of juvenile poems' in 1929, but his first serious book of verse was Poems *(1935). Apart from travel-books, a book on modern poetry, a study of Yeats and a translation of Goethe's* Faust, *his other publications were: a verse-translation,* The Agamemnon of Aeschylus *(1936); a poetic drama,* Out of the Picture *(1937), strongly influenced by the Auden–Isherwood plays;* The Dark Tower *(1947), a collection of plays for radio; and eight volumes of verse. These eight are* The Earth Compels *(1938),* Autumn Journal *(1939),* Plant and Phantom *(1941),* Springboard *(1944),* Holes in the Sky *(1948),* Ten Burnt Offerings *(1951),* Autumn Sequel *(1954), and* Visitations *(1957). His* Collected Poems *appeared in 1949. A new book of verse,* Solstices, *was published in 1961.*

I have represented MacNeice in this anthology by poems from all his books of verse published before 1948 except the verse-diary Autumn Journal *and* Holes in the Sky. *As the poems will show, there is not much development to record, certainly none of the conversions and re-conversions to be noticed in the poetic careers, say, of Auden or Day Lewis. It is hard to trace even a technical development in his work. He was attempting the eclogue and the long ode in* Poems *(1935), and even 'The Kingdom' in* Springboard *(1944) is no more ambitious than these and in the opinion of some critics (including myself) less successful. MacNeice's virtues include a fine sense of colour, a satirical and observant eye, and a lively interest in words, rhymes, and rhythms. All his collections contain good poems. The variety of this goodness is to be noted: he has written excellent love poetry, successful dramatic lyrics or character sketches like the 'Novelettes' of* Plant and Phantom *(from which I reprint 'Les Sylphides'), humorous and satirical verse like 'Bagpipe Music', argumentative and reflective poems like 'Plurality'. He can celebrate the ordinary and the everyday without putting his tongue in his cheek, because the imperviousness — except in time of* war – of the ordinary man to politics, creeds, and -isms strikes a sympathetic chord in MacNeice. He almost always writes well of Ireland. His best work was unequalled in the thirties for its gaiety, grace, and a lightness which was never silly or ostrich-like.

'The Kingdom' from Springboard seems to hint at a more serious defence of the individual as the safest repository of human values. This poem should be compared with Auden's 'September 1, 1939' from Another Time (1940), and both poems should be placed alongside Mr E. M. Forster's essay in the symposium, I Believe (1940). This essay sketches a philosophy of personal relations and employs ideas and even phrases which are repeated in the pieces by Auden and MacNeice.

The limitations of MacNeice's poetry, when it is thought of beside the best work of Auden and Spender, seem to be due to a certain devil-may-care lack of seriousness. ('A poet should not be afraid of being thought either sentimental or vulgar,' he has said.) He is too eager and impatient to accept his subject quietly and try to understand it. He grabs it, pats it into various shapes, and varnishes any cracks in the quality of his perception with his prestidigitatory skill with words and images.

On the whole this remark applies with equal force to the poet's later as to his earlier work, but it is important to note that Mac-Neice himself thought the poems in Visitations more concentrated and better organized – 'relying more on syntax and bony feature than on bloom or frill or the floating image'.

Snow

The room was suddenly rich and the great bay-window was
Spawning snow and pink roses against it
Soundlessly collateral and incompatible:
World is suddener than we fancy it.

World is crazier and more of it than we think,
Incorrigibly plural. I peel and portion
A tangerine and spit the pips and feel
The drunkenness of things being various.

And the fire flames with a bubbling sound for world
Is more spiteful and gay than one supposes –
On the tongue on the eyes on the ears in the palms of one's
 hands –
There is more than glass between the snow and the huge roses.

Bagpipe Music

It's no go the merrygoround, it's no go the rickshaw,
All we want is a limousine and a ticket for the peepshow.
Their knickers are made of crêpe-de-chine, their shoes are made
 of python,
Their halls are lined with tiger rugs and their walls with heads of
 bison.

John MacDonald found a corpse, put it under the sofa,
Waited till it came to life and hit it with a poker,
Sold its eyes for souvenirs, sold its blood for whiskey,
Kept its bones for dumb-bells to use when he was fifty.

It's no go the Yogi-Man, it's no go Blavatsky,
All we want is a bank balance and a bit of skirt in a taxi.

Annie MacDougall went to milk, caught her foot in the heather,
Woke to hear a dance record playing of Old Vienna.
It's no go your maidenheads, it's no go your culture,
All we want is a Dunlop tyre and the devil mend the puncture.

The Laird o' Phelps spent Hogmanay declaring he was sober,
Counted his feet to prove the fact and found he had one foot
 over.
Mrs Carmichael had her fifth, looked at the job with repulsion,
Said to the midwife 'Take it away; I'm through with over-
 production.'

It's no go the gossip column, it's no go the Ceilidh,
All we want is a mother's help and a sugar-stick for the baby.

Willie Murray cut his thumb, couldn't count the damage,
Took the hide of an Ayrshire cow and used it for a bandage.
His brother caught three hundred cran when the seas were
    lavish,
Threw the bleeders back in the sea and went upon the parish.

It's no go the Herring Board, it's no go the Bible,
All we want is a packet of fags when our hands are idle.

It's no go the picture palace, it's no go the stadium,
It's no go the country cot with a pot of pink geraniums.
It's no go the Government grants, it's no go the elections,
Sit on your arse for fifty years and hang your hat on a pension.

It's no go my honey love, it's no go my poppet;
Work your hands from day to day, the winds will blow the
    profit.
The glass is falling hour by hour, the glass will fall for ever,
But if you break the bloody glass you won't hold up the weather.

Les Sylphides

    Life in a day: he took his girl to the ballet;
    Being shortsighted himself could hardly see it –
        The white skirts in the grey
        Glade and the swell of the music
        Lifting the white sails.

    Calyx upon calyx, canterbury bells in the breeze
    The flowers on the left mirror to the flowers on the right
        And the naked arms above
        The powdered faces moving
        Like seaweed in a pool.

Now, he thought, we are floating – ageless, oarless –
Now there is no separation, from now on
  You will be wearing white
  Satin and a red sash
  Under the waltzing trees.

But the music stopped, the dancers took their curtain,
The river had come to a lock – a shuffle of programmes –
  And we cannot continue down-
  Stream unless we are ready
  To enter the lock and drop.

So they were married – to be the more together –
And found they were never again so much together,
  Divided by the morning tea,
  By the evening paper,
  By children and tradesmen's bills.

Waking at times in the night she found assurance
In his regular breathing but wondered whether
  It was really worth it and where
  The river had flowed away
  And where were the white flowers.

Prayer Before Birth

I am not yet born; O hear me.
Let not the bloodsucking bat or the rat or the stoat or the
 clubfooted ghoul come near me.

I am not yet born; console me.
I fear that the human race may with tall walls wall me,
 with strong drugs dope me, with wise lies lure me,
  on black racks rack me, in blood-baths roll me.

I am not yet born; provide me
With water to dandle me, grass to grow for me, trees to talk
   to me, sky to sing to me, birds and a white light
     In the back of my mind to guide me.

I am not yet born; forgive me
For the sins that in me the world shall commit, my words
     when they speak me, my thoughts when they think me,
       my treason engendered by traitors beyond me,
        my life when they murder by means of my
         hands, my death when they live me.

I am not yet born; rehearse me
In the parts I must play and the cues I must take when
     old men lecture me, bureaucrats hector me, mountains
       frown at me, lovers laugh at me, the white
        waves call me to folly and the desert calls
         me to doom and the beggar refuses
          my gift and my children curse me.

I am not yet born; O hear me,
Let not the man who is beast or who thinks he is God come
   near me.

I am not yet born; O fill me
With strength against those who would freeze my
     humanity, would dragoon me into a lethal automaton,
       would make me a cog in a machine, a thing with
        one face, a thing, and against all those
         who would dissipate my entirety, would
          blow me like thistledown hither and
           thither or hither and thither
            like water held in the
             hands would spill me
Let them not make me a stone and let them not spill me.
Otherwise kill me.

W. H. AUDEN

Wystan Hugh Auden was born at York in 1907, the son of George Auden M.D. and Constance Auden, and was educated at Gresham's School, Holt, and Christ Church, Oxford. After leaving the university he went to Berlin where he met Layard, psychologist and anthropologist, who

> *... fed*
> *New doctrines into my receptive head.*

> *Part came from Lane, and part from D. H. Lawrence,*
> *Gide, though I didn't know it then, gave part.*

These new doctrines can be found as a heavy deposit in Poems *(1930) and* The Orators *(1932), and more than traces of them survive even in* The Age of Anxiety *(1948) and later volumes. On his return from Germany Auden became a schoolmaster in England and Scotland before spending some time in documentary films – the verse commentary to* Night Mail, *made by the old G.P.O. Film Unit, was one result of this interest. 'Letter to Lord Byron' (Part IV) in* Letters from Iceland *(1937), a book written in collaboration with Louis MacNeice, is a short autobiography in verse up to 1936. Christopher Isherwood, who collaborated with Auden in three verse plays –* The Dog Beneath the Skin *(1935),* The Ascent of F6 *(1936), and* On the Frontier *(1938), as well as in a travel book about China,* Journey to a War *(1939), gives pictures of Auden at his prep. school and at Oxford in his autobiographical* Lions and Shadows *(1938). Auden himself has written about Gresham's School, Holt, in* The Old School, *a symposium edited by Graham Greene.*

During the Spanish Civil War Auden went to Spain and served as a stretcher-bearer and sanitary worker on the Republican side. (Those were days when 'Mr' Attlee could be photographed giving a clenched fist salute.) He has travelled widely in continental Europe apart from visits (see above) to Iceland and China. In the autumn of 1938 he went to the U.S.A. and is now an American citizen. He has taught and lectured at various schools and universities in America, but now occupies himself entirely with writing. In 1937 Auden was awarded the King's Medal for Poetry in this country, and in 1945 the American Academy of Arts and Letters bestowed their award on him. During the last war he served with the Strategic Bombing Survey of the American Army in Germany. In 1956 he was elected Professor of Poetry at Oxford in succession to Cecil Day Lewis, and his inaugural lecture has been published under the title of Making, Knowing and Judging. *He has visited England quite frequently in recent years, but when he is not in America he prefers to live on the Continent. 'On Installing an American Kitchen in Lower Austria' and 'Good-bye to the Mezzogiorno' from* Homage to Clio *(1960), Auden's most recent volume of poems, record a translation of domicile from Ischia to Austria.*

Auden is an extremely prolific (and uneven) writer. Apart from the books and plays already mentioned, he had published before his departure to the U.S.A. the following works: The Dance of Death *(1933) – drama;* Look, Stranger! *(1936) – poems; and two important anthologies,* The Poet's Tongue *(1935) – with John Garrett – and* The Oxford Book of Light Verse *(1938). Since that time he has issued the following books of verse:* Another Time *(1940),* New Year Letter *(1941),* For the Time Being *(1945),* The Age of Anxiety *(1948),* Nones *(1952),* The Shield of Achilles *(1955), and* Homage to Clio *(1960). His* Collected Shorter Poems, 1930–44 *was published in 1950. The epigraph to* Homage to Clio *is wry*

> Bullroarers cannot keep up the annual rain,
> The water-table of a once green champaign
> Sinks, will keep on sinking: but why complain? – Against odds,
> Methods of dry farming may still produce grain ...

but it certainly does not suggest that he has written himself out. The Auden double number of New Verse *contains a fairly complete list of Auden's writings up to the end of 1937, but I know nothing so full for the later years. The bibliographies in Richard Hoggart's excellent critical study,* Auden *(1951), and in his 1957 pamphlet for the British Council 'Writers and Their Work' series will be complete enough for most purposes.*

For criticism of Auden as a poet the reader should turn first to the two works by Hoggart noted above. Scarfe's Auden *(1948) and J. W. Beach's* The Making of the Auden Canon *(1958), which is concerned with Auden's revision of his poems and the reasons behind the various changes, should also be consulted. For other criticism of the poet, some of it early, reference may be made to the double number of* New Verse, *Spender's* Poetry *since 1939 and* World Within World, *Randall Jarrell's articles in the* Partisan Review *in 1945–6 (which are acute but too brightly written) and Geoffrey Grigson's excellent introduction to his* Poetry of the Present *(1949). There are some interesting remarks in Robert Conquest's introduction to* New Lines *(1956), which give some idea of how the 'Movement' poets feel about Auden. Donald Davie's 'Remembering the Thirties' (p. 325) is also instructive in this connexion.*

The chief influence in the poetic movement of the thirties was, as Spender says, undoubtedly the powerful intelligence and personality of W. H. Auden, 'the most brilliant poet of his generation'. Spender has characterized his work as 'the didactic, highly intellectualized, technically dazzling, at times wise poetry of an aloof commentator', but this is not in my view the whole truth. Auden is more involved in his subjects than this statement suggests, although he is less involved than Spender himself, who tends to identify the lyric with the subjective lyric and to carry the lyrical mood as far as possible even into satirical and didactic writing. And, after all, it was Auden's 'ice and wooden-faced acrobatics' which almost persuaded Wyndham Lewis in the thirties that the poet was 'the new guy who's got into the landscape'. Summing up, however, Spender remarks that he thinks Auden has qualities of greatness. With this I agree. As early as the collection Look, Stranger! *there are poems of astonishing truth and power. The sonnet sequence, 'In Time of War', in* Journey to a War *seems to me completely satisfying and quite free from the cleverness, tricks, and obscurity of some of the earlier work. After Auden left England there were for some years persistent attempts to write him off, to suggest that by so severing his roots his work had suffered in quality. These attempts were small-minded and silly, and the conclusions drawn from his departure were absurd. In some of the later work Auden has certainly become more abstract as a result of new moral, philosophical, and religious interests – or, better, new emphasis on these old interests – but the sequence 'The Quest'* from New Year Letter, *much of* For the Time Being *and* The Age of Anxiety, *'In Praise of Limestone' and 'The Managers' from* Nones, *and 'The Truest Poetry is the most Feigning', 'The Willow-wren and the Stare', several of the 'Bucolics', and the title-poem from* The Shield of Achilles *should demonstrate that Auden's brilliance is not simply a thirties phenomenon. There is no space here to discuss his development from a 'political' to a 'religious' point of view – to speak thus for economy's sake is to use dangerous simplifications – but the reader keen to know more about the matter is recommended to read in their chronological order Auden's prose contributions to G. Grigson's* The Arts Today, *to the symposium* I Believe *(referred to in the note on MacNeice), and to Stauffer's* The Intent of the Critic. *The last of these essays has been reprinted in* The Mint *No. 2 (1948). He should then read the poems again.*

I think it is true to say that no other poet writing in English to-day has attempted as much as Auden; just as no other poet of his generation can place beside his a body of work so exciting for its peculiar insight, its range of reference, and its skill in the use of language and rhythm. In the variety of subjects and manners he has used successfully, Auden has to be found a parallel outside contemporary poetry altogether – in the painter Picasso.

I must omit the usual paragraph in explanation of my selections, but for the understanding of 'Solo and Chorus' it is necessary to point out that it is from the 'Annunciation' section of For the Time Being, *which has the sub-title 'a Christmas Oratorio'. A revised version of the chorus from* The Dog Beneath the Skin *with the title 'Culture' will be found in Auden's* Collected Shorter Poems.

From *The Dog Beneath the Skin*

Chorus

Happy the hare at morning, for she cannot read
The Hunter's waking thoughts. Lucky the leaf
Unable to predict the fall. Lucky indeed
The rampant suffering suffocating jelly
Burgeoning in pools, lapping the grits of the desert,
The elementary sensual cures,
The hibernations and the growth of hair assuage:
Or best of all the mineral stars disintegrating quietly into light.
But what shall man do, who can whistle tunes by heart,
Know to the bar when death shall cut him short, like the cry of
    the shearwater?
We will show you what he has done.
How comely are his places of refuge and the tabernacles of his
    peace,
The new books upon the morning table, the lawns and the
    afternoon terraces!
Here are the playing-fields where he may forget his ignorance
To operate within a gentleman's agreement: twenty-two sins
    have here a certain licence.
Here are the thickets where accosted lovers combatant
May warm each other with their wicked hands,
Here are the avenues for incantation and workshops for the
    cunning engravers.
The galleries are full of music, the pianist is storming the keys,
    the great cellist is crucified over his instrument,
That none may hear the ejaculations of the sentinels
Nor the sigh of the most numerous and the most poor; the thud
    of their falling bodies
Who with their lives have banished hence the serpent and the
    faceless insect.

In Time of War

VIII

He turned his field into a meeting-place,
And grew the tolerant ironic eye,
And formed the mobile money-changer's face,
And found the notion of equality.

And strangers were as brothers to his clocks,
And with his spires he made a human sky;
Museums stored his learning like a box,
And paper watched his money like a spy.

It grew so fast his life was overgrown,
And he forgot what once it had been made for,
And gathered into crowds and was alone,

And lived expensively and did without,
And could not find the earth which he had paid for,
Nor feel the love that he knew all about.

Law Like Love

Law, say the gardeners, is the sun,
Law is the one
All gardeners obey
To-morrow, yesterday, to-day.

Law is the wisdom of the old
The impotent grandfathers shrilly scold;
The grandchildren put out a treble tongue,
Law is the senses of the young.

Law, says the priest with a priestly look,
Expounding to an unpriestly people,
Law is the words in my priestly book,
Law is my pulpit and my steeple.

Law, says the judge as he looks down his nose,
Speaking clearly and most severely,
Law is as I've told you before,
Law is as you know I suppose,
Law is but let me explain it once more,
Law is The Law.

Yet law-abiding scholars write;
Law is neither wrong nor right,
Law is only crimes
Punished by places and by times,
Law is the clothes men wear
Anytime, anywhere,
Law is Good-morning and Good-night.

Others say, Law is our Fate;
Others say, Law is our State;
Others say, others say
Law is no more
Law has gone away.

And always the loud angry crowd
Very angry and very loud
Law is We,
And always the soft idiot softly Me.

If we, dear, know we know no more
Than they about the law,
If I no more than you
Know what we should and should not do
Except that all agree
Gladly or miserably

That the law is
And that all know this,
If therefore thinking it absurd
To identify Law with some other word,
Unlike so many men
I cannot say Law is again,
No more than they can we suppress
The universal wish to guess
Or slip out of our own position
Into an unconcerned condition.

Although I can at least confine
Your vanity and mine
To stating timidly
A timid similarity,
We shall boast anyway:
Like love I say.

Like love we don't know where or why
Like love we can't compel or fly
Like love we often weep
Like love we seldom keep.

The Quest

II

All had been ordered weeks before the start
From the best firms at such work; instruments
To take the measure of all queer events,
And drugs to move the bowels or the heart.

A watch, of course, to watch impatience fly,
Lamps for the dark and shades against the sun;
Foreboding, too, insisted on a gun,
And coloured beads to soothe a savage eye.

In theory they were sound on Expectation
Had there been situations to be in;
Unluckily they were their situation:

One should not give a poisoner medicine,
A conjurer fine apparatus, nor
A rifle to a melancholic bore.

From *New Year Letter*

I

A weary Asia out of sight
Is tugging gently at the night
Uncovering a restless race;
Clocks shoo the childhood from its face,
And accurate machines begin
To concentrate its adults in
A narrow day to exercise
Their gifts in some cramped enterprise.
How few pretend to like it: O,
Three-quarters of these people know
Instinctively what ought to be
The nature of society
And how they'd live there if they could.
If it were easy to be good,
And cheap, and plain as evil how,
We all would be its members now:
How readily would we become
The seamless live continuum
Of supple and coherent stuff
Whose form is truth, whose content love.
Its pluralist interstices
The homes of happiness and peace,
Where in a unity of praise
The largest publicum's a res
And the least res a publicum;

How grandly would our virtues bloom
In a more conscionable dust
Where Freedom dwells because it must
Necessity because it can,
And men confederate in Man.

But wishes are not horses: this
Annus is not Mirabilis;
Day breaks upon the world we know
Of war and wastefulness and woe,
Ashamed civilians come to grief
In brotherhoods without belief,
Whose good intentions cannot cure
The actual evils they endure
Nor smooth their practical career
Nor bring the far horizon near.
The New Year brings an earth afraid,
Democracy a ready-made
And noisy tradesman's slogan, and
The poor betrayed into the hand
Of lackeys with ideas, and truth
Whipped by their elders out of youth,
The peaceful fainting in their tracks
With martyrs' tombstones on their backs,
And culture on all fours to greet
A butch and criminal élite
While in the vale of silly sheep
Rheumatic old patricians weep.

II

O Unicorn among the cedars
To whom no magic charm can lead us,
White childhood moving like a sigh
Through the green woods unharmed in thy
Sophisticated innocence
To call thy true love to the dance;
O Dove of science and of light

Upon the branches of the night;
O Icthus playful in the keep
Sea-lodges that for ever keep
Their secret of excitement hidden;
O sudden Wind that blows unbidden
Parting the quiet reeds; O Voice
Within the labyrinth of choice
Only the passive listener hears;
O Clock and Keeper of the years;
O Source of equity and rest,
Quando non fuerit, non est,
It without image, paradigm
Of matter, motion, number, time,
The grinning gap of Hell, the hill
Of Venus and the stairs of Will,
Disturb our negligence and chill,
Convict our pride of its offence
In all things, even penitence,
Instruct us in the civil art
Of making from the muddled heart
A desert and a city where
The thoughts that have to labour there
May find locality and peace,
And pent-up feelings their release.
Send strength sufficient for our day,
And point our knowledge on its way.
O da quod jubes, Domine.

From *For the Time Being*

Solo and Chorus

Let number and weight rejoice
In this hour of their translation
Into conscious happiness:
For the whole in every part,

The truth at the proper centre
(*There's a Way, There's a Voice.*)
Of language and distress
Is recognized in her heart
Singing and dancing.

Let even the great rejoice.
Though buffeted by admirers
And arrogant as noon,
The rich and the lovely have seen
For an infinitesimal moment
(*There's a Way. There's a Voice.*)
In another's eye till their own
Reflection came between,
Singing and dancing.

Let even the small rejoice
Though threatened from purple rostra
And dazed by the soldier's drum
Proclaiming total defeat,
The general loquacious Public
(*There's a Way. There's a Voice.*)
Have been puzzled and struck dumb,
Hearing in every street
Singing and dancing.

Let even the young rejoice
Lovers at their betrayal
Weeping alone in the night,
Have fallen asleep as they heard,
Though too far off to be certain
(*There's a Way. There's a Voice.*)
They had not imagined it,
Sounds that made grief absurd,
Singing and dancing.

Let even the old rejoice
The Bleak and the Dim abandoned
By impulse and regret,
Are startled out of their lives;
For to footsteps long expected
(*There's a Way. There's a Voice.*)
Their ruins echo, yet
The Demolisher arrives
Singing and dancing.

The Shield of Achilles

She looked over his shoulder
  For vines and olive trees,
Marble well-governed cities
  And ships upon untamed seas,
But there on the shining metal
  His hands had put instead
An artificial wilderness
  And a sky like lead.

A plain without a feature, bare and brown,
  No blade of grass, no sign of neighbourhood,
Nothing to eat and nowhere to sit down,
  Yet, congregated on its blankness, stood
  An unintelligible multitude.
A million eyes, a million boots in line,
Without expression, waiting for a sign.

Out of the air a voice without a face
  Proved by statistics that some cause was just
In tones as dry and level as the place:
  No one was cheered and nothing was discussed;
  Column by column in a cloud of dust
They marched away enduring a belief
Whose logic brought them, somewhere else, to grief.

She looked over his shoulder
   For ritual pieties,
White flower-garlanded heifers,
   Libation and sacrifice,
But there on the shining metal
   Where the altar should have been,
She saw by his flickering forge-light
   Quite another scene.

Barbed wire enclosed an arbitrary spot
   Where bored officials lounged (one cracked a joke)
And sentries sweated for the day was hot:
   A crowd of ordinary decent folk
   Watched from without and neither moved nor spoke
As three pale figures were led forth and bound
To three posts driven upright in the ground.

The mass and majesty of this world, all
   That carries weight and always weighs the same
Lay in the hands of others; they were small
   And could not hope for help and no help came:
   What their foes liked to do was done, their shame
Was all the worst could wish; they lost their pride
And died as men before their bodies died.

She looked over his shoulder
   For athletes at their games,
Men and women in a dance
   Moving their sweet limbs
Quick, quick, to music,
   But there on the shining shield
His hands had set no dancing-floor
   But a weed-choked field.

A ragged urchin, aimless and alone,
   Loitered about that vacancy, a bird
Flew up to safety from his well-aimed stone:

That girls are raped, that two boys knife a third,
Were axioms to him, who'd never heard
Of any world where promises were kept.
Or one could weep because another wept.

The thin-lipped armourer,
    Hephaestos, hobbled away,
Thetis of the shining breasts
    Cried out in dismay
At what the god had wrought
    To please her son, the strong
Iron-hearted man-slaying Achilles
    Who would not live long.

E. J. SCOVELL

*Edith Scovell was born at Sheffield in 1907 and educated at Caster-
ton School, Westmorland, and Somerville College, Oxford. She has
published the following volumes of verse:* Shadows of Chrysan-
themums (*1944*), The Midsummer Meadow (*1946*), *and* The
River Steamer (*1956*). The River Steamer *consists of two sec-
tions –* 'Earlier Poems', *drawn from her two earlier books, and*
'Recent Poems', *which have not previously been collected. The poet
acknowledges the help of Anne Ridler in selecting the poems for this
collected edition.*

*E. J. Scovell is a traditional poet in techniques and approach,
and also very much a woman poet in the domesticity of her muse.
Her poems constitute a sort of reticent emotional autobiography
with marriage and children pointing the passage of time, and with an
underlying continuity coming from the sympathetic truth of the ob-
servation of the natural world.* 'Child Waking', 'The Midsummer
Meadow', 'Day and Night', 'Mid-Winter Flowers', 'A Wife',
'In November', *and* 'Her Coughing Wakened Me' *illustrate her*

faithful exploration of a narrow range of subject-matter. She is particularly good on the effects of light. 'The Day of Widowhood', 'After Midsummer' and 'An Open-Air Performance of As You Like It' are achievements among the more ambitious pieces. 'After Midsummer', which is about the altered perspectives of middle age, reminds me of Walter de la Mare (whose influence on rhythm and phrasing may be felt in other poems) and rises to an admirable final quatrain:

> And whether we live or die, from this time on
> We must know death better; though here as we stand upon
> The rounded summit we think how softly the slope
> And the sky have changed, and the further dales come up.

Miss Scovell writes a poetry expressive of withdrawal from contemporary reality – the very occasional modern reference (for example, '... my parents' unplacated genes' in 'A Wife') always has a self-conscious ring – but the muted poetic world created by the poems is neither sentimentally false nor insipid.

Child Waking

The child sleeps in the daytime,
With his abandoned, with his jetsam look,
On the bare mattress, across the cot's corner;
Covers and toys thrown out, a routine labour.

Relaxed in sleep and light,
Face upwards, never so clear a prey to eyes;
Like a walled town, surprised out of the air
– All life called in, yet all laid bare

To the enemy above –
He has taken cover in daylight, gone to ground
In his own short length, his body strong in bleached
Blue cotton and his arms outstretched.

Now he opens eyes but not
To see at first; they reflect the light like snow
And I wait in doubt if he sleeps or wakes, till I see
Slight pain of effort at the boundary,

And hear how the trifling wound
Of bewilderment fetches a caverned cry
As he crosses out of sleep – at once to recover
His place and poise, and smile as I lift him over.

But I recall the blue-
White snowfield of his eyes empty of sight
High between dream and day, and think how there
The soul might rise visible as a flower.

JOHN LEHMANN

John Lehmann was born in 1907 and educated at Eton (King's Scholar) and Trinity College, Cambridge. (The novelist Rosamond Lehmann and the actress Beatrix Lehmann are his sisters.) He was the founder and editor of the influential New Writing *in the thirties, conducted* Penguin New Writing *during the war (copies of which were thumbed to pieces from Iceland to Burma), and was until recently – after some years as an independent publisher under his own name – editor of the* London Magazine *(1954–61). In 1952 he edited* New Soundings *for the Third Programme of the B.B.C., and from 1952 to 1958 he was Chairman of the Editorial Advisory Panel of the British Council. His position at the centre of the London literary scene from the mid thirties to the present time gives a high quality of interest to* The Whispering Gallery *(1955) and* I Am My Brother *(1960), two volumes of autobiography which bring Lehmann's own story down to the end of the Second World War and supply fascinating detail for the literary history of the*

thirties and forties. The autobiography, which has still to be com-
pleted, reveals Lehmann's feeling that his life has been a tug-of-war
between the desire to encourage new artistic talent as an editor and
publisher and the desire to find enough time to be a serious writer on
his own account. Apart from the autobiography, which is probably
his most important piece of writing so far, a novel, books of travel,
various anthologies, and much miscellaneous criticism, he has pro-
duced in the intervals of a busy literary life four books of verse: A
Garden Revisited (*1931*), The Noise of History (*1934*), Forty
Poems (*1942*), *and* The Sphere of Glass (*1944*). The Age of the
Dragon (*1951*) *selects from these four books and adds a few un-*
collected pieces. The best poems are to be found in the section
'Poems in Wartime and After', which contains such successes as
'The Summer Story', 'A Death in Hospital', and 'The Sphere of
Glass' (reprinted below). These pieces have a pleasing sobriety of
feeling, which degenerates in too many of the other poems into a
sort of emotional anaemia.

The Sphere of Glass

So through the sun-laced woods they went
Where no one walked but two that day,
And they were poets, and content
Sharing the one deep-vistaed way,
Sister and brother, to walk on
Where years like thickets round them lay.

It was the Roman dyke that ran
Between the bluebells and the fern,
The loam so fresh, they half began
To feel the bones deep under turn,
And, listening, dreamed their argument
Something from ancient death would learn.

One bird among the golden-green
Spangle of leaves was poised to sing:

They heard the opening trill, and then
Silence; as if its heart could bring
No note so pure but would disturb
The soundless fountain of the Spring.

Within the wood, within that hour
It seemed a sphere of glass had grown
That glittered round their lives, with power
To link what grief the dyke had known
With voices of their vaster war
The sun-shot bombers' homing drone,

And make one tragic harmony
Where still this theme, their hope, returned,
And still the Spring unchangeably
In fires of its own sap was burned,
And poetry, from love and death,
The peace their human contest earned.

It might have been all history
Without the sphere of wonder lay
And just beyond their colloquy
Some truth more pure than they could say,
While through the bluebells and the fern
Sister and brother made their way.

KATHLEEN RAINE

*Kathleen Raine was born in 1908 and educated at Girton College,
Cambridge, where she specialized in biology and took her Natural
Science tripos in 1929. She contributed to* New Verse *in the thirties,
but her first collection of poems was* Stone and Flower (*1943*),
*a book illustrated with drawings by Barbara Hepworth. Later
volumes of verse are* Living in Time (*1946*), The Pythoness *and*

Other Poems (*1949*), *and* The Year One (*1952*). *Her* Collected Poems *were published in 1956.*

A concern with religious ideas and religious vision, missing from her earliest 'periodical' poems, is apparent in Stone and Flower — *see 'Prayer', 'Good Friday', etc. — and finds expression in 'Ecce Homo', one of the best poems in* Living in Time. *From her poems, too, one might perhaps infer an interest in Blake and the 'visionary' Coleridge, writers whom she has introduced in the British Council 'Writers and Their Work' series. For her, Blake 'overtops all but the greatest men of genius that England … has known', combining, as for her he seems to do, 'the intellectual honesty of the scientist with a saint's sense of the holy'. It is the scientist in Kathleen Raine who writes of the 'maypole dance / Of chromosome and nucleus', but it is the stronger figure of the visionary who asserts that*

> *Behind the tree, behind the house, behind the stars*
> *Is the presence that I cannot see*
> *Otherwise than as house and stars and tree.*

Kathleen Raine is most at ease in the 'timeless' short lyric, and I have represented her by two lyrics, one from each of her first two collections. The reader will be able to see from these poems — and in these respects they are representative enough — that she writes musically in unaffected language and that she can express an apocalyptic element in feeling without inflation. To turn over the pages of her Collected Poems *is to be won to admire a narrow independent talent faithfully served.*

Passion

Full of desire I lay, the sky wounding me,
each cloud a ship without me sailing, each tree
possessing what my soul lacked, tranquillity.

Waiting for the longed-for voice to speak
through the mute telephone, my body grew weak
with the well-known and mortal death, heartbreak.

The language I knew best, my human speech
forsook my fingers, and out of reach
were Homer's ghosts, the savage conches of the beach.

Then the sky spoke to me in language clear,
familiar as the heart, than love more near.
The sky said to my soul, 'You have what you desire!

'Know now that you are born along with these
clouds, winds, and stars, and ever-moving seas
and forest dwellers. This your nature is.

'Lift up your heart again without fear,
sleep in the tomb, or breathe the living air,
this world you with the flower and with the tiger share.'

Then I saw every visible substance turn
into immortal, every cell new born
burned with the holy fire of passion.

This world I saw as on her judgement day
when the war ends, and the sky rolls away,
and all is light, love and eternity.

The Spring

(Song)

Out of hope's eternal spring
Bubbled once my mountain stream
Moss and sundew, fern and fell,
Valley, summer, tree and sun
All rose up, and all are gone.

By the spring I saw my love
(All who have parted once must meet,
First we live, and last forget),
With the stars about his head

With the future in his heart
Lay the green earth at my feet.

Now by the spring I stand alone
Still are its singing waters flowing;
Oh never thought I here to greet
Shadowy death who comes this way
Where hope's waters rise and play!

JAMES REEVES

*James Reeves was born in Middlesex in July 1909 and educated at
Stowe and Jesus College, Cambridge. He taught in schools and
teachers' training colleges for nearly twenty years before becoming a
'full-time author' in 1952. His first volume of poems* The Natural
Need *(1936) was published by the Seizin Press (which was run by
Robert Graves and Laura Riding in Majorca). Three later
volumes –* The Imprisoned Sea *(1949),* The Password *(1952),
and* The Talking Skull *(1958) – have appeared since the war, and*
Collected Poems *(1960) prints a generous selection of poems from
the four separate volumes and adds eight new pieces. Apart from the
books already mentioned and four books of poems for children he has
also published two collections of folk-song texts,* The Idiom of the
People *and* The Everlasting Circle, *based 'on the unpublished
mss. of collectors of about fifty years ago', and he is the general
editor of the useful Heinemann 'Poetry Bookshelf' series (being
personally responsible for the selections from D. H. Lawrence,
Donne, Clare, Hopkins, Browning, Coleridge, and Emily Dickin-
son). His two most recent books are an anthology of Georgian poetry
for Penguin Books and a short history of English poetry.*

*Robert Graves tells us that W. B. Yeats refused to include James
Reeves in* The Oxford Book of Modern Verse *on the grounds that
he was 'too reasonable, too truthful' and that the Muses always
prefer the embraces of 'gay, warty lads'. This was almost as unjust*

as the case made by Yeats for excluding Wilfred Owen, but there
is no denying that Reeves is a quiet poet not much given to self-
assertion – 'naïve', he says, is a favourite reviewers' epithet for his
poems. In the Introduction to his Collected Poems he writes:

> I remember the General Strike, mass unemployment, the
> Crisis of 1931, the premonitory rumblings of international
> war in the thirties. When the Nazis began their persecution of
> the Jews in Germany, I said to myself, 'One day there will
> have to be a war to put this right'. In 1940 when the news of
> the fall of France was announced, I was conscious of living
> through the worst day of history ... Nothing of all this has
> got into my poems ... To me poetry is rooted in the particular
> and the immediate.

'The Little Brother' originally appeared in The Password and
Other Poems (1952). The Talking Skull (1958) contains a poem
about Norman Cameron, who with Robert Graves has had some
influence on Mr Reeves's poetic manner. 'Old Crabbed Men' has a
touch of Cameron, for example, and 'Primadonna' is Gravesian.
Both of these are good poems, in no sense mere imitations.

The Little Brother

God! how they plague his life, the three damned sisters,
  Throwing stones at him out of the cherry trees,
Pulling his hair, smudging his exercises,
  Whispering. How passionately he sees
His spilt minnows flounder in the grass.

There will be sisters subtler far than these,
Baleful and dark, with slender, cared-for hands,
  Who will not grin and babble in the trees,
But feed him with sweet words and provocations,
  And in his sleep practise their sorceries,
Appearing in the form of ragged clouds
  And at the corners of malignant seas.

As with his wounded life he goes alone
　　To the world's end, where even tears freeze,
He will in bitter memory and remorse
　　Hear the lost sisters innocently tease.

STEPHEN SPENDER

Stephen Spender was born in 1909 and educated at University College School, London, and University College, Oxford. At Oxford he was a contemporary of Auden and MacNeice, editing Oxford Poetry *with the latter in 1929 and with Bernard Spencer in 1930. On his mother's side he is partly of German descent, and his father, Harold Spender, was a Liberal writer and speaker. Spender went to Germany for a couple of years after leaving Oxford and he has since travelled widely both in Europe and outside it. During the last war he was a fireman for a while in the N.F.S. in London and then (in his own words)* 'a small hack of a war-time branch of the Foreign Office'. *Between 1939 and 1941 he helped Cyril Connolly to edit* Horizon. *In 1947 he was a Counsellor for the Section of Letters, Unesco. Since 1953 he has been a co-editor of* Encounter. *He held the Chair of Poetry at the University of Cincinnati in 1953 and was a visiting professor at the University of California in 1959. He has an honorary degree of D.Litt. from Montpellier. His autobiography,* World Within World (1951), *is well worth reading for its candour and general literary interest.*

　　During the thirties Stephen Spender was a regular contributor to New Verse *and* New Writing. *The growth and development of his political opinions can be traced by reading first* Forward from Liberalism (1937), *which explores reasons for accepting Marxism as a working creed, and then* Life and the Poet (1942), *which finds better reasons for rejecting it.* 'I was always interested in politics,' *he wrote in* New Verse *in 1937, but I think it would be true to say that Spender's attachment to Communism derived less from an acceptance of dialectical materialism than from an active, angry pity for the underdog and an eager embracing of the Marxist millenial hope. In* Life and the Poet *he declares: 'The ultimate aim of politics is not politics, but the activities which can be practised within the political framework of the State. Therefore an effective statement of these activities – such as science, art, religion – is in itself a declaration of ultimate aims around which the political means will crystallize … A society with no values outside politics is a machine carrying its human cargo, with no purpose in its institutions reflecting their cares, eternal aspirations, loneliness, need for love …' It is possible to present the change in Spender's views too dramatically, and perhaps he lends himself to this misrepresentation when he speaks in* Poetry Since 1939 *(1946) of the war compelling him to turn from outward events to search for 'a universal experience through subjective contemplation'. He is here referring to poems in* Ruins and Visions *(1942), but already in* The Still Centre *(1939) he had included a section of poems in which 'I have deliberately turned back to a kind of writing which is more personal, and … have included within my subjects weakness and fantasy and illusion'. Apart from the books of verse mentioned Spender has written* Poems *(1933),* Vienna *(1934),* Poems of Dedication *(1947),* The Edge of Being *(1949), and the verse-play* Trial of a Judge *(1938). His* Collected Poems, 1928–53 *appeared in 1954.*

With the exception of Auden, Spender is to me the most interesting poet of his generation. An exceptional, at times almost painful, honesty about himself and the world, allied to a very personal lyrical gift of expression, result in a tension in his work which gives the reader of it the sensation of walking through unfamiliar country where paradoxically the landmarks are all known. The poet is a co-discoverer with the reader, rather than a tutor (as Auden so often is). 'The Poetry is in the pity' as often for Spender as for Wilfred Owen, and he has written movingly about elementary school-children, the unemployed, the defeated in the Spanish Civil War. In spite of this I would describe his finest work as personal – for example the love-poems of 'A Separation' (Part I of Ruins and Visions) *and the sequence 'Elegy for Margaret' in* Poems of Dedication. *Attention should also be drawn to 'Spiritual Explorations' in the same volume. The second and third sonnets of this group rank with the best of Auden's sonnets in 'In Time of War'. Some critics speak of a falling off in the quality of his poetry after the outbreak of the Second World War, but I do not think that it can be demonstrated. These remarks should not be taken to imply a failure to recognize Spender's weaknesses, but he has often had a bad press in recent years, and at present his achievement is undervalued.*

Besides the books mentioned above, Spender has also written a novel, short stories, a travel book, and much criticism. The Destructive Element (*1935*) *and* The Making of a Poem (*1955*) *contain his best critical prose, but all his literary criticism is worth a second glance in spite of its uneven quality. Among his most recent publications are* Engaged in Writing, *short stories, and a translation of Schiller's* Mary Stuart, *both of 1958. There is an attractive and amusing glimpse of Spender in Isherwood's* Lions and Shadows, *and the best article in Scarfe's* Auden and After *is devoted to him.*

'The Landscape near an Aerodrome' is from the early Poems. *It displays Spender's long, apparently careless, rhythmical breath, his descriptive power, and his desire at this time to force his imagery to point a moral (see the last verse-paragraph). 'Fall of a City' is from the third part of* The Still Centre *'when I was preoccupied with various kinds of political activity ... written directly and fairly quickly from the experiences which suggested them'. 'The Double Shame' is from Part I of* Ruins and Visions *and 'Elegy for Margaret', IV from* Poems of Dedication. *These groups of lyrics have already been referred to in this note. 'The Double Shame' seems to me one of Spender's finest poems.*

The Landscape near an Aerodrome

More beautiful and soft than any moth
With burring furred antennae feeling its huge path
Through dusk, the air-liner with shut-off engines
Glides over suburbs and the sleeves set trailing tall
To point the wind. Gently, broadly, she falls
Scarcely disturbing charted currents of air.

Lulled by descent, the travellers across sea
And across feminine land indulging its easy limbs
In miles of softness, now let their eyes trained by watching
Penetrate through dusk the outskirts of this town
Here where industry shows a fraying edge.
Here they may see what is being done.

Beyond the winking masthead light
And the landing-ground, they observe the outposts
Of work: chimneys like lank black fingers
Or figures frightening and mad: and squat buildings
With their strange air behind trees, like women's faces
Shattered by grief. Here where few houses
Moan with faint light behind their blinds
They remark the unhomely sense of complaint, like a dog
Shut out and shivering at the foreign moon.

In the last sweep of love, they pass over fields
Behind the aerodrome, where boys play all day
Hacking dead grass: whose cries, like wild birds,
Settle upon the nearest roofs
But soon are hid under the loud city.

Then, as they land, they hear the tolling bell
Reaching across the landscape of hysteria
To where, larger than all the charcoaled batteries
And imaged towers against that dying sky,
Religion stands, the church blocking the sun.

Fall of a City

All the posters on the walls
All the leaflets in the streets
Are mutilated, destroyed or run in rain,
Their words blotted out with tears,
Skins peeling from their bodies
In the victorious hurricane.

All the names of heroes in the hall
Where the feet thundered and the bronze throats roared,
F o x and L o r c a claimed as history on the walls,
Are now angrily deleted
Or to dust surrender their dust,
From golden praise excluded.

All the badges and salutes
Torn from lapels and from hands
Are thrown away with human sacks they wore
Or in the deepest bed of mind
They are washed over with a smile
Which launches the victors when they win.

All the lessons learned, unlearnt;
The young, who learned to read, now blind
Their eyes with an archaic film;
The peasant relapses to a stumbling tune
Following the donkey's bray;
These only remember to forget.

But somewhere some word presses
On the high door of a skull, and in some corner
Of an irrefrangible eye
Some old man's memory jumps to a child
– Spark from the days of energy.
And the child hoards it like a bitter toy.

The Double Shame

You must live through the time when everything hurts
When the space of the ripe, loaded afternoon
Expands to a landscape of white heat frozen
And trees are weighed down with hearts of stone
And green stares back where you stare alone,

And the walking eyes throw flinty comments
And the words which carry most knives are the blind
Phrases searching to be kind.

Solid and usual objects are ghosts,
The furniture carries cargoes of memory,
The staircase has corners which remember
As fire blows red in gusty embers,
And each empty dress cuts out an image
In fur and evening and summer and gold
Of her who was different in each.

Pull down the blind and lie on the bed
And clasp the hour in the glass of one room
Against your mouth like a crystal doom.
Take up the book and look at the letters
Hieroglyphs on sand and as meaningless –
Here birds crossed once and cries were uttered
In a mist where sight and sound are blurred.

For the story of those who made mistakes
Of one whose happiness pierced like a star
Eludes and evades between sentences
And the letters break into eyes which read
What the blood is now writing in your head,
As though the characters sought for some clue
To their being so perfectly living and dead
In your story, worse than theirs, but true.

Set in the mind of their poet, they compare
Their tragic bliss with your trivial despair
And they have fingers which accuse
You of the double way of shame.
At first you did not love enough
And afterwards you loved too much
And you lacked the confidence to choose
And you have only yourself to blame.

Elegy for Margaret

IV

Poor girl, inhabitant of a strange land
Where death stares through your gaze,
As though a distant moon
Shone through midsummer days
With the skull-like glitter of night:

Poor child, you wear your summer dress
And your shoes striped with gold
As the earth wears a variegated cover
Of grass and flowers
Covering caverns of destruction over
Where hollow deaths are told.

I look into your sunk eyes,
Shafts of wells to both our hearts,
Which cannot take part in the lies
Of acting these gay parts.
Under our lips, our minds
Become one with the weeping
Of the mortality
Which through sleep is unsleeping.

Of what use is my weeping?
It does not carry a surgeon's knife
To cut the wrongly multiplying cells
At the root of your life.
It can only prove
That extremes of love
Stretch beyond the flesh to hideous bone
Howling in hyena dark alone.

Oh, but my grief is thought, a dream,
Tomorrow's gale will sweep away.

It does not wake every day
To the facts which are and do not only seem:
The granite facts around your bed,
Poverty-stricken hopeless ugliness
Of the fact that you will soon be dead.

W. R. RODGERS

*W. R. Rodgers was born in Ulster in 1909 and educated at
Queen's University, Belfast. After twelve years spent as a clergy-
man in County Armagh, he resigned his parish in 1946 and joined
the B.B.C. Features Department in London. His first collection of
verse,* Awake! and Other Poems, *was published in 1941 (after a
first printing in 1940 had been entirely destroyed by enemy action),
and his second,* Europa and the Bull, *after a long interval in 1952.
He began to write poetry rather late. 'I was schooled,' he explains,
'in a backwater of literature out of sight of the running stream of
contemporary verse. Some rumours of course I heard, but I was
singularly ignorant of its extent and character. It was in the late
thirties that I came to contemporary poetry, and I no longer stood
dumb in the tied shops of speech or felt stifled in the stale air of
convention.'*

I wrote in 1948:

Awake! and Other Poems *attracted attention on its publi-
cation and several reviewers spoke of it as the most promising
first book of poetry since Auden's* Poems. *Although I appre-
ciate Rodgers's work, I cannot accept this opinion. The in-
fluence of the technique of Hopkins is apparent in the bold
alliteration and sometimes in the speed of movement, as the
influence of Auden is felt in the use of personification (see 'End
of a World', for example), but it may be questioned whether
here these are good influences. ... Generally Rodgers's use of
language is individual: he has at beck and call a wide voca-*

bulary which he deploys with an Irish exuberance. His subject-matter is the appearance of things rendered vividly and directly – in a manner that sometimes reminds us of MacNeice – with a quick eye for the arresting detail. 'Summer Holidays' with its fluency, its neat observation, and its long conveyor-belt of 'story' illustrates most of his virtues as a poet and one obvious weakness: the rather commonplace ideas which have been organized for expression by his observation and technical skill.

Europa and the Bull *does not mark a poetic development on Rodgers's first volume. In subject there is less of Ireland and more of myth, which is in keeping with the decade when the poems were being composed, but the handling of words is of the same order (though, sometimes, more tactful). 'Neither Here nor There' is one of the best poems in the later collection. With more room I should have been glad to include it in my selection.*

Stormy Day

O look how the loops and balloons of bloom
Bobbing on long strings from the finger-ends
And knuckles of the lurching cherry-tree
Heap and hug, elbow and part, this wild day,
Like a careless carillon cavorting;
And the beaded whips of the beeches splay
And dip like anchored weed round a drowned rock,
And hovering effortlessly the rooks
Hang on the wind's effrontery as if
On hooks, then loose their hold and slide away
Like sleet sidewards down the warm swimming sweep
Of wind. O it is a lovely time when
Out of the sunk and rigid sumps of thought
Our hearts rise and race with new sounds and sights
And signs, tingling delightedly at the sting
And crunch of springless carts on gritty roads,

The caught kite dangling in the skinny wires,
The swipe of a swallow across the eyes,
Striped awnings stretched on lawns. New things surprise
And stop us everywhere. In the parks
The fountains scoop and flower like rockets
Over the oval ponds whose even skin
Is pocked and goosefleshed by their niggling rain
That frocks a naked core of statuary.
And at jetty's jut, roped and ripe for hire,
The yellow boats lie yielding and lolling,
Jilted and jolted like jellies. But look!
There! Do you see, crucified on palings,
Motionless news-posters announcing
That now the frozen armies melt and meet
And smash? Go home now, for, try as you may,
You will not shake off that fact today.
Behind you limps that dog with tarry paw,
As behind him, perfectly-timed, follows
The dumb shadow that mimes him all the way.

Life's Circumnavigators

Here, where the taut wave hangs
Its tented tons, we steer
Through rocking arch of eye
And creaking reach of ear,
Anchored to flying sky,
And chained to changing fear.

O when shall we, all spent,
Row in to some far strand,
And find, to our content,
The original land
From which our boat once went,
Though not the one we planned.

Us on that happy day
This fierce sea will release,
On our rough face of clay,
The final glaze of peace.
Our oars we all will lay
Down, and desire will cease.

BERNARD SPENCER

*Bernard Spencer was born in 1909 and educated at Marlborough
and Corpus Christi College, Oxford. He was twice editor of* Oxford
Poetry *and, after leaving the university, for a number of years
worked as a schoolmaster, then on film-scripts and in an advertising
agency. After 1941 he lectured for the British Council in Greece,
Egypt, Spain, and Italy, and he also gave talks on travel and
literature for the B.B.C. He died in 1963.*

Many of his earlier poems were published in New Verse, *which
he helped Geoffrey Grigson to edit in the late thirties, and between
1942 and 1945 he did a similar job (with Lawrence Durrell and
Robin Fedden) for* Personal Landscape, *the poetry magazine in the
Middle East. His only book of verse is* Aegean Islands (1946), *but
he also edited (with Durrell and Nanos Valoritis) a book of
translations from modern Greek,* The King of Asine.

'Allotments: April' was first published in New Verse *in 1936
and 'On the Road' in* Penguin New Writing *in 1947. Both seem
to me to have an unpretentious clarity and directness and to be good
poems. 'Allotments: April' might very well represent the kind of
poem for which* New Verse *stood: straightforward but unpedestrian
language, feeling expressed through observation, intelligence reflect-
ing on observation and awake to the implications of feeling. Like
other* New Verse *poets, Bernard Spencer was influenced by Auden,
Spender, and MacNeice. He had mild left-wing sympathies in the
thirties – these come out in a few poems – but was not really of a*

political temper at all. His love poems in the thirties and forties seem to me his best pieces.

Allotments: April

Cobbled with rough stone which rings my tread
The path twists through the squared allotments.
Blinking to glimpse the lark in the warming sun,
In what sense am I joining in
Such a hallooing, rousing April day,
Now that the hedges are so gracious and
Stick out at me moist buds, small hands, their opening scrolls
     and fans?

Lost to some of us the festival joy
At the bursting of the tomb, the seasonal mystery,
God walking again who lay all winter
As if in those long barrows built in the fields
To keep the root-crops warm. On squires' lawns
The booted dancers twirl. But what I hear
Is spade slice in pebbled earth swinging the nigger-coloured
     loam.

And the love-songs, the medieval grace,
The fluting lyrics, 'The only pretty ring-time',
These have stopped singing. For love detonates like sap
Up into the limbs of men and bears all the seasons
And the starving and the cutting and hunts terribly through
     lives
To find its peace. But April comes as
Beast-smell flung from the fields, the hammers, the loud-
     speaking weir.

The rough voices of boys playing by the hedge,
As manly as possible, their laughter, the big veins
Sprawled over the beet-leaf, light-red fires

Of flower pots heaped by the huts; they make a pause in
The wireless voice repeating pacts, persecutions,
And imprisonments and deaths and heaped violent deaths,
Impersonal now as figures in the city news.

Behind me, the town curves. Its parapeted edge,
With its burnt look, guards towards the river.
The worry about money, the eyeless work
Of those who do not believe, real poverty,
The sour doorways of the poor; April which
Delights the trees and fills the roads to the South,
Does not deny or conceal. Rather it adds

What more I am; excites the deep glands
And warms my animal bones as I go walking
Past the allotments and the singing water-meadows
Where hooves of cattle have plodded and cratered, and
Watch today go up like a single breath
Holding in its applause at masts of height
Two elms and their balanced attitude like dancers, their arms
    like dancers.

On the Road

Our roof was grapes and the broad hands of the vine
as we two drank in the vine-chinky shade
of harvest France;
and wherever the white road led we could not care,
it had brought us there
to the arbour built on a valley side where time,
if time any more existed, was that river
of so profound a current, it at once
both flowed and stayed.

We two. And nothing in the whole world was lacking.
It is later one realizes. I forget

the exact year or what we said. But the place
for a lifetime glows with noon. There are the rustic
table and the benches set; beyond the river
forests as soft as fallen clouds, and in
our wine and eyes I remember other noons.
It is a lot to say, nothing was lacking;
river, sun and leaves, and I am making
words to say 'grapes' and 'her skin'.

FRANCIS SCARFE

Francis Scarfe was born in 1911 and educated at King's College, Durham University, and Fitzwilliam House, Cambridge. He has also studied at the Sorbonne. Before the war he became a lecturer in French at Glasgow University, and he returned there after war service in the army (when he was stationed in the Orkneys and Faroes) and peace service in adult education for Oxford University. He is now director of the British Institute in Paris. He gives some details of himself and his attitude to poetry in Auden and After *(1942), but the book was put together too quickly under difficult war conditions and is not much more than topical journalism. More serious criticism can be found in* Auden *(1948) and* The Art of Paul Valéry *(1954). He has also published three novels and various translations from the French.*

Scarfe has several collections of verse to his name, but the only one that the reader is likely to come across is Underworlds *(1950), from which 'Tyne Dock' is reprinted. It is a piece of autobiographical nostalgia, unequal, like much of Scarfe's work, but emotionally honest. Scarfe inclines to think that the poetic gifts possessed by Spender are the most important ones – it does not embarrass him to walk naked. His best poem is 'The Land of Corners' – surrealist, loosely shaped and unpolished, oddly memorable.*

Tyne Dock

The summer season at Tyne Dock
Lifted my boyhood in a crane
Above the shaggy mining town,
Above the slaghills and the rocks,
Above the middens in backlanes
And wooden hen-huts falling down.

Grass grew vermilion in the streets
Where the blind pit-ponies pranced
And poppies screamed by butchers' stalls
Where bulls kicked sparks with dying feet,
And in the naked larks I sensed
A cruel god beneath it all.

Over the pithead wheel the moon
Was clean as a girl's face in school;
I envied the remote old man
Who lived there, quiet and alone,
While in the kitchen the mad spool
Unwound, as Annie's treadle ran.

The boyish season is still there
For clapping hands and leaping feet
Across the slagheaps and the dunes,
And still it breaks into my care
Though I will never find the street,
Nor find the old, impulsive tune,
Nor ever lose that child's despair.

NORMAN MACCAIG

*Norman MacCaig was born at Edinburgh in 1910 and educated at
Edinburgh University, where he read Classics. By profession he is a
schoolmaster, and he is married, with two children. He was asso-
ciated in his poetic beginnings with the 'Apocalyptic' movement and
published two books of verse in the forties –* Far Cry *(1943) and*
The Inward Eye *(1946) – but his present reputation rests on the
poems in three more recent collections:* Riding Lights *(1955),* The
Sinai Sort *(1957), and* A Common Grace *(1960). 'Nude in the
Fountain', a representative poem in his developed manner, is re-
printed from the last volume.*

Louis MacNeice said of Riding Lights, *which won an Arts
Council award for Scotland, that it showed that its author had 'both
a mind on the one hand and a heart and senses on the other'. With-
out wishing in the least to deny this, I think it is the poet's 'lust of
looking', as he calls it in 'Inverkirkaig Bay' (from* A Common
Grace), *and his linking of it with his almost obsessive preoccupation
with the philosophical problems of appearance and reality, that will
strike the reader most forcibly. The world impresses the poet with
its 'clarity of seeming', but his metaphysical questioning of its
reality –*

> *I see a rose, that strange thing, and what's there
> But a seeming coloured something on the air
> With the transparencies that make up me,
> Thickened to existence by my notice ...*
>
> *('Ego')*

*– causes him to refine his observation in an impossible attempt (like
that of trying to see behind mirror images by going round to the
back of the mirror) to catch perceptions at their point of emergence
from sensation:*

> *That blueness is what pine-tips, weathered thus
> And backed with pine-tips, make of air,
> Region of compromise which they two share.*

The 'lust of looking' is enough to notice roebuck who 'stilt and leap sideways', but wit is involved in writing

> *An invisible drone boomed by*
> *With a beetle in it …*

— a neat separation of a perception from the conclusion to be drawn from it. Of course there are disadvantages in Mr MacCaig's obsession: as when abstractions and paradoxes are so densely packed that they squeeze the sensuous life out of what might have been poems. The best poems plant themselves mid-way between the polar extremes of the abstract 'In No Time at All' and the pleasantly descriptive 'Clachtoll'. 'Ego', 'A Glass of Summer', 'Feeding Ducks', 'Bloom on Pine-trees in August', 'Blue Chair in a Sunny Day', 'Goat', and 'Nude in a Fountain' are a few examples. Literary influences are a matter of guesswork, but Wallace Stevens is certainly one — see the delightful 'Jug' in A Common Grace *and various other pieces which, more obviously than 'Jug', underpin Yankee frivolity with Scottish weight. Mr MacCaig is often a difficult poet, but the quality of the writing in his best poems needs proper recognition.*

Nude in a Fountain

Clip-clop go water-drops and bridles ring –
Or, visually, a gauze of water, blown
About and falling and blown about, discloses
Pudicity herself in shameless stone,
In an unlikely world of shells and roses.

On shaven grass a summer's litter lies
Of paper bags and people. One o'clock
Booms on the leaves with which the trees are quilted
And wades away through air, making it rock
On flower-beds that have blazed and dazed and wilted.

Light perches, preening, on the handle of a pram
And gasps on paths and runs along a rail
And whitely, brightly in a soft diffusion
Veils and unveils the naked figure, pale
As marble in her stone and stilled confusion.

And nothing moves except one dog that runs,
A red rag in a black rag, round and round
And that long helmet plume of water waving,
In which the four elements, hoisted from the ground,
Become this grace, the form of their enslaving.

Meeting and marrying in the midmost air
Is mineral assurance of them all;
White doldrum on blue sky; a pose of meaning
Whose pose is what is explicit; a miracle
Made, and made bearable, by the water's screening.

The drops sigh, singing, and, still sighing, sing
Gently a leaning song. She makes no sound.
They veil her, not with shadows, but with brightness;
Till, gleam within a glitter, they expound
What a tall shadow is when it is whiteness.

A perpetual modification of itself
Going on around her is her; her hand is curled
Round more than a stone breast; and she discloses
The more than likely in an unlikely world
Of dogs and people and stone shells and roses.

CHARLES MADGE

Charles Madge was born at Johannesburg, South Africa, in 1912 and educated at Winchester and Magdalene College, Cambridge. After a year in Fleet Street as a reporter, he helped to found Mass Observation. Later he did social and economic research under the guidance of Lord Keynes and for P.E.P. He was a director of the Pilot Press for three years and edited Pilot Papers. *In 1948 he was Social Development Officer for the new Stevenage, and he is now Professor of Social Science at Birmingham University. His publications include two collections of verse:* The Disappearing Castle *(1937) and* The Father Found *(1941).*

In approaching Charles Madge's work it is useful to remember two things: (i) that he went to Cambridge and was an admirer of William Empson; and (ii) that political sympathies brought him for a time under the influence of the 'social' poets of the thirties – there are early Audenesque verses by Madge in Michael Roberts's New Country *(1933), and he was a regular contributor to* New Verse. *Madge is often an obscure poet (like Empson) in the sense that he does not seem to be caring very much whether the reader is following him, and he uses scientific references, not in Auden's popular way, but accurately and professionally. Yet it would give a false impression to imply that his work is generally obscure, or that it has anything like the same degree of complication as Empson's. 'Loss' from* The Father Found *is fairly representative. It uses a metrical pattern which Empson might have chosen, opens with a scientific image –*

> *Like the dark germs across the filter clean*

– then moves on to speak of Vienna and its 'wounded walls', a reference to the bombardment of the workers' flats by Dollfuss. Again, apart from the social poets and Cambridge, it is useful to bear in mind Madge's interest in the literature of the quarter-century preceding the Romantic Revival. The sequence 'Delusions'

would hardly have been written without Gray. In Madge's first volume the short pieces 'In Conjunction', 'Fortune', and 'Solar Creation' (which is particularly fine) have been appreciated, and there are pieces with a similar appeal in The Father Found. *One trouble for the anthologist is that Madge has definite ideas about his best poems, and has failed to collect, and refuses to allow to be reprinted, certain pieces which now disappoint him, e.g. 'Drawing Room Experience'* (The Year's Poetry, 1938). *It is an attractive poem.*

'Ode' is from The Father Found. *'Inscription I', an uncollected poem, is more typical of his imagery and rhythms.*

Ode

The lesson of our time is sore:
Having and to have no more,
Within the smoky reference
Of life and its indifference.

Whether in want, whether in wealth,
There is no peace, there is no health.
To enact the plot we're fated
In the world that we've created.

The innumerable heart-beats
Of the traffic and the streets,
The impassive architecture
And the whole colossal structure

But elaborately disguise
Confusion and the nest of spies:
Always the policeman stands
With the baton in his hands.

Those from whom the industrial vulture
Draws the sinews of its culture,

For whom the evil choice is small,
If it is a choice at all,

Badly housed, badly fed
And abominably misled,
In the lottery of life
Can lose a job or choose a wife.

Those who love the time of play
Or to drink the time away
Or the curls and smiles that vie
In the wineshop of the eye

May win bitterness and pain
May win happiness again
And from the nature of the odds
Authenticate their various gods.

Still the million fires burn
Still the million souls can learn,
Ever loving and reviling,
Hating and then reconciling,

Ever finding and concealing
The diversity of feeling,
Life is irretrievable
But death is inconceivable.

Inscription I

Here cries chisel-parted stone
High, dry and wingless.

In hollow warning like the moon
Her own appearing ghost.

The wind blows, the wind blows away
From the small piping glottis
Words, airy and small
The wind blows, the wind blows away
Scuttering messages into darkness
And among muffled feet

But these remain from time again
Departed relatives
Ignored, yet they persist
And will not easily dissolve
In the hard rain and gentle rain.

These had a resonance, it seems
An engram, as a leaf
Is mottled in its fall.
They cut them square, as though they did not feel,
And finding nature, left a line,
Line upon line, a pale and crooked line
The shadowless wall people

Good grooves for lichen spores and chance connexions.

HENRY TREECE

*Henry Treece was born of Welsh origin in the Midlands in 1912
and was educated at Birmingham University before becoming a
schoolmaster. At various times he has also been a university exten-
sion lecturer, an artist's model, and a pianist in a dance band. When
war broke out he became an A.R.P. Control-Room Officer and later
a pilot-officer in the R.A.F. With J. F. Hendry he was joint-leader
of the wartime Apocalyptic movement in literature, and he was co-
editor of the two Apocalyptic anthologies –* The New Apocalypse
(1939) *and* The White Horseman (1941). *In recent years he has*

devoted himself to writing novels, 'juvenile novels', and short stories, but he has also published Dylan Thomas: 'Dog Among the Fairies' *(1949, revised edition 1956) and the following collections of verse:* Thirty-Eight Poems *(1940),* Invitation and Warning *(1942),* The Black Seasons *(1945),* The Haunted Garden *(1947), and* Exiles *(1952).*

The Apocalyptic movement, which is now quite dead (if one is generous enough to admit that it was ever alive), was a reaction against political elements in the literature of the thirties and specifically against 'social reporting' in poetry. The movement had negative political and social aims, disclaiming any political allegiance to existing groups, disliking the machine-age, and calling loudly for a revival of myth. It was in fact a rather barmy 'fringe' form of neo-romanticism. Literary ancestors of the movement – this was in imitation of some of the sweeping claims of the Surrealists – were said to be the author of the Book of Revelation, Shakespeare, Webster, Blake, and Kafka, a suspiciously miscellaneous crew, but it was the head of Dylan Thomas that topped the tallest totem-pole. ('Dylan Thomas was a dedicated poet, in the sense that he was called, spoken to from elsewhere, made to utter' *– Treece's emphasis.) None of this would have mattered had the Apocalyptics included a few real poets and short-story writers. Names associated with the movement were those of J. F. Hendry, Nicholas Moore, Tom Scott, Norman MacCaig, and G. S. Fraser. Some of these were writers of talent – specimens of the work of most of them can be found in M. J. Tambimuttu's* Poetry in Wartime *(1942) – but the body of verse produced by them at the time (with the exception of some early pieces by G. S. Fraser and Norman MacCaig) was tame, second-hand, and derivative; and it is often difficult to see why it should be called Apocalyptic. Of the poets mentioned only MacCaig – and then it is for his later work – is included in this anthology. The Apocalyptic movement is therefore represented by a single poem by Henry Treece, who seems to me the best of its 'typical' writers (although I do not like what he is trying to do and find myself repelled by the touch of whimsy in many of his pieces).*

'Legend' is reprinted from the section 'Mystic Numbers' of Invitation and Warning.

Legend

There was a man
With a coloured coat of rags
Who left his body and blood on a tree.
But the thieves at his side gave the bones to the dogs,
And the black-thorn cock sang merrily.

The lads of the town
Drank down to the dregs
Then took a sharp axe to lop the tree.
But the thieves had been there first gathering logs,
And the black-thorn cock sang steadily.

One day at dawn
Upon their nags
Twelve tinkers came and their hearts were free,
For they cut twelve whistles from the knuckles of the dogs,
To bear the black cock company.

ANNE RIDLER

*Anne Ridler (née Bradby) was born in 1912 at Rugby, where her
father and uncle were housemasters of Rugby School, and educated
at Downe House School and King's College, London. In 1938 she
married Vivian Ridler, who became the Oxford University Printer
in 1958, and they now have a family of four children. She published
her first important collection of poems,* The Nine Bright Shiners,
in 1943 – this was preceded by smaller books, Poems (1939) *and*
A Dream Observed (1941), *and followed by two verse-plays,*
Cain (1944) *and* The Shadow Factory (1946), *the latter pro-
duced by Martin Browne in a season of plays by poets at the Mer-
cury Theatre. Her later publications include* The Golden Bird

(*1951*), Henry Bly and Other Plays (*1951*), The Trial of
Thomas Cranmer (*1956*), *and* A Matter of Life and Death
(*1959*). *She has also edited* Shakespeare Criticism 1919–35, A
Little Book of Modern Verse (*1942*), *a revised edition* (1951) *of*
The Faber Book of Modern Verse, *and* The Image of the City
and Other Essays (*1958*), *a collection of uncollected essays by
Charles Williams.*

*The subjects of Mrs Ridler's poems are domestic and religious,
so that it was inevitable that some critics should talk of Patmore,
particularly as she has intelligence and a verbal wit expressing itself
with the utmost neatness rhythmically. To* Focus Three, *a sym-
posium on T. S. Eliot, she contributed an excellent article, 'A Ques-
tion of Speech', from which I extract the following:*

> *For myself, I should say it was Eliot who first made me
> despair of becoming a poet; Auden (with, of course, dead poets,
> notably Sir Thomas Wyatt) who first made me think I saw
> how to become one.*
>
> *An age can afford a few good poets who stand aside from
> this battle for the colloquial idiom in poetry, and continue to
> use the artificial diction of an earlier generation – as, in our
> own day, are such diverse poets as Walter de la Mare and
> Charles Williams – but not many; and with these, the young
> must 'admire and do otherwise', as Hopkins put it. It can also
> afford a different kind of poet, who treats words as though he
> were present at their creation – a Dylan Thomas or a George
> Barker – but only if the main channel is kept clear. These are
> the luxury of a strong tradition.*

*As these sensible remarks might suggest, Anne Ridler is an able
reviewer of new poetry.*

At Parting

Since we through war awhile must part
Sweetheart, and learn to lose
Daily use
Of all that satisfied our heart:

Lay up those secrets and those powers
Wherewith you pleased and cherished me these two years:

Now we must draw, as plants would,
On tubers stored in a better season,
Our honey and heaven;
Only our love can store such food.
Is this to make a god of absence?
A new-born monster to steal our sustenance?

We cannot quite cast out lack and pain.
Let him remain – what he may devour
We can well spare:
He never can tap this, the true vein.
I have no words to tell you what you were,
But when you are sad, think, Heaven could give no more.

For a Child Expected

Lovers whose lifted hands are candles in winter,
Whose gentle ways like streams in the easy summer,
Lying together
For secret setting of a child, love what they do,
Thinking they make that candle immortal, those streams forever
        flow,
And yet do better than they know.

So the first flutter of a baby felt in the womb,
Its little signal and promise of riches to come,
Is taken in its father's name;
Its life is the body of his love, like his caress,
First delicate and strange, that daily use
Makes dearer and priceless.

Our baby was to be the living sign of our joy,
Restore to each the other's lost infancy;

To a painter's pillaging eye
Poet's coiled hearing, add the heart we might earn
By the help of love; all that our passion would yield
We put to planning our child.

The world flowed in; whatever we liked we took:
For its hair, the gold curls of the November oak
We saw on our walk;
Snowberries that make a Milky Way in the wood
For its tender hands; calm screen of the frozen flood
For our care of its childhood.

But the birth of a child is an uncontrollable glory;
Cat's cradle of hopes will hold no living baby,
Long though it lay quietly.
And when our baby stirs and struggles to be born
It compels humility: what we began
Is now its own.

For *as the sun that shines through glass*
So Jesus in His Mother was.
Therefore every human creature,
Since it shares in His nature,
In candle-gold passion or white
Sharp star should show its own way of light.
May no parental dread or dream
Darken our darling's early beam:
May she grow to her right powers
Unperturbed by passion of ours.

KENNETH ALLOTT

Kenneth Allott was born in 1912 and educated at various schools and at King's College, Durham University, and St Edmund Hall, Oxford. He has worked as a journalist, schoolmaster, and staff tutor in adult education, but since 1947 he has been at Liverpool University, where he is now A. C. Bradley Professor of Modern English Literature. In 1960 he was a Visiting Professor in New Zealand.

In the thirties Kenneth Allott was a regular contributor to New Verse, *which he helped Geoffrey Grigson to edit in 1938-9. He is also the author of a novel and several plays (the last of which, written in collaboration with Stephen Tait, was produced by the Group Theatre in London in 1953); of two collections of verse,* Poems *(1938) and* The Ventriloquist's Doll *(1943); and of a biography of Jules Verne (1940), a study of Graham Greene's novels (1951), and critical editions of Habington (1948) and Praed (1953). For Penguin Books he has edited a selection of Matthew Arnold's poems (1954) and, in collaboration with Miriam Allott in 1956, the Victorian volume of* The Pelican Book of English Prose: *1550-1880 (of which he was also general editor). His most recent publications are a large annotated edition of Matthew Arnold's poems (1965), and a volume of selections of Browning's poems (1967).*

'Lament for a Cricket Eleven' is reprinted from Poems, *'Two Ages' from* The Ventriloquist's Doll.

Lament for a Cricket Eleven

Beyond the edge of the sepia
Rises the weak photographer
With the moist moustaches and the made-up tie.
He looked with his mechanical eye,
And the upshot was that they had to die.

Portrait of the Eleven nineteen-o-five
To show when these missing persons were last alive.
Two sit in Threadneedle Street like gnomes.
One is a careless schoolmaster
Busy with carved desks, honour and lines.
He is eaten by a wicked cancer.
They have detectives to watch their homes.

From the camera hood he looks at the faces
Like the spectral pose of the praying mantis.
Watch for the dicky-bird. But, O my dear,
That bird will not migrate this year.
Oh for a parasol, oh for a fan
To hide my weak chin from the little man.

One climbs mountains in a storm of fear,
Begs to be unroped and left alone.
One went mad by a tape-machine.
One laughed for a fortnight and went to sea.
Like a sun one follows the *jeunesse dorée*.

With his hand on the bulb he looks at them.
The smiles on their faces are upside down.
'I'll turn my head and spoil the plate.'
'Thank you, gentlemen.' Too late. Too late.

One greyhead was beaten in a prison riot.
He needs injections to keep him quiet.
Another was a handsome clergyman,
But mortification has long set in.
One keeps six dogs in an unlit cellar.
The last is a randy bachelor.

The photographer in the norfolk jacket
Sits upstairs in his darkroom attic.
His hand is expert at scissors and pin.
The shadows lengthen, the days draw in,

And the mice come out round the iron stove.
'What I am doing, I am doing for love.
When shall I burn this negative
And hang the receiver up on grief?'

Two Ages

Ballet of Fahrenheit and Réaumur,
The swarm of bees round time's thermometer,
The Sheffield edge of summer where,
Baffled at every cardinal point with cuckoos,
Sturdy as dandelion, tanned juventus
Straddles on river-bank to arch his piss
Into a rainbow cataract of sun,
Ears pricked for sexual music, view-halloos
To a death-brush with sense
So glittering, so glittering
After the glory-leap down the ravine.
He may be happy even once,
Or think he is,
Away from home's maternal echoes,
As innocent as a clock
Before time's shipwreck.

But when the rowdy summer is kaput
And birds must emigrate
From unfond headlands; when skies shiver
To stream blind windows and to raise gooseflesh
And everything is over:
He will transmogrify the wish
And set up house
And burn his own coal in the hearth
And have a good address
Religiously for ever;
Prefer the sun's low course,
Creating his own snow,

A walking Greenland now,
To his own children marking good and evil,
Becoming his own devil,
As usual, as usual.

F. T. PRINCE

Frank Templeton Prince was born at Kimberley in 1912 and edu-cated at schools in South Africa and at Balliol College, Oxford. He did some literary research in America before 1939 and became a captain in the Intelligence Corps during the war. From it he returned to lecturing at Southampton University, where he has been Profes-sor of English since 1957. His first book of verse, Poems, *was pub-lished in 1938; his second,* Soldiers Bathing, *in 1954. The Italian Element in Milton's Verse (1954) is a piece of scholarly literary criticism that has been highly and deservedly praised. More recently (1960) Prince has edited the* Poems *(excluding the sonnets) for the New Arden edition of Shakespeare.*

Stephen Spender, who was one of the first people to recognize F. T. Prince's merits as a poet, has spoken highly of his work in Poetry *since 1939. 'Soldiers Bathing' has appeared in several anthologies and is his most considerable poem.*

Soldiers Bathing

The sea at evening moves across the sand,
And under a sunset sky I watch the freedom of a band
Of soldiers who belong to me: stripped bare
For bathing in the sea, they shout and run in the warm air.
Their flesh, worn by the trade of war, revives
And watching them, my mind towards the meaning of it strives.

All's pathos now. The body that was gross,
Rank, ravening, disgusting in the act and in repose,
All fever, filth and sweat, all bestial strength
And bestial decay, by pain and labour grows at length
Fragile and luminous. 'Poor bare forked animal',
Conscious of his desires and needs and flesh that rise and fall,
Stands in the soft air, tasting after toil
The sweetness of his nakedness: letting the sea-waves coil
Their frothy tongues about his feet, forgets
His hatred of the war, its terrible pressure that begets
A machinery of death and slavery,
Each being a slave and making slaves of others: finds that he
Remembers his old freedom in a game
Mocking himself, and comically mimics fear and shame.

He plays with death and animality,
And reading in the shadows of his pallid flesh, I see
The idea of Michelangelo's cartoon
Of soldiers bathing, breaking off before they were half done
At some sortie of the enemy, an episode
Of the Pisan wars with Florence. I remember how he showed
Their muscular limbs that clamber from the water
And heads that turn across the shoulder, eager for the slaughter,
Forgetful of their bodies that are bare,
And hot to buckle on and use the weapons lying there.
And I think too of the theme another found
When, shadowing lean bodies on a sinister red ground –
Was it Antonio Pollaiuolo? –
Painted a naked battle: warriors straddled, hacked the foe,
Dug their bare toes into the soil and slew
The brother-naked man who lay between their feet and drew
His lips back from his teeth in a grimace.
They were Italians who knew war's sorrow and disgrace
And showed the thing suspended, stripped, a theme
Born out of the experience of war's horrible extreme
Beneath a sky where even the air flows
With *Lachrimae Christi*; and that rage, that bitterness, those blows,

That hatred of the slain, what could it be
But indirectly or brutally a commentary
On the Crucifixion? for the picture burns
With indignation and pity and despair and love by turns
Because it is the obverse of the scene
Where Christ hangs murdered, stripped, upon the Cross:
    I mean,
That is the explanation of its rage.

And we too have our bitterness and pity that engage
Thought, horror in this war. But night begins,
Night of the mind: who nowadays is conscious of our sins?
Though every human deed concerns our blood,
And even we must know what no one yet has understood,
That some great love is over what we do,
And that is what has driven us to this fury, for so few
Can suffer all the terror of that love:
The terror of that love has set us spinning in this groove
Greased with our blood.

                     These dry themselves and dress,
Resume their shirts, forget the fear and shame of nakedness.
Because to love is frightening we prefer
The freedom of our crimes. Yet as I drink the dusky air,
I feel a strange delight that fills me full,
A gratitude, as if evil itself were beautiful;
And kiss the wound in thought, while in the west
I watch a streak of red that might have issued from Christ's
    breast.

ROY FULLER

Roy Fuller was born in 1912 at Oldham, Lancashire. He served in the Royal Navy from 1941 to 1946, most of the time in the Fleet Air Arm. Before the war he had become a solicitor in London, and he is now solicitor to the Woolwich Equitable Building Society and legal adviser to the Building Societies Association. He has published five novels, which include the fine Image of a Society *(1956),* The Ruined Boys *(1959), and* The Father's Comedy *(1961); two books for children; and six collections of verse:* Poems *(1939),* The Middle of a War *(1942),* A Lost Season *(1944),* Epitaphs and Occasions *(1949),* Counterparts *(1954), and* Brutus's Orchard *(1957).*

As a poet Roy Fuller developed more slowly than other poets who began writing in the thirties. He was then a regular contributor to New Verse *and* Twentieth Century Verse *(edited by Julian Symons), and his early poems faithfully echo the social mood of that decade as – say – the early work of John Heath-Stubbs echoes the neo-romantic mood of the forties. When neo-romanticism goes bad, it dissolves into a nasty pool of feeling in which swim faint, evocative fishes; when the social poetry of the thirties went bad, it was dull, prosy, as powder-dry as a country lane in a heat-wave. Fuller's earliest work was sometimes prosy, although it was clear even then that Auden had taught him to observe and to arrange his observations in support of a serious interpretation of social reality. The war extended his range by giving him more to observe and made him a better poet, but* Epitaphs and Occasions *(1949) perhaps marks a new confidence and maturity in various scathing satirical verses about post-war life –*

> *How completely we have slipped into the same old world of cod,*
> *Our companions Henry James or cats or God ...*

– and post-war literature –

> Quite often he was heard to babble
> 'Poets should be intelligible.'

The maturity is more strongly in evidence in Counterparts, but
neither of his post-war volumes really prepares us for the authority
of the writing in Brutus's Orchard, which seems to me one of the
most important books of verse to be published since the war. The
only reviewer to note this clearly was Alan Brownjohn in Listen
(Winter 1958). I dislike his attempt to write down Auden's
'Bucolics' by comparing them unfavourably with Fuller's 'Mytho-
logical Sonnets', but I soberly agree with him that much in Brutus's
Orchard has 'the wide view and generous compassion of major
poetry'. The distance that Fuller has travelled since 1942 may be
measured by comparing 'Poem' and 'Harbour Ferry' below, which
are from The Middle of a War (1942), with 'At a Warwickshire
Mansion' and 'The Final Period'. Fuller himself thinks that in
these and similar pieces in his last collection of poems there may be
an enlargement of vocabulary and a partial escape from 'the tyranny
of the personal lyric', the latter assisted perhaps by the writing of
prose fiction.

Of 'At a Warwickshire Mansion' Roy Fuller remarks that it
has 'a good wadding of general ideas which, I hope, raises it above
the level of personal yearnings and fears'. His commentary on the
poem will be helpful to the reader.

> I say that in the conflict between human art and human
> society it is society that seems to be the more permanent, be-
> cause evil and passion dominate the world, not the ordered
> ideas of art. Perhaps I do not develop this notion sufficiently –
> the last three lines of the last stanza seem paradoxical, though
> I think they follow from the previous stanza which emphasizes
> the weakness of the artist and points out that his natural audi-
> ence is the insane, who crave 'magic and mystery' – a classic
> symptom of schizophrenia, according to the textbooks.

'The Final Period' is almost entirely impersonal – here the poet's
mask is clearly compounded of late Yeats and late Shakespeare, the
former recalling his political poems which 'sent men out' to be

killed in the Irish Revolution, the latter thinking in retirement at
Stratford of Measure for Measure, Troilus and Cressida, *and*
other plays that deal with lust.

Poem

Reading the shorthand on a barber's sheet
In a warm and chromium basement in Cannon Street
I discovered again the message of the city,
That without power there is no place for pity.

The barber with a flat and scented hand
Moved the dummy's head in its collar band.
'What will you do with the discarded hair?'

The mirror showed a John the Baptist's face,
Detached and sideways. 'Can you tell me how,'
It said, 'I may recover grace?'

'Make me a merchant, make me a manager.'
His scissors mournfully declined the task.
'Will you do nothing that I ask?'

'It is no use,' he said, 'I cannot speak
To you as one in a similar position.
For me you are the stern employer,
Of wealth the accumulator.
I must ignore your singular disposition.'

He brushed my shoulders and under his practised touch
I knew his words were only a deceit.
'You spoke to me according to the rules
Laid down for dealing with madmen and with fools.'

'I do my best,' he said, 'my best is sufficient.
If I have offended it is because
I never formulate the ideal action
Which depends on observation.'

'And do you never observe and never feel
Regret at the destruction of wealth by war?
Do you never sharpen your razor on your heel
And draw it across selected throats?'

He smiled and turned away to the row of coats.
'This is your mackintosh,' he said, 'you had no hat.
Turn left for the station and remember the barber.
There is just time enough for that.'

Harbour Ferry

The oldest and simplest thoughts
Rise with the antique moon:
How she enamels men
And artillery under her sphere,
Eyelids and hair and throats
Rigid in love and war;
How this has happened before.

And how the lonely man
Raises his head and shudders
With a brilliant sense of the madness,
The age and shape of his planet,
Wherever his human hand
Whatever his set of tenets,
The long and crucial minute.

Tonight the moon has risen
Over a quiet harbour,
Through twisted iron and labour,

Lighting the half-drowned ships.
Oh surely the fatal chasm
Is closer, the furious steps
Swifter? The silver drips

From the angle of the wake:
The moon is flooding the faces.
The moment is over: the forces
Controlling lion nature
Look out of the eyes and speak:
Can you believe in a future
Left only to rock and creature?

At a Warwickshire Mansion

Mad world, mad kings, mad composition – King John

Cycles of ulcers, insomnia, poetry –
Badges of office; wished, detested tensions.
Seeing the parsley-like autumnal trees
Unmoving in the mist, I long to be
The marvellous painter who with art could freeze
Their transitory look: the vast dissensions
Between the human and his world arise
And plead with me to sew the hurt with eyes.

Horn calls on ostinato strings: the birds
Sweep level out of the umbrageous wood.
The sun towards the unconsidered west
Floats red, enormous, still. For these the words
Come pat, but for society possessed
With frontal lobes for evil, rear for good,
They are incongruous as the poisoner's
Remorse or as anaemia in furs.

In the dank garden of the ugly house
A group of leaden statuary perspires;
Moss grows between the ideal rumps and paps
Cast by the dead Victorian; the mouse
Starves behind massive panels; paths relapse
Like moral principles; the surrounding shires
Darken beneath the bombers' crawling wings,
The terrible simplifiers jerk the strings.

But art is never innocent although
It dreams it may be; and the red in caves
Is left by cripples of the happy hunt.
Between the action and the song I know
Too well the sleight of hand which points the blunt,
Compresses, lies. The schizophrenic craves
Magic and mystery, the rest the sane
Reject: what force and audience remain?

The house is dark upon the darkening sky:
I note the blue for which I never shall
Find the equivalent. I have been acting
The poet's role for quite as long as I
Can, at a stretch, without it being exacting:
I must return to less ephemeral
Affairs – to those controlled by love and power;
Builders of realms, their tenants for an hour.

The Final Period

I watch across the desk the slight
Shape of my daughter on the lawn.
With youth's desire my fingers write
And then contain an old man's yawn.

At first my only verb was 'give',
In middle age sought out a god:
Ugly and impotent I live
The myth of a final period.

I see within the tetrastich
A jealousy as gross, intense,
As ulcered that real love of which
Art's tragedies alone make sense.

He pulses still the man of force –
The armoured chest, the boar-thick yards;
And here the woman-nature, coarse
Beneath the dainty silks and fards.

Appalling that should still arise
All that is dead and was untrue,
That my imagination flies
Where now my flesh may not pursue.

Life goes on offering alarms
To be imprisoned in the cage
Of art. I must invent more charms
To still the girl's erotic rage:

Frozen in their betrothal kiss,
The innocent boy will never move
To loose the codpiece, and his miss
Stays spellbound in her father's love –

And yet the actual girl will sigh
And cross the garden with her flowers;
And I will leave the desk, and try
To live with ordinary powers.

Bermuda or Byzantium –
To some utopia of forgiving
And of acceptance I have come.
But still rebellious, still living.

The first absurd haphazard meeting
With one loved unrequitedly,
The insurrection caused by fleeting
Words of my own, while I stood by –

Those fatal and recorded times
Return like heartburn, and I see
Behind heroic plangent rhymes
Unutterable deficiency.

Even this noon of greens and blues;
June's badges, roses of human red;
Birds in the cavern of the yews;
A lark's quaver figure in my head;

The car in the lane that circumvents
The archipelagos of dung –
These trivial concomitants
Of feeling, these, too, must be sung.

And in the song all will be whole,
Immortal, though the author pass –
Ended his little speaking role –
On to the doomed and venal mass.

She comes whom I would marble through
Her painful and tumultuous years,
So she would wake at last in true
Epochs, to music of the spheres.

GEORGE BARKER

George Barker was born in Essex in 1913 and educated at an L.C.C. school in Chelsea and the Regent Street Polytechnic. He taught English Literature at a Japanese university in 1939 and lived in America from 1940 to 1943. His home is now in the country near Haslemere, halfway up Blackdown (at the top of which Tennyson once lived at Aldworth, his last hiding-place). He is married, has several children, and writes for a living. His first book of poems, Thirty Preliminary Poems, was published when he was twenty. He followed this up with Poems (1935), Calamiterror (1937), Lament and Triumph (1940), Eros in Dogma (1944), News of the World (1950), The True Confession of George Barker (1950), and A Vision of Beasts and Gods (1954). His Collected Poems, which excludes various poems (among them, at the publisher's request, 'The True Confession of George Barker'), appeared in 1957. Prose works include Alanna Autumnal (1933), Janus (1935), The Dead Seagull (1950).

Edwin Muir described Barker in 1939 as 'a poet of genius still at the unformed stage', and Calamiterror as 'a pouring out of all sorts of material, good and bad, deep and shallow'. There have been much less favourable judgements. The truth, as I see it, is that few modern poets have written so well and so badly inside the covers of one volume, sometimes inside a single poem. Reading his longer pieces is therefore rather like riding a switchback, continually being jerked and bucketed from some well-phrased perception into the bathetic and the grotesque. In a serious sense Barker is still an unformed poet, and is likely to remain one.

To characterize his work the reader needs to image a contention between unequal elements of the visceral and the moral-didactic, or, to put it another way, between a clumsier Dylan Thomas and a less intelligent Spender. In the thirties he was more of a moralist-politician than Thomas –

> *... by being miserable for myself, I began*
> *And now am miserable for the mass of man ...*

– and Calamiterror *was directly inspired by the Spanish Civil War.
The didactic is, on the whole, his strength. See, for example,
'Allegory of the Adolescent and the Adult' and 'Resolution of De-
pendence' in* Lament and Triumph, *from which 'Battersea Park'
is reprinted. But even in this book he can write:*

> *Of James O' Hanlon who died at the hand*
> *Of the Black with Blood, the with sin Tan ...*

*with an excruciating punning irrelevancy amounting to monumental
bad taste. A similar absurdity disfigures the 'Pacific Sonnets' in*
Eros in Dogma. *For example, the last two lines of 'Sonnet X'
read:*

> *Renders it as wretched as the mistletoe minute*
> *To the statuesque Balderdash in it.*

*Yet 'To My Mother', from the same volume and reprinted here,
seems to me a real achievement in the tender-comic, beautifully writ-
ten until the unfortunate pun in the last line. In still later work the
nonsense phrasing persists. 'At the Wake of Dylan Thomas' con-
tains the absurd line:*

> *The brainstruck harp lies with its bright wings furled ...*

*which one would expect almost any poet to remove at once. There is
enough 'statuesque Balderdash' in Barker's poetic writing to make
us understand why the* New Lines *poets regard him with suspicion.
To sum up, George Barker must be called a hit-or-miss artist, but
at least in* Lament and Triumph, *his best volume, and* Eros and
Dogma *there are hits to record.*

Battersea Park

Now it is November and mist wreathes the trees,
The horses cough their white blooms in the street,
Dogs shiver and boys run; the barges on the Thames
Lie like leviathans in the fog; and I meet

A world of lost wonders as I loiter in the haze
Where fog and sorrow cross my April days.

I recollect it was so often thus; with
Diamonds and pearls like mineral water pointing
The Park railings and the gardens' evergreens:
I spent my winters in summer's disappointments.
The things that burned so bright in my Augusts
Scattering me with their November dusts.

Now I marvel that I am again investigating
The fringes of the bare gardens in the winter.
I had expected to be otherwhere now,
Where the worm curls about the bone's splinter.
Now what good is the great world where I walk
That only revives desire to live once more?

How in the fog of failure and distress
Glitter of things seen in a flicker can
Paralyse will and deter determination,
Make a man afraid of the ghost of a man.
It is the wile of the world of crystal things
That catch the eye and keep me in their rings.

What I saw was Sorrow loitering along by
The Thames near the tall bridge by Battersea Park;
He had in his hand Pavlova or a swan,
And I heard him singing softly in the dark:
My twin, he sang to me, whatever of thine
Is sad and sorry, shall be glad of mine.

And he went on, singing a gay tune.
And now I know that the sorrow is this,
Not that the world a space of sorrow is
But that it's glad. O so gay a grief!
How can I ever be at home here
Where Sorrow sings of Joy in my ear?

How can I ever be happy here, where
The cock robin whistles with a gun at his breast;
Here where the flower has for bud a tear,
Here where Beauty breeds fodder for the Beast?
How can I here be happy when I know
I can be happy only here and now?

To My Mother

Most near, most dear, most loved and most far,
Under the window where I often found her
Sitting as huge as Asia, seismic with laughter,
Gin and chicken helpless in her Irish hand,
Irresistible as Rabelais, but most tender for
The lame dogs and hurt birds that surround her, –
She is a procession no one can follow after
But be like a little dog following a brass band.

She will not glance up at the bomber, or condescend
To drop her gin and scuttle to a cellar,
But lean on the mahogany table like a mountain
Whom only faith can move, and so I send
O all my faith and all my love to tell her
That she will move from mourning into morning.

R. S. THOMAS

*R. S. Thomas was born at Cardiff in 1913 and took a degree in
Latin from the University College of North Wales at Bangor. He
is a clergyman and was Rector of Manafon, Montgomeryshire,
where he wrote many of the poems in* Song at the Year's Turning
(1956), for twelve years between 1942 and 1954. He is now Vicar

*of Eglwys Fach, Machynlleth, Cardiganshire. His latest collection
of poems is* Poetry for Supper (*1958*). *Mr Thomas was brought
up to speak English and taught himself Welsh when he was adult.*
Song at the Year's Turning, *which is dedicated to the novelist
James Hanley and has an informative introduction by John Betje-
man, is a selection from poems published earlier in three small books
at Carmarthen and Newtown:* The Stones of the Field (*1946*),
An Acre of Land (*1952*), *and* The Minister (*1953*). *The poems
were not widely known until they were praised by Alan Pryce-Jones
on a B.B.C. programme in 1952.*

*R. S. Thomas is a traditional and local poet, but he is not in the
ordinary sense a nature-poet. Nor is topography his real concern. As
Betjeman says, Thomas is 'not at all literary and even remoter
from the neo-Georgians than he is from the pastoral poets of the
eighteenth century'. Indeed it is the harshness of the hill-country
life that comes out most strongly in his poetry — that and the hard-
ness of men dulled and impoverished by it. The priest is tied to his
people in a love–hate knot. He can love them, but it is almost too
difficult for him to like them.*

> *Men of the hills, wantoners, men of Wales,*
> *With your sheep and your pigs and your ponies, your sweaty*
>   *females,*
> *How I have hated you for your irreverence, your scorn even*
> *Of the refinements of art and the mysteries of the Church …*

*To the end they 'affront, bewilder, yet compel' his gaze. They
sharpen his vision and form his style; and he complains of their
barren ignorance, knowing that all the same their speech contains
'the source of all poetry'. 'A Priest to His People', from which I
have been quoting, 'The Airy Tomb', 'The Hill Farmer Speaks',
'Welsh Landscape' ('You cannot live in the present | At least not
in Wales'), 'Priest and Peasant' are a few of the poems that bear
on Thomas's central poetic subject, namely, growth into a know-
ledge of the real and the illusory in oneself and others from an en-
forced intimacy, like that of locked wrestlers, with what at first
seemed intolerably alien. 'A Peasant' is from* Song at the Year's
Turning (*originally from* The Stones of the Field), *'Iago Pry-*

therch' from Poetry for Supper. *One poem interprets the other.*
Both tell us as much of the poet as of the peasant.

A Peasant

Iago Prytherch his name, though, be it allowed,
Just an ordinary man of the bald Welsh hills,
Who pens a few sheep in a gap of cloud.
Docking mangels, chipping the green skin
From the yellow bones with a half-witted grin
Of satisfaction, or churning the crude earth
To a stiff sea of clods that glint in the wind –
So are his days spent, his spittled mirth
Rarer than the sun that cracks the cheeks
Of the gaunt sky perhaps once in a week.
And then at night see him fixed in his chair
Motionless, except when he leans to gob in the fire.
There is something frightening in the vacancy of his mind.
His clothes, sour with years of sweat
And animal contact, shock the refined,
But affected, sense with their stark naturalness.
Yet this is your prototype, who, season by season
Against siege of rain and the wind's attrition,
Preserves his stock, an impregnable fortress
Not to be stormed, even in death's confusion.
Remember him, then, for he, too, is a winner of wars,
Enduring like a tree under the curious stars.

Iago Prytherch

Iago Prytherch, forgive my naming you.
You are so far in your small fields
From the world's eye, sharpening your blade
On a cloud's edge, no one will tell you
How I made fun of you, or pitied either

Your long soliloquies, crouched at your slow
And patient surgery under the faint
November rays of the sun's lamp.

Made fun of you? That was their graceless
Accusation, because I took
Your rags for theme, because I showed them
Your thought's bareness; science and art,
The mind's furniture, having no chance
To install themselves, because of the great
Draught of nature sweeping the skull.

Fun? Pity? No word can describe
My true feelings. I passed and saw you
Labouring there, your dark figure
Marring the simple geometry
Of the square fields with its gaunt question.
My poems were made in its long shadow
Falling coldly across the page.

LAWRENCE DURRELL

Lawrence Durrell was born in India in 1914 and educated at Dar-jeeling and St Edmund's School, Canterbury. For several years after leaving school he led a bohemian life in London, at one time playing the piano in a nightclub for a living, at another working in a photographer's studio, but for the last twenty years or so he has lived abroad, chiefly around the Mediterranean, and he now writes his books at his home in Provence. During the bad troubles of the fifties he was Director of Public Relations for the Government of Cyprus – his Bitter Lemons *has life on the island as its subject – and earlier he had held appointments as Foreign Service Press officer at Athens and Cairo (where he worked at the British Embassy during part of the war); as a Press attaché at Alexandria and*

Belgrade; and as Director of Public Relations for the Dodecanese islands. Before the war he lived for a while in Corfu, and in the intervals between some of the appointments listed he has been Director of British Council Institutes at Kalamata (Greece) and Cordoba (Argentina).

Since the completion of The Alexandria Quartet *(1957–60), a 'word continuum' consisting of the four novels* Justine, Balthazar, Mountolive, *and* Clea, *Durrell is probably better known as a novelist than as a poet, but it was as a poet that he began writing, and it is his poetry that still seems to me his central achievement. His first poetic collection – if we disregard a preliminary* Poems *(1938), edited by O. Blakeston – was* A Private Country *(1943). Later volumes are:* Cities, Plains and People *(1946),* On Seeming to Presume *(1948), and* The Tree of Idleness *(1955). Collected Poems appeared in 1960. Other publications than those already mentioned include* Prospero's Cell *(1947) and* Reflections on a Marine Venus *(1953), which he describes as 'companions to the landscapes of Corfu and Rhodes', a verse play* Sappho *(1950), and a single work of literary criticism,* A Key to Modern Poetry *(1952).*

Lawrence Durrell's work, in which the evocation of the landscapes of the Aegean Islands and of the Near East plays an important part as a background to feeling, has a sensuousness nicely kept in control by wit and a satirical temperament. I find this combination exhilarating and satisfying. His weaknesses are occasional carelessness about making his meaning clear and, in some of the earlier poems, a kind of undergraduate brashness. Carols I, III, and V from 'The Death of General Uncebunke' and 'A Ballad of the Good Lord Nelson' appeared originally in A Private Country, *'Deus Loci' in* The Tree of Idleness. *'The Death of General Uncebunke', a biography in little, consists of fourteen carols and five soliloquies with this preliminary note:*

Not satire but an exercise in ironic compassion, celebrating a simplicity of heart which is proof against superiority or the tooth of the dog ... After all, we may have had other criteria, but they were only criteria.

I should have liked to print all fourteen carols and, lacking space, I ought perhaps to have chosen something else complete in itself. But these poems please me and a few other people whose opinions I value. 'A Ballad of the Good Lord Nelson' is good, not so clean, fun. 'Deus Loci' was suggested by Mr Durrell for inclusion so that his 'Mediterranean' self as well as his 'Cockney' self might be represented.

The Death of General Uncebunke

I

My uncle sleeps in the image of death.
In the greenhouse and in the potting-shed
The wrens junket: the old girl with the trowel
Is a pillar of salt, insufferably brittle.
His not to reason why, though a thinking man.
Beside his mesmeric incomprehension
The little mouse mopping and mowing,
The giraffe and the spin-turtle, these can
On my picture-book look insufferably little
But knowing, incredibly Knowing.

III

Aunt Prudence, she was the eye of the needle.
Sleeping, a shepherdess of ghostly sheep.
'Thy will be done in Baden Baden.
In Ouchy, Lord, and in Vichy.'
In the garden of the vicarage sorting stamps
Was given merit of the poor in spirit
For dusting a cinquefoil, tuning the little lamps.

Well, God sends weather, the English apple,
The weeping willow.
Grum lies the consort of Prudence quite:
Mum as a long fiddle in regimentals:

This sudden IT between two tropical thumbs.
Unwrinkle him, Lord, unriddle this strange gorgon,
For tall Prudence who softens the small lamps,
Gives humble air to the organ that it hums.

v

My uncle has gone beyond astronomy.
His sleep is of the Babylonian deep-sea
Darker than bitumen, defter than devil's alliances.
He has seen Golgotha in carnival:
Now in the shin-bone the smart worm
Presides at the death of the sciences,
The Trinity sleeps in his knee.

Curse Orion who pins my man like moth,
Who sleeps in the monotony of his zone,
Who is a daft ankle-bone among stars,
O shame on the beggar by silent lands
Who has nothing but carbon for his own.

Uncouple the flutes! Strike with the black rod!
Our song is no more plural, the bones
Are hollow without your air, Lord God.
Give us the language of diamonds or
The speech of the little stones.

A Ballad of the Good Lord Nelson

The Good Lord Nelson had a swollen gland,
Little of the scripture did he understand
Till a woman led him to the promised land
    Aboard the Victory, Victory O.

Adam and Evil and a bushel of figs
Meant nothing to Nelson who was keeping pigs,
Till a woman showed him the various rigs
    Aboard the Victory, Victory O.

His heart was softer than a new laid egg,
Too poor for loving and ashamed to beg,
Till Nelson was taken by the Dancing Leg
　　Aboard the Victory, Victory O.

Now he up and did up his little tin trunk
And he took to the ocean on his English junk,
Turning like the hour-glass in his lonely bunk
　　Aboard the Victory, Victory O.

The Frenchmen saw him a-coming there
With the one-piece eye and the valentine hair,
With the safety-pin sleeve and occupied air
　　Aboard the Victory, Victory O.

Now you all remember the message he sent
As an answer to Hamilton's discontent –
There were questions asked about it in the Parliament
　　Aboard the Victory, Victory O.

Now the blacker the berry, the thicker comes the juice.
Think of Good Lord Nelson and avoid self-abuse,
For the empty sleeve was no mere excuse
　　Aboard the Victory, Victory O.

'England Expects' was the motto he gave
When he thought of little Emma out on Biscay's wave,
And remembered working on her like a galley-slave
　　Aboard the Victory, Victory O.

The first Great Lord in our English land
To honour the Freudian command,
For a cast in the bush is worth two in the hand
　　Aboard the Victory, Victory O.

Now the Frenchman shot him there as he stood
In the rage of battle in a silk-lined hood
And he heard the whistle of his own hot blood
    Aboard the Victory, Victory O.

Now stiff on a pillar with a phallic air
Nelson stylites in Trafalgar Square
Reminds the British what once they were
    Aboard the Victory, Victory O.

If they'd treat their women in the Nelson way
There'd be fewer frigid husbands every day
And many more heroes on the Bay of Biscay
    Aboard the Victory, Victory O.

Deus Loci

1

All our religions founder, you
remain, small sunburnt *deus loci*
safe in your natal shrine,
landscape of the precocious southern heart,
continuously revived in passion's common
tragic and yet incorrigible spring:
in every special laughter overheard,
your specimen is everything –
accents of the little cackling god,
part animal, part insect, and part bird.

2

This dust, this royal dust, our mother
modelled by spring-belonging rain
whose soft blank drops console
a single vineyard's fever or a region
falls now in soft percussion on the earth's
old stretched and wrinkled vellum skin:

each drop could make one think
a footprint of the god, but out of season,
yet in your sudden coming know
life lives itself without recourse to reason.

3

On how many of your clement springs
the fishermen set forth, the foresters
resign their empty glasses, rise,
confront the morning star, accept
the motiveless patronage of all you are –
desire recaptured on the sea or land
in the fables of fish, or grapes held up,
a fistful of some champion wine
glowing like a stained-glass window
in a drunkard's trembling hand.

4

All the religions of the dust can tell –
this body of damp clay that cumbered so
Adam, and those before, was given him,
material for his lamp and spoon and body;
to renovate your terra cotta shrines
whose cupids unashamed
to make a fable of the common lot
curled up like watchsprings in a kiss,
or turned to *putti* for a lover's bed,
or *amorini* for a shepherd's little cot.

5

Known before the expurgation of gods
wherever nature's carelessness exposed
her children to the fear of the unknown –
in families gathered by hopeless sickness
about a dying candle, or in sailors
on tilting decks and under shrouded planets:

wherever the unknown has displaced the known
you encouraged in the fellowship of wine
of love and husbandry: and in despair
only to think of you and you were there.

6

The saddle-nose, the hairy thighs
composed these vines, these humble vines,
so dedicated to themselves yet offering
in the black froth of grapes their increment
to pleasure or to sadness where a poor
peasant at a husky church-bell's chime
crosses himself: on some cracked pedestal
by the sighing sea sets eternally up,
item by item, his small mid-day meal,
garlic and bread, the wine-can and the cup.

7

Image of our own dust in wine!
drinkers of that royal dust pressed out
drop by cool drop in science and in love
into a model of the absconding god's
image – human like our own. Or else in other
mixtures, of breath in kisses dropped
under the fig's dark noonday lantern, yes,
lovers like tenants of a wishing-well
whose heartbeats labour though all time has stopped.

8

Your panic fellowship is everywhere,
not only in love's first great illness known,
but in the exile of objects lost
to context, broken hearts, spilt milk,
oaths disregarded, laws forgotten:

or on the seashore some old pilot's
capital in rags of sail, snapped oars,
water-jars choked with sand,
and further on, half hidden, the fatal letter
in the cold fingers of some marble hand.

9

Deus loci your provinces extend
throughout the domains of logic,
beyond the eyes watching from dusty murals
or the philosopher's critical impatience
to understand, to be done with life:
beyond beyond even the mind's dark spools
in a vine-wreath or an old wax cross
you can become the nurse and wife of fools,
their actions and their nakedness –
all the heart's profit or the loss.

10

So today, after many years, we meet
at this high window overlooking
the best of Italy, smiling under rain,
that rattles down the leaves like sparrow-shot,
scatters the reapers, the sunburnt girls,
rises in the sour dust of this table,
these books, unfinished letters – all
refreshed again in you O spirit of place,
Presence long since divined, delayed, and waited for,
And here met face to face.

DYLAN THOMAS

Dylan Thomas was born in 1914 at Swansea and educated at Swansea Grammar School. The main facts of his life – even if they have been decorated with a good deal of legendary material – are now so well known that they hardly need to be repeated here except in the most summary form. When Thomas first came up to London he lived by his journalistic wits, doing reviewing and other jobs for newspapers and magazines. Later he married (and 'life with Caitlin', too, is now part of the legend). During the war he tackled B.B.C. and film work after being rejected for the army, and in those fields he rapidly made a deserved reputation then and in the post-war years as a script-writer for screen and radio and as a broadcaster ('The poor man's Charles Laughton' was how he described his own 'poetry' voice and manner). The Sunday Referee *prize, Rimbaud-isms and alcoholisms in London and elsewhere before and after the war, home life at Laugharne, the lecture tours in the U.S.A. – these and other elements in his story can be read about in* Dylan Thomas: the Legend and the Poet *(1960), a miscellaneous collection of reminiscences and appraisals edited by E. W. Tedlock, and in the earlier books by John Malcolm Brinnin (1956) and Caitlin Thomas (1957) – to mention only three obvious sources. Brinnin's* Dylan Thomas in America *is an honest and convincing piece of work in spite of the accusations that have been made of muckraking: as D. J. Enright has pointed out, the death of Dylan Thomas, which took place in New York in November 1953, was 'the occasion of a general leave-taking of senses, even on the part of normally reasonable people' and the lapse of time before Brinnin's book appeared was not enough to prevent resentment at well-intentioned candour. (The high peak of earlier hysteria is probably George Barker's peculiar notion that Thomas's death represented 'the undisguised intervention of the powers of darkness in our affairs'.) Sometimes it seems that almost everyone has one good 'Dylan'* story, *usually a drinking story, which he cannot wait to put into circulation, but if one goes back to the poems it is fairly clear that the really important time for Dylan Thomas, almost as much as for Walter de la Mare, was his childhood – his own memories of it, pointed up with picturesque extravagance and soaked in broad humour, can be found in a brilliant collection of radio scripts,* Quite Early One Morning, *edited by Aneirin Davies in 1954. During his life Dylan Thomas published the following books of poems:* 18 Poems (*1934*), Twenty-Five Poems (*1936*), Deaths and Entrances (*1946*), Collected Poems, 1934–52 (*1952*); *and two prose works,* The Map of Love (*1939*), *which also contains some poems, and* Portrait of the Artist as a Young Dog (*1940*). *Apart from* Quite Early One Morning, *posthumously there have appeared* Under Milk Wood (*1954*), *the highly popular but also in many parts genuinely funny and moving 'play for voices',* A Prospect of the Sea (*1955*), *uncollected stories and other prose writings, and the unfinished fantastic novel,* Adventures in the Skin Trade (*1955*). *The last has an interesting foreword by Vernon Watkins. There was a memorable first production of* Under Milk Wood *by the B.B.C. with an all-Welsh cast in January 1954.*

The poetry of Dylan Thomas has been widely acclaimed and with particular emphasis by Sir Herbert Read ('... the most absolute poetry that has been written in our time ...') and Dame Edith Sitwell ('A new poet has arisen who shows every sign of greatness. His work is on a huge scale both in theme and structurally'). Stephen Spender is more reserved but still positive ('Dylan Thomas is a poet of whom, at times, we can use the word "genius" '). Geoffrey Grigson, who printed Thomas's early work in New Verse *and recognized its promise, dissents from these judgements. He attacks Thomas for his neglect of a continuous line of meaning and for being, at times, fantastic and slovenly. There is, of course, a real disagreement here, but it is less than it at first sight appears. On the promise of Thomas's early poems there is agreement, but the rhetoric was too drunken, the insight too fragmentary, the lack of unity in most of the pieces too obvious, for his first two books to be spoken of as positive achievements. Certain poems did break through into real life before* The Map of Love (*1939*), *for example*

'*In Memory of Anne Jones*' (*reprinted there, first published in 1938*), *but much more frequent were poems like* '*A Grief Ago*', *full of towering phrases and* '*vertebrate*', *but arbitrarily obscure for lack of a central theme or any clear impulse on the poet's part beyond that of wishing to produce a poem. It is to be noted that Spender reserves his real praise of Dylan Thomas for the work produced after 1943 and collected in* Deaths and Entrances (*1946*). *It is also to be noted that the carping note in Mr Grigson's criticism is due not only to what he considers faults in Thomas's work, but to the use of Thomas as a spearhead in the attack on the kind of poetry written by Auden. It is a fact that Dylan Thomas fathered the* '*Apocalyptic*' *movement and with it a lot of bad thinking and bad writing, but the sins of the children should not always be visited on their fathers. In my opinion Thomas moved in his later work towards the decorum of a more continuous* '*narrative*' *of meaning, and both* '*The Hunchback in the Park*' *and* '*Poem in October*' (*reprinted here from* Deaths and Entrances) *are satisfactory in this respect. His real poetic achievement, which in the heat of battle the* '*Movement*' *poets of the fifties were reluctant to recognize, consists of these and perhaps another dozen of his later poems (including* '*Do not go gentle into that good night*', '*Fern Hill*', *and the finished sections of the projected* '*In Country Heaven*'). *Very few of the poems produced before the war stand up with the same certainty, but* '*After the Funeral*' (*alias* '*In Memory of Anne Jones*') *is one of them. The worst of Thomas's poetic writing is the* '*Altar-wise by owl-light*' *sequence, which has, however, been eccentrically championed by the Chicago critic, Elder Olson. More useful than Olson's book, which I am reluctant to advertise further by naming it, is Henry Treece's enthusiastic* Dylan Thomas: 'Dog among the Fairies' (*1949, revised edition 1956*). *For all its rather juvenile snarling at* '*uncommitted*' *readers and critics and its innocence of critical approach, this book furnishes helpful information to those about to tackle Thomas for the first time and should not be ignored even by more sophisticated readers.*

A Grief Ago

A grief ago,
She who was who I hold, the fats and flower,
Or, water-lammed, from the scythe-sided thorn,
Hell wind and sea,
A stem cementing, wrestled up the tower,
Rose maid and male,
Or, masted venus, through the paddler's bowl
Sailed up the sun;

Who is my grief,
A chrysalis unwrinkling on the iron,
Wrenched by my fingerman, the leaden bud
Shot through the leaf,
Was who was folded on the rod the aaron
Rose cast to plague,
The horn and ball of water on the frog
Housed in the side.

And she who lies,
Like exodus a chapter from the garden,
Brand of the lily's anger on her ring,
Tugged through the days
Her ropes of heritage, the wars of pardon,
On field and sand
The twelve triangles of the cherub wind
Engraving going.

Who then is she,
She holding me? The people's sea drives on her,
Drives out the father from the caesared camp;
The dens of shape
Shape all her whelps with the long voice of water,
That she I have,
The country-handed grave boxed into love,
Rise before dark.

The night is near,
A nitric shape that leaps her, time and acid;
I tell her this: before the suncock cast
Her bone to fire.
Let her inhale her dead, through seed and solid
Draw in their seas,
So cross her hand with their grave gipsy eyes,
And close her fist.

After the Funeral

After the funeral, mule praises, brays,
Windshake of sailshaped ears, muffle-toed tap
Tap happily of one peg in the thick
Grave's foot, blinds down the lids, the teeth in black,
The spittled eyes, the salt ponds in the sleeves,
Morning smack of the spade that wakes up sleep,
Shakes a desolate boy who slits his throat
In the dark of the coffin and sheds dry leaves,
That breaks one bone to light with a judgement clout,
After the feast of tear-stuffed time and thistles
In a room with a stuffed fox and a stale fern,
I stand, for this memorial's sake, alone
In the snivelling hours with dead, humped Ann
Whose hooded, fountain heart once fell in puddles
Round the parched worlds of Wales and drowned each sun,
(Though this for her is a monstrous image blindly
Magnified out of praise; her death was a still drop;
She would not have me sinking in the holy
Flood of her heart's fame; she would lie dumb and deep
And need no druid of her broken body).
But I, Ann's bard on a raised hearth, call all
The seas to service that her wood-tongued virtue
Babble like a bellbuoy over the hymning heads,
Bow down the walls of the ferned and foxy woods
That her love sing and swing through a brown chapel,

Bless her bent spirit with four, crossing birds.
Her flesh was meek as milk, but this skyward statue
With the wild breast and blessed and giant skull
Is carved from her in a room with a wet window
In a fiercely mourning house in a crooked year.
I know her scrubbed and sour humble hands
Lie with religion in their cramp, her threadbare
Whisper in a damp word, her wits drilled hollow,
Her fist of a face died clenched on a round pain;
And sculptured Ann is seventy years of stone.
These cloud-sopped, marble hands, this monumental
Argument of the hewn voice, gesture and psalm
Storm me for ever over her grave until
The stuffed lung of the fox twitch and cry Love
And the strutting fern lay seeds on the black sill.

The Hunchback in the Park

The hunchback in the park
A solitary mister
Propped between trees and water
From the opening of the garden lock
That lets the trees and water enter
Until the Sunday sombre bell at dark

Eating bread from a newspaper
Drinking water from the chained cup
That the children filled with gravel
In the fountain basin where I sailed my ship
Slept at night in a dog kennel
But nobody chained him up.

Like the park birds he came early
Like the water he sat down
And Mister they called Hey mister
The truant boys from the town

Running when he had heard them clearly
On out of sound

Past lake and rockery
Laughing when he shook his paper
Hunchbacked in mockery
Through the loud zoo of the willow groves
Dodging the park keeper
With his stick that picked up leaves.

And the old dog sleeper
Alone between nurses and swans
While the boys among willows
Made the tigers jump out of their eyes
To roar on the rockery stones
And the groves were blue with sailors

Made all day until bell time
A woman figure without fault
Straight as a young elm
Straight and tall from his crooked bones
That she might stand in the night
After the locks and chains

All night in the unmade park
After the railings and shrubberies
The birds the grass the trees the lake
And the wild boys innocent as strawberries
Had followed the hunchback
To his kennel in the dark.

Poem in October

It was my thirtieth year to heaven
Woke to my hearing from harbour and neighbour wood
And the mussel pooled and the heron
Priested shore

The morning beckon
With water praying and call of seagull and rook
And the knock of sailing boats on the net webbed wall
         Myself to set foot
         That second
In the still sleeping town and set forth.

         My birthday began with the water-
Birds and the birds of the winged trees flying my name
         Above the farms and the white horses
                  And I rose
                  In rainy autumn
And walked abroad in a shower of all my days.
High tide and the heron dived when I took the road
         Over the border
                  And the gates
Of the town closed as the town awoke.

         A springful of larks in a rolling
Cloud and the roadside bushes brimming with whistling
         Blackbirds and the sun of October
                  Summery
         On the hill's shoulder,
Here were fond climates and sweet singers suddenly
Come in the morning where I wandered and listened
         To the rain wringing
                  Wind blow cold
In the wood faraway under me.

         Pale rain over the dwindling harbour
And over the sea wet church the size of a snail
         With its horns through mist and the castle
                  Brown as owls
         But all the gardens
Of spring and summer were blooming in the tall tales
Beyond the border and under the lark full cloud.

There could I marvel
My birthday
Away but the weather turned around.

It turned away from the blithe country
And down the other air and the blue altered sky
Streamed again a wonder of summer
With apples
Pears and red currants
And I saw in the turning so clearly a child's
Forgotten mornings when he walked with his mother
Through the parables
Of sunlight
And the legends of the green chapels

And the twice told fields of infancy
That his tears burned my cheeks and his heart moved in mine.
These were the woods the river and sea
Where a boy
In the listening
Summertime of the dead whispered the truth of his joy
To the trees and the stones and the fish in the tide.
And the mystery
Sang alive
Still in the water and singingbirds.

And there could I marvel my birthday
Away but the weather turned around. And the true
Joy of the long dead child sang burning
In the sun.
It was my thirtieth
Year to heaven stood there then in the summer noon
Though the town below lay leaved with October blood.
O may my heart's truth
Still be sung
On this high hill in a year's turning.

NORMAN NICHOLSON

Norman Nicholson was born in 1914 at Millom, Cumberland, where he has lived all his life, and was educated at local schools. He earns his living by writing and is known as a book-critic and broad-caster. He is married. In 1959 he became an Honorary M.A. of Manchester University. His first independent collection of verse, Five Rivers *(1944), was preceded by* Selected Poems *(in which his work was accompanied by that of J. C. Hall and Keith Douglas) and followed by* Rock Face *(1948) and* The Pot Geranium *(1954). He has also published three verse plays:* The Old Man of the Mountains *(1946),* Prophesy to the Wind *(1950), and* A Match for the Devil *(1955), the last of which was produced at the Edinburgh Festival in 1953. Other publications include* William Cowper *(1951),* The Lakers *(1955), and* Provincial Pleasures *(1959).*

The Old Man of the Mountains *is the story of Elijah and the raven transferred to modern times and a Cumberland setting. Nicholson's poetry is built around two main elements – his religious beliefs and his affection for his own region (which is not the Lake District, but the industrial belt of Cumberland along the coast). He is very much a local poet. 'Whatever critics may say about my technique,' he has claimed, 'they cannot find fault with my topography.' He is stimulated by what is near at hand, familiar, and apparently commonplace. This makes me think that it was probably a mistake not to choose a poem of place from* Five Rivers *to represent his earlier work rather than 'A Poem for Epiphany', a religious lyric tinged – quite untypically for Nicholson – with the neo-romantic 'strangeness' of the forties. What is typical of Nicholson is the solidity, colour, and energy that he gets into his poetic scenes, and these qualities are present from the beginning – which is another way of saying that there is no striking development to record in passing from* Five Rivers *to* The Pot Geranium. *'A Turn for the Better',*

*which exemplifies the religious and local elements in his verse, is from
this last volume. Other good poems in* The Pot Geranium *are 'The
Buzzer', 'Millom Old Quarry', 'The Undiscovered Planet', and
'Ravenglass Railway Station'.*

Poem for Epiphany

Three Kings stepped out of my body,
Walked across the sand by the wild sea
From December into January.

A King stepped out of my head,
And before him the sand was red
And the sea gold,
And he beheld
The landscape like an empire and found in
Even a sycamore leaf the plan of his domain.
And he offered the gold of his sight
The regimen of his thought
To the Child born that night.

A King stepped out of my breast
Who had the bearing of a priest.
To him the moon's movement
Was a sacrament,
And the taste of water and of wine,
The touch of bread and the weight of a stone.
And he offered the frankincense of the heart,
Prayer swung in the censer on the charcoal alight,
To the Child born that night.

A King stepped out of my loins,
And black as grapes were his skin and his veins.
In him was the anger of sex
Where the blood like a sea on the shingle breaks,
The pride of living, the longing for further birth

Because of the presentiment of death.
And he offered the myrrh of tiredness, the untight'ning of the
      fingers from the nerve's root
To the Child born that night.

Three Kings stepped out of my body
But only my two eyes between the three —
Only my two eyes and the wild skies to see.

A Turn for the Better

'Now I Joseph was walking, and I walked not.'
     Book of James or Protevangelium

Now I Joseph was walking, and I walked not,
Between the allotments on a December morning.
The clouds were mauve as a crocus, peeling back petals,
And a sparse pollen of snow came parping down
On the bare ground and green-house groins and dun
Tight-head chrysanthemums crumpled by the frost.
The cock in the hen-run blustered to its perch
On the lid of the swill bucket, rattled its red
At the fluttering flakes, levered its throat open —
And not a croak creaked out.

                I looked about me:
The snow was stock-still in the sky like pluckings
Of cottonwool glued on a grocer's window,
And down in the brown of the dyke, a smoky feather
Lit on a robin's head, between the black
Glass-ally eyes and the gimlet beak,
And never a flick it gave to shake it off.
Workmen on the electric cable track
Swung picks in the air and held them there, rigid,
Raised bait to mouths and never took a bite.
One, putting up a hand to scratch his head,
Shifted the peak of his cap a couple of inch,

And never scratched. A dead leaf drifting
Hung bracketed against the wire netting
Like a pin caught on a magnet.

                       For at that minute,
Making was made, history rolled
Backward and forward into time, memory was unfolded
Like a quick discovery, old habits were invented,
Old phrases coined. The tree grew down
Into its sapling self, the sapling into the seed.
Cobbles of wall and slate of rafters
Were cleft and stratified again as rock,
And the rock un-weathered itself a cloud-height higher,
And the sea flowered over it. A brand-new now
Stretched on either hand to then and someday,
Might have and perhaps.

                       Then suddenly the cock
Coughed up its crow, the robin skittered off,
And the snow fell like a million pound of shillings.
And out in the beginning always of the world
I heard the cry of a child.

HENRY REED

Henry Reed was born in Birmingham in 1914 and educated at the King Edward VI School, Birmingham, and Birmingham University. Between 1937 and 1941 he did some teaching and became a free-lance journalist. He is glad, he has said, to have been in Birmingham 'one of a group of people which included Auden and Mac-Neice, John Hampson and Walter Allen, the painter John Melville, the critic Robert Melville, and the sculptor Gordon Herrick'. He was called up in 1941, but was released from the army in 1942 and went to work at the Foreign Office (1942–5). At the end of the war he returned to writing for a living. Since then he has done a good deal of work for broadcasting, including a radio version of Moby Dick, *which was published in 1947, and some widely praised humorous scripts for the Third Programme of the B.B.C. ('Hilda Tablet', etc.).*

A Map of Verona (1946), his only book of verse, has great competence in its varied metres and manners. There are good things in the less colloquial poems such as 'Philoctetes' and the 'Tintagel' sequence, but there can be no question that 'Naming of Parts' and 'Judging Distances' are the best poems in the book, as they are among the best and most intelligent poems produced during the war. I should also have liked to print 'Chard Whitlow', the wickedest and funniest parody of Mr Eliot known to me.

Lessons of the War

Vixi duellis nuper idoneus
Et militavi non sine gloria

I. Naming of Parts

Today we have naming of parts. Yesterday,
We had daily cleaning. And tomorrow morning,
We shall have what to do after firing. But today,
Today we have naming of parts. Japonica
Glistens like coral in all of the neighbouring gardens,
    And today we have naming of parts.

This is the lower sling swivel. And this
Is the upper sling swivel, whose use you will see,
When you are given your slings. And this is the piling swivel,
Which in your case you have not got. The branches
Hold in the gardens their silent, eloquent gestures,
    Which in our case we have not got.

This is the safety-catch, which is always released
With an easy flick of the thumb. And please do not let me
See anyone using his finger. You can do it quite easy
If you have any strength in your thumb. The blossoms
Are fragile and motionless, never letting anyone see
    Any of them using their finger.

And this you can see is the bolt. The purpose of this
Is to open the breech, as you see. We can slide it
Rapidly backwards and forwards: we call this
Easing the spring. And rapidly backwards and forwards
The early bees are assaulting and fumbling the flowers:
    They call it easing the Spring.

They call it easing the Spring: it is perfectly easy
If you have any strength in your thumb: like the bolt,
And the breech, and the cocking-piece, and the point of balance,
Which in our case we have not got; and the almond-blossom
Silent in all of the gardens and the bees going backwards and
    forwards,
    For today we have naming of parts.

II. Judging Distances

Not only how far away, but the way that you say it
Is very important. Perhaps you may never get
The knack of judging a distance, but at least you know
How to report on a landscape: the central sector,
The right of arc and that, which we had last Tuesday,
    And at least you know

That maps are of time, not place, so far as the army
Happens to be concerned – the reason being,
Is one which need not delay us. Again, you know
There are three kinds of tree, three only, the fir and the poplar,
And those which have bushy tops to; and lastly
    That things only seem to be things.

A barn is not called a barn, to put it more plainly,
Or a field in the distance, where sheep may be safely grazing.
You must never be over-sure. You must say, when reporting:
At five o'clock in the central sector is a dozen
Of what appear to be animals; whatever you do,
          Don't call the bleeders *sheep*.

I am sure that's quite clear; and suppose, for the sake of example,
The one at the end, asleep, endeavours to tell us
What he sees over there to the west, and how far away,
After first having come to attention. There to the west,
On the fields of summer the sun and the shadows bestow
          Vestments of purple and gold.

The still white dwellings are like a mirage in the heat,
And under the swaying elms a man and a woman
Lie gently together. Which is, perhaps, only to say
That there is a row of houses to the left of arc,
And that under some poplars a pair of what appear to be humans
          Appear to be loving.

Well that, for an answer, is what we might rightly call
Moderately satisfactory only, the reason being,
Is that two things have been omitted, and those are important.
The human beings, now: in what direction are they,
And how far away, would you say? And do not forget
          There may be dead ground in between.

There may be dead ground in between; and I may not have got
The knack of judging a distance; I will only venture
A guess that perhaps between me and the apparent lovers,
(Who, incidentally, appear by now to have finished,)
At seven o'clock from the houses, is roughly a distance
          Of about one year and a half.

LAURIE LEE

Laurie Lee was born in 1914 in the Cotswolds and educated at a village school and Stroud Central School. He travelled in the Mediterranean between 1935 and 1939 and worked with the G.P.O. Film Unit in 1939–40 and with the Crown Film Unit from then until 1943. From 1944 to 1946 he was Publications Editor at the Ministry of Information and then worked for a year with the Green Park Film Unit. He wrote captions for the Festival of Britain in 1951 and was awarded the M.B.E. in 1952. He was represented in Poets of Tomorrow, Third Selection *(1942), but his first complete volume was* The Sun My Monument *(1944), which shows that he had learnt something from Lorca. His second book of verse,* The Bloom of Candles *(1947), which is sub-titled 'verses from a poet's year' and consists of twelve short poems, is at the same time less ambitious and from the point of view of craftsmanship a much more finished job than* The Sun My Monument. *A third collection,* My Many-Coated Man *(1955), is like its predecessor quite literally 'a slim volume' – it consists of fifteen short poems printed on one side of the paper only to create an illusion of what even then could hardly be called bulk. The manner is similar to that of* The Bloom of Candles. *Laurie Lee has also published* The Voyage of Magellan *(1948), a verse play originally written for the B.B.C. Third Programme, and* Cider with Rosie *(1959), an autobiographical best-seller that has been awarded a literary prize.*

There is euphuism, I suggest, in the poet's combination of sophisticated recording of sensation with simple feeling, and perhaps a wilfulness in his romantic determination to avoid the least tincture of modernity, but the best poems in The Bloom of Candles *and* My Many-Coated Man *have perhaps as much simplicity as Tennysonian simplesse.*

April Rise

If ever I saw blessing in the air
　I see it now in this still early day
Where lemon-green the vaporous morning drips
　Wet sunlight on the powder of my eye.

Blown bubble-film of blue, the sky wraps round
　Weeds of warm light whose every root and rod
Splutters with soapy green, and all the world
　Sweats with the bead of summer in its bud.

If ever I heard blessing it is there
　Where birds in trees that shoals and shadows are
Splash with their hidden wings and drops of sound
　Break on my ears their crests of throbbing air.

Pure in the haze the emerald sun dilates,
　The lips of sparrows milk the mossy stones,
While white as water by the lake a girl
　Swims her green hand among the gathered swans.

Now, as the almond burns its smoking wick,
　Dropping small flames to light the candled grass;
Now, as my low blood scales its second chance,
　If ever world were blessed, now it is.

ALUN LEWIS

*Alun Lewis, who was born in 1915, came from a mining area of
South Wales. He read medieval history at the University of Wales
and took his M.A. degree in 1939. Having joined the army, he went
out to India in 1942 as a lieutenant in The South Wales Borderers.
Something of his physical existence there and more of his mental life*

and of the things which were important to him (his marriage, his Welsh descent — 'I know more Urdu than Welsh: it's very sad' — his ambitions for future stories and poems) can be learnt from Letters from India (*1946*), *selected by Gweno Lewis and Gwyn Jones with a brief preface by A. L. Rowse. He was killed in an accident in Arakan early in 1944.*

'Thinking back on my own writing,' he had said in June 1943, 'it all seemed to mature of a sudden between the winter of 1939 and the following autumn. Can't make it out. Was it Gweno [his wife] and the Army? What a combination!!! Beauty and the Beast!' His first collection of poems, Raiders' Dawn, *containing the much-quoted 'All Day it has Rained' and revelatory of his devotion to Edward Thomas, came out in 1942 and was well received, as was* The Last Inspection, *a book of short stories. His second book of poems,* Ha! Ha! among the Trumpets, *appeared posthumously in 1944 with a foreword by Robert Graves, who had read the manuscript at the poet's request and advised on the revision and exclusion of certain poems.*

The name of Alun Lewis has often been bracketed with that of Sidney Keyes when critics and columnists have discussed the best poets thrown up by the war, but it is possible that Lewis, had he lived, would have developed rather as a prose-writer than as a poet, and that his gift was only temporarily sharpened into poetic expression by war, love, and separation. One cannot be sure of this, and Robert Graves's opinion certainly shakes me. In all Lewis's writing there is a most attractive honesty and unpretentiousness — 'My longing,' he said, 'is more and more for one thing only, integrity, and I discount the other qualities in people far too ruthlessly if they lack that fundamental sincerity and wholeness.' 'The Mahratta Ghats', which comes from the third part of Ha! Ha! among the Trumpets, *has the directness and solidity which are to me the most positive of his qualities as a poet.*

The Mahratta Ghats

The valleys crack and burn, the exhausted plains
Sink their black teeth into the horny veins
Straggling the hills' red thighs, the bleating goats
– Dry bents and bitter thistles in their throats –
Thread the loose rocks by immemorial tracks.
Dark peasants drag the sun upon their backs.

High on the ghat the new turned soil is red,
The sun has ground it to the finest red,
It lies like gold within each horny hand.
Siva has spilt his seed upon this land.

Will she who burns and withers on the plain
Leave, ere too late, her scraggy herds of pain,
The cow-dung fire and the trembling beasts,
The little wicked gods, the grinning priests,
And climb, before a thousand years have fled,
High as the eagle to her mountain bed
Whose soil is fine as flour and blood-red?
But no! She cannot move. Each arid patch
Owns the lean folk who plough and scythe and thatch
Its grudging yield and scratch its stubborn stones.
The small gods suck the marrow from their bones.

Who is it climbs the summit of the road?
Only the beggar bumming his dark load.
Who was it cried to see the falling star?
Only the landless soldier lost in war.

And did a thousand years go by in vain?
And does another thousand start again?

DAVID GASCOYNE

David Gascoyne was born in 1916 and educated at Salisbury Cathedral Choir School and the Regent Street Polytechnic. He began to write early. His first book of poems was published when he was sixteen and his first novel in the following year. He spent some time in France, met certain surrealist poets and artists, and was influenced to produce A Short Survey of Surrealism *(1935) and a volume of poems,* Man's Life Is This Meat *(1936). At this time he also contributed many translations of Éluard, Aragon, Tzara, and other French poets, to the literary magazines. Among other pre-war publications may be mentioned* Hölderlin's Madness *(1938), translations with prose and verse commentary. Later work, which began to point in a new direction, appeared in* Poets of Tomorrow, Third Selection *(1942); and his collection,* Poems 1937–42 *(1943), illustrated with drawings by Graham Sutherland, exemplifies the style which has emerged from earlier experimentation. Perhaps I should have written 'styles', for the book has several manners. It contains translations from Jouve and Supervielle, a few poems written in French, much work that in its freedom and boldness of imagery – though not in its organization – still recalls his surrealist verse, and a section of religious poems, which have been much praised, entitled 'Miserere'. The best of these in my opinion are 'Pieta' and 'Lachrymae', but in most of them there is a sense of strain, not apparent in 'A Wartime Dawn' by which he is represented here.*

Gascoyne's later volumes, A Vagrant *(1950) and* Night Thoughts *(1956) mark no new development and are in other ways rather disappointing. Too much of* A Vagrant *consists of inoffensive but low-powered 'thinkings-aloud', and only in a few pieces, notably 'The Sacred Hearth', do we get the sense of a real attempt to shape the raw poetic material into a satisfying form.* Night Thoughts *is a long poem in three sections composed for broadcasting. Various 'voices' ruminate weakly.*

A Wartime Dawn

Dulled by the slow glare of the yellow bulb;
As far from sleep still as at any hour
Since distant midnight; with a hollow skull
In which white vapours seem to reel
Among limp muddles of old thought; till eyes
Collapse into themselves like clams in mud ...
Hand paws the wall to reach the chilly switch;
Then nerve-shot darkness gradually shakes
Throughout the room. *Lie still* ... Limbs twitch;
Relapse to immobility's faint ache. And time
A while relaxes; space turns wholly black.

But deep in the velvet crater of the ear
A chip of sound abruptly irritates.
A second, a third chirp; and then another far
Emphatic trill and chirrup shrills in answer; notes
From all directions round pluck at the strings
Of hearing with frail finely-sharpened claws.
And in an instant, every wakened bird
Across surrounding miles of air
Outside, is sowing like a scintillating sand
Its throat's incessantly replenished store
Of tuneless singsong, timeless, aimless, blind.

Draw now with prickling hand the curtains back;
Unpin the blackout-cloth; let in
Grim crack-of-dawn's first glimmer through the glass.
All's yet half sunk in Yesterday's stale death,
Obscurely still beneath a moist-tinged blank
Sky like the inside of a deaf mute's mouth ...
Nearest within the window's sight, ash-pale
Against a cinder coloured wall, the white
Pearblossom hovers like a stare; rain-wet
The further housetops weakly shine; and there,
Beyond, hangs flaccidly a lone barrage-balloon.

An incommunicable desolation weighs
Like depths of stagnant water on this break of day. –
Long meditation without thought. – Until a breeze,
From some pure Nowhere straying, stirs
A pang of poignant odour from the earth, an unheard sigh
Pregnant with sap's sweet tang and raw soil's fine
Aroma, smell of stone, and acrid breath
Of gravel puddles. While the brooding green
Of nearby gardens' grass and trees, and quiet flat
Blue leaves, the distant lilac mirages, are made
Clear by increasing daylight, and intensified.

Now head sinks into pillows in retreat
Before this morning's hovering advance;
(Behind loose lids, in sleep's warm porch, half hears
White hollow clink of bottles, – dragging crunch
Of milk-cart wheels, – and presently a snatch
Of windy whistling as the newsboy's bike winds near,
Distributing to neighbour's peaceful steps
Reports of last-night's battles); at last sleeps.
While early guns on Norway's bitter coast
Where faceless troops are landing, renew fire:
And one more day of War starts everywhere.

TERENCE TILLER

Terence Tiller was born in Cornwall in 1916 and educated in London and at Jesus College, Cambridge. He was awarded the Chancellor's Medal for English verse in 1936 and lectured in history at Cambridge between 1937 and 1939. From 1939 until 1946 he was a Lecturer in English Literature at Fuad I University, Cairo, and at the same time gave talks to troops and did cipher work for G.H.Q., Middle East. On his return to England he worked under

Patric Dickinson at the B.B.C. as Assistant Poetry Editor for a
short time before joining the B.B.C. Features Department as a
writer and producer. He has published the following books of
poems: Poems (*1941*), The Inward Animal (*1943*), Unarm,
Eros (*1948*), and Reading a Medal (*1957*). The 'intellectual com-
ponent' is not missing in Tiller's best work, which is characterized
by an agreeable tautness and economy of effect.

'Egyptian Beggar' is reprinted from Unarm, Eros. With more
space I should have liked to include 'Tropical Aquarium' from
Reading a Medal.

Egyptian Beggar

Old as a coat on a chair; and his crushed hand,
as unexpressive as a bird's face, held
out like an offering, symbol of the blind,
he gropes our noise for charity. You could build
his long-deserted face up out of sand,
    or bear his weakness as a child.

Shuffling the seconds of a drugged watch, he
attends no answer to his rote; for soul's
and body's terrible humility,
stripped year by year a little barer, wills
nothing: he claims no selfhood in his cry:
    his body is an age that feels.

As if a mask, a tattered blanket, should
live for a little before falling, when
the body leaves it: so briefly in his dead
feathers of rags, and rags of body, and in
his crumpled mind, the awful and afraid
    stirs and pretends to be a man.

Earth's degradation and the voice of earth;
colour of earth and clothed in it; his eyes

white pebbles blind with deserts; the long growth
of landscape in his body: as if these
or these dead acres horribly gave birth:
here will fall from him like disguise.

Only a sad and humble motion keeps
the little space he is, himself: to row
his mindless caves with ritual hand and lips,
and wonder dimly at his guilt: with no
memory of it now: it was perhaps
too fearful, or too long ago.

THOMAS BLACKBURN

*Thomas Blackburn was born in Cumberland in 1916 and educated
at Bromsgrove School and Durham University. He is now – after
teaching at St Marylebone Grammar School for ten years – a
Lecturer in English at the College of St Mark and St John,
Chelsea. He held the Gregory Poetry Fellowship at Leeds Univer-
sity for two years in the late fifties, and, although his first collection
of verses,* The Outer Darkness (*1952*), *did not appear until he was
thirty-five, he has published four volumes of poems since then:* The
Holy Stone (*1954*), In the Fire (*1956*), The Next Word (*1958*),
and A Smell of Burning (*1960*). *Other publications are* 45–60
(*1960*), *an anthology of post-war English poetry, and* The Price
of an Eye (*1961*), *which is literary criticism. He is married, with
one daughter.*

In the preface to 45–60 *Mr Blackburn writes that 'poems are
often concerned with the struggle to understand the complexities of
ourselves ... They try to make articulate what one might call the
growing pains of life.' This is near enough to Dylan Thomas's view
of poetry as a 'spiritual unravelling' of the self to make it clear that
Mr Blackburn is on the romantic side of the fence, disliking both*

'cross-word puzzles which rhyme' and verse that insists on technique and 'purity of diction' at the expense of the poetic subject. Indeed Dylan Thomas, whom he admires, has influenced Mr Blackburn's writing — although less than Yeats, whose sonorities are rather too obviously reproduced in In the Fire. *This is the poet's least satisfactory volume (although it contains one poem, 'Spring-Heeled Jack', which I thought of representing him by), and elsewhere the Yeatsian influence is more adequately digested. It is present, for example, in 'Hospital for Defectives', which may be Mr Blackburn's best poem. The poems on classical themes, which seem to take off from Yeats's 'Leda and the Swan', have been admired by some critics and reviewers, but 'Oedipus' and 'Pasiphae' — to cite two of the best known — strike me as strained.*

Hospital for Defectives

By your unnumbered charities
A miracle disclose,
Lord of the Images, whose love,
The eyelid and the rose
Takes for a language, and today
Tell to me what is said
By these men in a turnip field
And their unleavened bread.

For all things seem to figure out
The stirrings of your heart,
And two men pick the turnips up
And two men pull the cart;
And yet between the four of them
No word is ever said
Because the yeast was not put in
Which makes the human bread.
But three men stare on vacancy
And one man strokes his knees;
What is the meaning to be found
In such dark vowels as these?

Lord of the Images, whose love,
The eyelid and the rose
Takes for a metaphor, today,
Beneath the warder's blows,
The unleavened man did not cry out
Or turn his face away;
Through such men in a turnip field
What is it that you say?

ROBERT CONQUEST

Robert Conquest was born at Malvern in 1917 and educated at Winchester and Magdalen College, Oxford. Between 1939 and 1946 he was an infantry officer – he served in the Oxford and Bucks. Light Infantry – and after the war a diplomat 'in the Balkans and at the U.N.'. Lately he has varied free-lance writing with a Research Fellowship in Soviet Politics at the London School of Economics and a lectureship in English at Buffalo University. Since 1946 he has been a member of the British Interplanetary Society, and, apart from his poems, his publications include A World of Difference, *a piece of science fiction,* Back to Life, *a collection of verse from the 'Soviet-bloc' countries, several works on Soviet subjects, and, of course,* New Lines (1956), *the anthology that introduced Larkin, Gunn, Amis, Wain, Elizabeth Jennings, and other poets of the 'Movement' to the poetry-reading general public. His own first collection of verse,* Poems, *appeared in 1955. In 1961 he published a book on 'the disgrace and death' of Boris Pasternak and he is now planning a new collection of poems.*

From covering roughly the same ground in preparing to revise the present anthology I have been made aware how well chosen were the poems included in New Lines, *and Mr Conquest's introduction to his anthology may be said to explain the 'new poetry' of the fifties much as pronouncements by Michael Roberts and Geoffrey Grigson explained the new poetry of the thirties a generation ago. Robert Conquest has something of Grigson's pungency and pointed manner of expression in this introduction, which is essential reading for those who want to understand in broad terms how a new poetic generation regarded Messrs Eliot, Auden, and Dylan Thomas, and what new ideals of subject-matter and expression they proposed. (This is true enough to be worth saying, although I am aware that Mr Conquest committed nobody but himself; that the New Lines contributors were individuals who differed at the time over many things and have since diverged even further from any conceivable common centre.) Mr Conquest also resembles Geoffrey Grigson in having some positive bugbears: Ezra Pound, Edith Sitwell, Christopher Logue. His confessed likings include Graves, Auden, Roy Fuller, Dylan Thomas (in part) and, among younger poets, Larkin, Thom Gunn, and Amis. The firm intelligence behind the introductory essay and the choice of poems in New Lines is evident in Mr Conquest's own poetry, which is elegantly vertebrate. He speaks of establishing in a poem 'a sort of structural wholeness involving both the sensuous world and the practice of art' – which seems to explain his pleasure in the poetry of André Chénier. The same remark reminds me of distich in 'For the 1956 Opposition of Mars', a piece written too late to be included in Poems:*

> Pure joy of knowledge rides as high as art.
> The whole heart cannot keep alive on either.

It is a comment that illuminates the nice poise of 'A Problem', in which reflections rise easily and naturally (that is, with unobtrusive artifice) out of the set description. Other poems that tempted me were 'Near Jakobselv', which I particularly like, 'The Rokeby Venus', and 'Epistemology of Poetry'.

A Problem

Liguria tingles with peculiar light.
The sea and sky exchange their various blues.
The asphodel that even goats refuse
 Glows dryly on each rocky height,
Whose foothills' wooded convolutions rise
 Through a heavy, luminous air. And here
 Man might, as well as anywhere,
Combine his landscapes and philosophies.

There Sestri crammed into its littoral shelf
Seems motionless with distance; motionless
Green flames pour up, the pines and cypresses
 Beyond the stream. The stream itself
Ripples and ripens to a falling sun
 Whose light makes metal at this hour
 Its golden froth of leaf and flower.
A dragonfly is basking on a stone.

Foam spurts between the pebbles; currents swirl;
It slides, a shining film, over rock
Smooth as itself, or into pools of dark.
 Where wood and sea and sky and hill
Give static broad simplicities, its course
 At once more complex and more simple
 Appears to thought as an example,
Like the complex, simple movement of great verse.

Gaze in that liquid crystal; let it run,
Some simple, fluent structure of the all,
No many-corridored dark Escorial,
 But, poem or stream, a Parthenon:
The clear completeness of a gnomic rhyme;
 Or, off the beat of pure despair
 But purer to the subtle ear,
The assonance of eternity with time.

How would it come? This war gave nothing. If
No abstract thought can generate its laws
Unless some special impulse cracks or thaws
   The present icefields of belief:
– Perhaps from the strange new telepathic data,
   Or when the first craft, fairly soon,
   Its rockets flaring, eases down
To total strangeness under Deimos' glitter.

Till then, or till forever, those who've sought
Philosophies like verse, evoking verse,
Must take, as I beneath these junipers,
   Empiric rules of joy and thought,
And be content to break the idiot calm;
   While many poems that dare not guide
   Yet bring the violent world inside
Some girl's ephemeral happiness and charm.

JOHN HEATH-STUBBS

*John Heath-Stubbs was born in London in 1918 and spent his
childhood in Hampshire and the Isle of Wight. Between 1939 and
1943 he studied English at Queen's College, Oxford, where he met
and became the friend of Sidney Keyes. Since then he has worked as
a private tutor, schoolmaster, and publisher's reader, and has held
the following appointments: Gregory Fellow in Poetry, Leeds Uni-
versity (1952–5), Visiting Professor of English at Alexandria
University (1955–8), Visiting Professor at Michigan University
(1960–1). He has published six books of poems –* Wounded
Thammuz *(1942),* Beauty and the Beast *(1944),* The Divided
Ways *(1946),* The Swarming of the Bees *(1950),* A Charm
Against the Toothache *(1954), and* The Triumph of the Muse
(1958), as well as a volume of translations, Poems from Giacomo

Leopardi (*1946*), *a collection of plays*, Helen in Egypt and Other Plays (*1958*), *and a critical study 'of the later fortunes of romanticism in English poetry from George Darley to W. B. Yeats's*, The Darkling Plain (*1950*). *In 1950 he edited* The Forsaken Garden, *an anthology of nineteenth-century poetry, and in 1953 – in collaboration with David Wright* – The Faber Book of Twentieth Century Verse.

In his earlier poetic work John Heath-Stubbs can properly be called a neo-romantic, although he would probably – as Keyes did – disclaim attachment to the 'new and overwrought romanticism' that began early in the forties to replace the 'social' poetry of the thirties in the little magazines. 'The Divided Ways' is one of the more disciplined of these early poems, but even so there is some 1890-ish posturing ('My long white fingers on a small carved lute') and some Sitwellian phrases ('red-clawed Sun', etc.). The other two poems, which are both from A Charm against the Toothache (*1954*), *represent another order of achievement. In 'A Charm against the Toothache' what might have been a sad fancy triumphantly comes off because of its rhythmical and verbal delicacy. 'Epitaph' with its sardonic humour is equally successful. Mr Heath-Stubbs has not denied the romanticism of his poetic impulse in his mature work, but a degree of self-consciousness and a certain formality in the writing have given this later romanticism muscles and intelligence.*

The Divided Ways

In memory of Sidney Keyes

He has gone down into the dark cellar
To talk with the bright-faced Spirit with silver hair;
But I shall never know what word was spoken there.

.   .   .   .   .

My friend is out of earshot; our ways divided
Before we even knew we had missed each other.
For he advanced

Into a stony wilderness of the heart,
Under a hostile and a red-clawed Sun;
All that dry day, until the darkness fell,
I heard him going, and shouting among the canyons.
But I, struck backward from the Eastern Gate,
Had turned aside, obscure,
Beneath the unfriendly silence of the Moon,
My long white fingers on a small carved lute.
There was a forest, and faces known in childhood
Rose unexpected from the mirrored pools;
The trees had hands to clutch my velvet shoulders,
And birds of fever sang among the branches;
Till the dark vine-boughs, breaking as I seized them,
And dripping blood, cried out with my own voice:
'I also have known thirst, and the wanderer's terror! ...'
But I had lost my friend and the mountain paths.
And if there might have been another meeting –
The new Sun rising in a different sky,
Having repaired his light in the streams of Ocean,
And the Moon, white and maternal, going down
Over the virgin hills – it is too late
Ever to find it now.

And though it was in May that the reptile guns
And breeze-fly bullets took my friend away,
It is no time to forge a delicate idyll
Of the young shepherd, stricken, prone among
The flowers of Spring, heavy with morning dew,
And emblematic blood of dying gods:
Or that head pillowed on a wave's white fleece,
Softly drowning in a Celtic sea.
This was more harsh and meaningless than Winter.

But now, at last, I dare avow my terror
Of the pale vampire by the cooling grate;
The enemy face that doubled every loved one;'
My secret fear of him and his cold heroes;

The meaning of the dream
Which was so fraught with trouble for us both;
And how, through this long autumn
(Sick and tempestuous with another sorrow)
His spirit, vexed, fluttered among my thoughts,
A bird returning to the darkened window –
The hard-eyed albatross with scissor bill.
And I would ask his pardon for this weakness.

But he is gone where no hallooing voice
Or beckoning hand may ever call him back;
And what is ours of him
Must speak impartially for all the world.
There is no personal word remains for me,
And I pretend to find no meaning here.
Though I might guess that other Singer's wisdom
Who saw in Death a dark immaculate flower
And tenderness in every falling Autumn,
This abstract music will not bring again
My friend to his warm room.
Inscrutable the darkness covers him.

A Charm against the Toothache

Venerable Mother Toothache
Climb down from the white battlements,
Stop twisting in your yellow fingers
The fourfold rope of nerves;
And tomorrow I will give you a tot of whisky
To hold in your cupped hands,
A garland of anise-flowers,
And three cloves like nails.

And tell the attendant gnomes
It is time to knock off now,
To shoulder their little pick-axes,
Their cold-chisels and drills.

And you may mount by a silver ladder
Into the sky, to grind
In the cracked polished mortar
Of the hollow moon.

By the lapse of warm waters,
And the poppies nodding like red coals,
The paths on the granite mountains,
And the plantation of my dreams.

Epitaph

Mr Heath-Stubbs as you must understand
Came of a gentleman's family out of Staffordshire
Of as good blood as any in England
But he was wall-eyed and his legs too spare.

His elbows and finger-joints could bend more ways than one
And in frosty weather would creak audibly
As to delight his friends he would give demonstration
Which he might have done in public for a small fee.

Amongst the more learned persons of his time
Having had his schooling in the University of Oxford
In Anglo-Saxon Latin ornithology and crime
Yet after four years he was finally not preferred.

Orthodox in beliefs as following the English Church
Barring some heresies he would have for recreation
Yet too often left these sound principles (as I am told) in the
    lurch
Being troubled with idleness, lechery, pride and dissipation.

In his youth he would compose poems in prose and verse
In a classical romantic manner which was pastoral
To which the best judges of the Age were not averse
And the public also but his profit was not financial.

Now having outlived his friends and most of his reputation
He is content to take his rest under these stones and grass
Not expecting but hoping that the Resurrection
Will not catch him unawares whenever it takes place.

W. S. GRAHAM

*W. S. Graham was born on Clydeside in 1918 and educated at
Greenock High School before serving his time as a structural en-
gineer. At a later date he studied literature and philosophy at New-
battle Abbey College, a centre for adult education near Edinburgh.
In 1947–8 he held an Atlantic Award for Literature, and he has
twice visited the U.S.A., in 1948 and 1951, to lecture and give
readings of his own poetry. In all he has published five books of verse*
– Cage Without Grievance (*1942*), The Seven Journeys (*1943*),
2nd Poems (*1945*), The White Threshold (*1949*), *and* The
Nightfishing (*1955*) – *but he is now chiefly known by the last two
of these, and his claim to be a poet rests most firmly on* The Night-
fishing. The White Threshold *shows Mr Graham temporarily
possessed by the spirit of Dylan Thomas: exaggerating the Welsh
poet's mannerisms and cultivating oddity at the expense of intelligi-
bility.* The Nightfishing *is certainly superior. It consists of the
title-poem, seven 'Letters', and two ballads. There is still too much
of whatever is the Scots equivalent of 'hwyl' –*

> *I, in Time's grace, the grace of change, sail surely
> Moved off the land and the skilled keel sails
> The darkness burning under where I go ...*

*– but there is an attempt at the discipline of meaning in a more per
sonal style. On the basis of this volume W. S. Graham is probably
a poet, although one who cherishes some bad poetic habits and is ex-
cessively literary under all the toughness of 'The Broad Close' and
'Baldy Bane'. Letter III echoes Dylan Thomas again ('... O my*

strayed dear ...') and leans on a famous elegiac passage in Finne-
gan's Wake ('... What a dark | Rush goes under it all | Here we
inherit ...'), but it carries a romantic charge of feeling in its pub,
fishing-boat, and sea imagery.

Letter III

As Mooney's calls Time this moment
Amazed faces me with that
Face Love lashed and lashed
I love and wend me always
To death with. O my strayed dear,

Find me. I find you fairly
Wandered under every eye
Yet fondly near me among
Them all in all the harp-hung
Tara of the drinking time
And the drink talking. What a dark
Rush goes under it all
Here we inherit. We'll drink
Ourselves here face to face
A one for the road across
More than these words. Here's us,
And may tonight's nets stroll
Where the herring are. We'll see.
Come nearer to hear. He's high
Singing on the top and gallant
Grace-notes of his longing.
O you are tonight as first
As ever you were then I
Set eyes on you one summer
Gazing your younglashed eyes
On me and playing shyness
And torment, and then you even
Made me buttercup your chin.
Clearly it seems no time.

There's nothing. Not anything
More. Love swells my tongue.
Let the signs start and peer
Us into light. We drift
Above fathoms that move
Their friendly thunders through
This breathless thoroughfare.
And never fear here under
The light of the brandished gale
Of Michael risen double
Sworded with the salt word
Reeking his tongue. Who hears?
Who sees us? Surely only
A drop or two of the spray
That the main deep may favour.

Mooney's called Closing and
Three standing men in a sculled
Boat brimming slowly the night
Skinned harbour calms, move out
To the riding port and star
Board of their trade. Now let
The sail creak and talk
Over us and the light
Swing at the slow mast-head.
We shall lie held here
In the moving hull of Love
Face to face making
The perfect couple perfect.
So, under every eye,
Who shall we perish to?
Here it's endlessly us
Face to face across
The nine-waved and the berry-
Stained kiss of the moved sea.
And not one word we merge in

Here shall we unmarvel
From its true home. My dear,

Easy. We'll keep a good
Watch for the fresh on the salt
As the river moves through
In a stain of calm on the sea.

Easy. Move as I move
Through this breathless sea
Rended openly. The deck
Bleeds sudden fire and
The binnacle like a clutch
Of glow-worms glows. See.
This night moves and this language
Moves over slightly
To meet another's need
Or make another's need.

Move here. We'll choose inshore,
But that's not their concern.

JOHN HOLLOWAY

*John Holloway was born 'on the Kentish fringe' of London in 1919
and attended a local grammar school before going up to Oxford with
a history scholarship. After war service he taught philosophy for a
time at New College and became a Prize Fellow of All Souls. His
first book,* Language and Intelligence, *was the product of these
years. He then transferred his interest to English studies and in
1949 was appointed a Lecturer in English at Aberdeen University.
Since 1954 he has taught English literature at Cambridge (where
he is a Fellow of Queens' College). The* Victorian Sage *(1953) and*

The Charted Mirror (*1960*), *which is a collection of critical essays on a wide range of subjects, reflect his professional interest in English literature. He has also published* The Minute (*1956*), *a book of poems from which 'Warning to a Guest' is taken.*

John Holloway was a contributor to New Lines *and deserved his place in the anthology, but he has a less individual voice than several of the anthology's contributors. For example, he does not stake out a claim to a particular territory like Elizabeth Jennings, and he has not Robert Conquest's ease or architectural sense.* The Minute *is an interesting collection with a fair quota of successes, but it is curiously uneven. The two ambitious longer poems, 'The Life and Adventures of Heroic Mr Clubman' and 'A Voice for Winter' do not really come off, and there are other pieces – 'Toper's Poem', 'The Petty Testament of Peter the Clerk', and 'Recognition Scene' – which betray too obviously their origins in the work of other poets: in these instances, Yeats, the Auden–MacNeice Testament in* Journey to Iceland, *and Eliot's interview with the compound ghost in* Little Gidding. *'Warning to a Guest' illustrates a level of expression achieved in half-a-dozen poems. The best poem in* The Minute *is in my opinion 'Journey Through the Night', but some good judges prefer 'Apollonian Poem'. None of Mr Holloway's pieces falls below a decent standard of organization and coherence – he has all the minor virtues of 'Movement' writing.*

Warning to a Guest

Against the flare and descant of the gas
I heard an old woman in a shop maintain
This fog comes when the moon is on the wane:
    And ten full days must pass
Before the crescent mows it in like grass.
  Shun the black puddles, the scrub hedge
Down to the sea. Keep to the wet streets where
Mercury and sodium flood their sullen fire.
Tonight, do not disturb the water's edge.

There'll be no storm, I know: having often gone,
In storm or calm, where the strong tide has flowed
Right to the tunnel underneath the road
    Along the formless dune.
But this is the third quarter of the moon
  In fog. There'll be no drench and roar
Of breakers: the quiet tide will drift
Idly among the pebbles, and then sift
Back to the sea. Yet shun that dark foreshore.

There'll be no sound: except the echoing
Horn of a baffled ship, shut out from home,
And the small birds that skirt the stranded foam.
    Dunlin and sanderling
Feed through the night, or lightly they take wing
  Down the soft fog. So sharp their pulse
Trills, and their dram of blood burns up so clear,
Each minute, in their bright sight, makes a year.
But you may catch the note of something else.

I have watched you, as you have visited at this house,
And know, from knowing myself, that you will be
Quick to people the shore, the fog, the sea,
    With all the fabulous
Things of the moon's dark side. No, stay with us.
  Do not demand a walk tonight
Down to the sea. It makes no place for those
Like you and me who, to sustain our pose,
Need wine and conversation, colour and light.

D. J. ENRIGHT

Dennis Joseph Enright was born at Leamington in 1920 and edu-
cated at Leamington College and Downing College, Cambridge. He
has been an extension lecturer in England and has lectured abroad
at the Free University of Berlin and at universities in Egypt, Japan
and Thailand. He is now Professor of English at Singapore, where
his inaugural lecture in 1960 huffed the Government and created a
political rumpus. His travels in various parts of the world feature in
his writings, so that the novel Academic Year *has amusing side-*
lights on Egyptian society, and the travel book The World of Dew
and the poems in Bread Rather Than Blossoms *(1956) deal with*
life in Japan. Again, Some Men Are Brothers *(1960) contains*
sections of poems labelled 'Siam', 'Berlin', and 'Japan'. An earlier
collection of poems than the two already mentioned was The Laugh-
ing Hyena *(1953). Mr Enright has also published some lively*
literary criticism and edited an interesting anthology, Poets of the
1950s *(Tokyo, 1955), which anticipated Robert Conquest's* New
Lines *(1956) by bringing together the same group of poets (with*
the exception of Thom Gunn).

Mr Enright was himself a contributor to New Lines, *but he has*
not much really in common with Mr Conquest's other poets. He is,
I think it is fair to say, a self-confident, unsubtle, and rather sprawl-
ing poet, whose successes are therefore mainly in his broadly satiri-
cal, comic or comic-tender pieces, where to simplify people or issues
for the sake of point and vigour is justifiable. In such pieces – 'No
Offence', which is a smack at Teutonic thoroughness and hygiene,
'The Interpreters: or, How To Bury Yourself in a Book', 'Akiko
San', 'A Poor Little Lonely Child Whose Parents Have Gone to a
Cultural Festival', and the group of poems entitled 'Nasty Thoughts
of a Nasty Fellow' give some idea of their variety and range of
feeling – the derivation of a personal manner from the lighter
'social' Auden and the Ezra Pound of Lustra *is evident. The*

'serious' poems are less successful on the whole, as I have already implied, but 'Blue Umbrellas', which is reprinted from Bread Rather Than Blossoms, *and a few other pieces show what Mr Enright can achieve in this kind of writing.*

Blue Umbrellas

'The thing that makes a blue umbrella with its tail –
How do you call it?' you ask. Poorly and pale
Comes my answer. For all I can call it is peacock.

Now that you go to school, you will learn how we call all sorts
    of things;
How we mar great works by our mean recital.
You will learn, for instance, that Head Monster is not the gentle-
    man's accepted title;
The blue-tailed eccentrics will be merely peacocks; the dead
    bird will no longer doze
Off till tomorrow's lark, for the letter has killed him.
The dictionary is opening, the gay umbrellas close.

   Oh our mistaken teachers! –
It was not a proper respect for words that we need,
But a decent regard for things, those older creatures and more
    real.
Later you may even resort to writing verse
To prove the dishonesty of names and their black greed –
To confess your ignorance, to expiate your crime, seeking one
    spell to lift another curse.
Or you may, more commodiously, spy on your children, busy
    discoverers,
Without the dubious benefit of rhyme.

HILARY CORKE

Hilary Corke was born in 1921 at Malvern and educated at Charterhouse and Christ Church, Oxford. During the Second World War he served in the Royal Artillery (1941–5) and subsequently became a lecturer in Medieval English studies, first at Cairo University and then at the University of Edinburgh. His poems, which are interesting in their variety and have a distinct individual tang, have appeared in many English and American magazines (including Encounter, The London Magazine, *and* The New Yorker) *but have not yet been collected.*

'*O Castle Heart*' *is reprinted from a special* Poetry Supplement (*July 1956*) *edited by G. S. Fraser for the Poetry Book Society.*

O Castle Heart

Fell is the cullis-ʒett of my hertes castell-steade.
Chatterton

O castle heart your walls are down,
Your cullis sprawled, your turrets broken,
Your bridge to household drumskin drawn
With pattering feet and greetings spoken;
    Your runnels that once boiling lead
    Now pour soft rainwater instead.

Your battlements, that marched amain
As granite soldiers on the sky,
Tossed in a heap of dusty slain
Like tumbled chessmen useless lie;
    Though long the cry and long the glare
    Have ceased reflecting on the air.

Your bannered arms that every breath
Blew more defiant, brighter gules,
Your foul-mouthed cannon arguing death,
Your iron maiden ripe for fools –
    Victorious love with deeper thunder
    Has danced the breach and spurned them under.

The blue-tit in the cannon's mouth
Broods on her sheltered eggs at peace;
From every cranny facing south
The swallows eye the skeining geese;
    And round the lily-studded moat
    The swan drives on with restless foot.

Confetti-stars, that on the breeze
Blew in like spies from neighbour farms,
Lay down their peacock-train of eyes;
And love's convolvulus in streams
    Over the crumpled ramparts pours
    And binds them fallen down in flowers.

Glass castle melting in the sun,
How soon your angry heart is still
How swiftly to fine air you run,
To nothing but a fair green hill
    When earth receives her rocks again
    And only flowers and birds remain!

SIDNEY KEYES

Sidney Keyes was born at Dartford in Kent in 1922 and educated at Dartford Grammar School, Tonbridge School, and Oxford. He was commissioned in the Queen's Own Royal West Kent Regiment in September 1942, left England in the following March, and died during the last days of the Tunisian campaign in April 1943 after only a fortnight's active service. He saw his first book of poems, The Iron Laurel *(1942), in print, but his second collection,* The Cruel Solstice *(1944), appeared posthumously and won the award of the Hawthornden Prize.* Collected Poems *(1945), edited by Michael Meyer, contains a valuable memoir with quotations from letters by Keyes expressing some of his ideas about poetry and the death-wish (a recurrent theme in all his work).* Minos of Crete *(1948), also edited by Michael Meyer, is a collection of plays and stories with selections from Keyes's notebooks and a few early poems.*

Sidney Keyes, who died before he was twenty-one, was considered by general critical consent at the time of the award of the Hawthornden Prize (1944) the most promising of the younger war-poets. A re-reading of his poems – in spite of much that is naturally fragmentary and imitative – confirms this judgement (although it is possible to prefer Alun Lewis, and it may be wisest to connect these two very different poets together in achievement). Of living writers, Keyes wrote during the war, he accepted 'Eliot, Williams, Graves (to some extent), my great friend John Heath-Stubbs'. The most important poets of the last hundred years to him were Yeats and Rilke. Like the early Heath-Stubbs he may be labelled a neo-romantic, but it is impossible to say how he might have developed had he lived even a few years longer. The two poems given here date from the autumn of 1941 before the writing of 'The Foreign Gate', a poem which was in Meyer's words 'the great turning-point in his life'. 'I feel myself rather isolated as a writer,' Keyes declared, and again, 'I am not a man but a voice.' Something of this isolation and necessary loneliness is expressed in 'The Bards'. 'William Wordsworth' was suggested by the death-mask of the poet reproduced as a frontispiece in Sir Herbert Read's study of Wordsworth.

The Bards

Now it is time to remember the winter festivals
Of the old world, and see their raftered halls
Hung with hard holly; tongues' confusion; slow
Beat of the heated blood in those great palaces
Decked with the pale and sickled mistletoe;
And voices dying when the blind bard rises
Robed in his servitude, and the high harp
Of sorrow sounding, stills those upturned faces.

O it is such long learning, loneliness
And dark despite to master
The bard's blind craft; in bitterness
Of heart to strike the strings and muster
The shards of pain to harmony, not sharp
With anger to insult the merry guest.
O it is glory for the old man singing
Dead valour and his own days coldly cursed.

How ten men fell by one heroic sword
And of fierce foray by the unwatched ford,
Sing, blinded face; quick hands in darkness groping
Pluck the sad harp; sad heart forever hoping
Valhalla may be songless, enter
The moment of your glory, out of clamour
Moulding your vision to such harmony
That drunken heroes cannot choose but honour
Your stubborn blinded pride, your inward winter.

William Wordsworth

No room for mourning: he's gone out
Into the noisy glen, or stands between the stones
Of the gaunt ridge, or you'll hear his shout
Rolling among the screes, he being a boy again.
He'll never fail nor die
And if they laid his bones
In the wet vaults or iron sarcophagi
Of fame, he'd rise at the first summer rain
And stride across the hills to seek
His rest among the broken lands and clouds.
He was a stormy day, a granite peak
Spearing the sky; and look, about its base
Words flower like crocuses in the hanging woods,
Blank though the dalehead and the bony face.

DONALD DAVIE

*Donald Davie was born at Barnsley in 1922 and educated at
Barnsley Grammar School and St Catherine's College, Cambridge.
During the war he served in the Royal Navy from 1941 to 1946,
including eighteen months in North Russia and six months in India
and Ceylon. From 1950 to 1957 he was a Lecturer in English at
Trinity College, Dublin (becoming a Fellow of the college in 1954).
During 1957–8 he was a visiting professor at the University of
California. Later in 1958 he was appointed Lecturer in English at
Cambridge University, and in 1959 he became a Fellow of Gonville
and Caius College, Cambridge. He is married, with three children.
His publications include* Purity of Diction in English Verse
(1952) *and* Articulate Energy: An Enquiry into the Syntax of
English Poetry (1957), *two important books of criticism, and the
following books of verse:* Brides of Reason (1955), A Winter

Talent (*1957*), *and* The Forests of Lithuania (*1959*), *the last a long poem adapted from the* Pan Tadeusz *of the Polish poet Adam Mickiewicz* (*1798–1855*). *His latest publications are a book about Sir Walter Scott* (*1961*) *and a new book of poems,* A Sequence for Francis Parkman (*1961*).

Mr Davie is, after Philip Larkin, the New Lines *poet who has given me most pleasure, and* A Winter Talent *is one of the most satisfying collections of poems to be published since the Second World War. Mr Davie is extremely intelligent in both his verse and prose, but what I notice particularly is the way intelligence and sensibility rest on a more equable disposition than most poets are lucky enough to possess – it comes out in his warm commendation of other poets (Larkin, Tomlinson, Kinsella, Lowell) and also, perhaps, in the tone of some of his poems – for example, the very charming 'Woodpigeons at Raheny', 'Time Passing, Beloved' (but this is more than charming in the elegance and justice of its expression), and the splendid 'Heigh-ho on a Winter Afternoon', with which I am so taken that I have preferred it to the more ambitiously architectural but almost equally successful 'Obiter Dicta', 'Mens Sana in Corpore Sano', and 'A Gathered Church' from the sequence 'Dissentient Voice'. The failures in* A Winter Talent *are few: 'Under St Paul's', which tries too hard and is obscure, some of the short art-poems in the section 'Italy', and 'The Pacer in the Fresco' from the same section, which looks like an exercise in Mr Tomlinson's manner. Mr Davie is a distinguished poet already in several modes, and the anthologist's chief difficulty is to do him justice in less than half-a-dozen poems. 'The Garden Party' from* Brides of Reason *claims inclusion here as a representative specimen of an early manner that survives into* A Winter Talent *in such pieces as 'At Knaresborough'. It is not enough to describe the author of this poem as (in his own ironic phrase) 'A pasticheur of late-Augustan styles' – the surefootedness is distinctly personal. 'Remembering the Thirties', a more developed example of the same manner, is also from* Brides of Reason. *I feel guilty about not resisting it in favour of maturer work, but it is so informative about the attitude of the fifties to the thirties, and so polished a performance with its 'rhymes that strike, exploding like a whip', that I have* let my choice stand. It is in this early work that the evidence is clearest of Mr Davie's desire 'to reinstate some of the traditional disciplines' of English poetry ('chaste' diction, strict metric). What he was after can be given in his own words.

> In particular, I have tried to get force into my poems, not by concentration of highly figurative language, nor by dislocation of traditional syntax, but by making syntax, while flawlessly correct, as compact and rapid as possible ...

The surprising thing is that so much self-conscious critical study of what his poetry should be and do did not dry Mr Davie up poetically. On the contrary, the poems in A Winter Talent give us the feeling that an apprenticeship has been faithfully served and that certain poetic liberties may now be taken. In 'Rejoinder to a Critic' Mr Davie rounds on those who dare him as a constipated 'Movement' poet to the more open expression of feeling with the debating reply that the atom-bomb was also an expression of feeling —

> Not love, but hate? Well, both are versions of
> The 'feeling' that you dare me to. Be dumb!
> Appear concerned only to make it scan!
> How dare we now be anything but numb?

— but this was hardly more than a reflex of distaste: already in 1955 he was admitting that the new poetry seemed to him 'rather unambitious, too limited in its scope, insufficiently various and adventurous', although he still felt strongly — it was a matter on which all the New Lines poets agreed — that poets 'were in duty bound to write as if Edith Sitwell, Dylan Thomas, and George Barker had never existed'. A Winter Talent might be thought to contain sufficiently adventurous poems — apart from pieces already mentioned there are others ('The Mushroom Gatherers', 'The Wind at Penistone', 'The Fountain', 'Samuel Beckett's Dublin', and 'Under a Skylight' to cite a few titles) that succeed by their 'formal mastery' in conveying the sense of elation that the poet rightly judges to be important — but Mr Davie would probably rather have the adventurousness of The Forests of Lithuania recognized. He sees it as a blow struck for the emancipation of the poetic subject from ingrowing *provincialism.* The Forests of Lithuania *is a poem that I have enjoyed and found full of good things on successive readings, but I hope that he will not allow what must remain in large measure a literary exercise (enabling him to experiment and 'keep his hand in') to usurp the place of poetry based on more immediate experience. Fortunately it seems unlikely. Indeed Mr Davie is already moving on. He tells me that he thinks he may have discovered in his study of Robert Lowell's recent poems a hint for a profitable way of treating in verse the social and political subjects that were rather frowned on in Mr Conquest's introduction to* New Lines. *This eagerness to experiment and try out something new seems to be Mr Davie's most recognizable call-note as a poet. In his case it illustrates not uncertainty and immaturity but a reasonable wish to enlarge, even at some risk, the boundaries of his art.*

The Garden Party

Above a stretch of still unravaged weald
In our black country, in a cedar shade,
I found, shared out in tennis-courts, a field
Where children of the local magnates played.

And I grew envious of their moneyed ease
In Scott Fitzgerald's unembarrassed vein:
Let prigs, I thought, fool others as they please;
I only wish I had my time again.

To crown a situation as contrived
As any in 'The Beautiful and Damned',
The phantom of my earliest love appeared.
(I shook absurdly as I shook her hand.)

As dusk drew in on cultivated cries,
Faces hung pearls upon a cedar bough.
And gin could blur the glitter of her eyes;
But it's too late to learn to tango now.

My father, of a more submissive school,
Remarks the rich themselves are always sad.
There is that sort of equalizing rule;
But theirs is all the youth we might have had.

Remembering the Thirties

I

Hearing one saga, we enact the next.
We please our elders when we sit enthralled;
But then they're puzzled; and at last they're vexed
To have their youth so avidly recalled.

It dawns upon the veterans after all
That what for them were agonies, to us
Are high-brow thrillers, though historical;
And all their feats quite strictly fabulous.

This novel written fifteen years ago,
Set in my boyhood and my boyhood home,
These poems about 'abandoned workings', show
Worlds more remote than Ithaca or Rome.

The Anschluss, Guernica – all the names
At which those poets thrilled, or were afraid,
For me mean schools and schoolmasters and games;
And in the process someone is betrayed.

Ourselves perhaps. The Devil for a joke
Might carve his own initials on our desk,
And still we'd miss the point, because he spoke
An idiom too dated, Audenesque.

Ralegh's Guiana also killed his son.
A pretty pickle if we came to see
The tallest story really packed a gun,
The Telemachiad an Odyssey.

II

Even to them the tales were not so true
As not to be ridiculous as well:
The ironmaster met his Waterloo,
But Rider Haggard rode along the fell.

'Leave for Cape Wrath to-night!' They lounged away
On Fleming's trek or Isherwood's ascent.
England expected every man that day
To show his motives were ambivalent.

They played the fool, not to appear as fools
In time's long glass. A deprecating air
Disarmed, they thought, the jeers of later schools:
Yet irony itself is doctrinaire.

And, curiously, nothing now betrays
Their type to time's derision like this coy
Insistence on the quizzical, their craze
For showing Hector was a mother's boy.

A neutral tone is nowadays preferred.
And yet it may be better, if we must,
To find the stance impressive and absurd
Than not to see the hero for the dust.

For courage is the vegetable king,
The sprig of all ontologies, the weed
That beards the slag-heap with its hectoring,
Whose green adventure is to run to seed.

Heigh-ho on a Winter Afternoon

There is a heigh-ho in these glowing coals
By which I sit wrapped in my overcoat
As if for a portrait by Whistler. And there is

A heigh-ho in the bird that noiselessly
Flew just now past my window, to alight
On winter's moulding, snow; and an alas,
A heigh-ho, and a desultory chip,
Chip, chip on stone from somewhere down below.

Yes I have 'mellowed', as you said I would,
And that's a heigh-ho too for any man;
Heigh-ho that means we fall short of alas
Which sprigs the grave of higher hopes than ours.
Yet heigh-ho too has its own luxuries,
And salts with courage to be jocular
Disreputable sweets of wistfulness,
By deprecation made presentable.

What should we do to rate the long alas
But skeeter down a steeper gradient?
And then some falls are still more fortunate,
The meteors spent, the tragic heroes stunned
Who go out like a light. But here the chip,
Chip, chip will flake the stone by slow degrees,
For hour on hour the fire will gutter down,
The bird will call at longer intervals.

KINGSLEY AMIS

Kingsley Amis was born in Clapham in 1922 and educated at the City of London School and St John's College, Oxford. He served in the army between 1942 and 1945, and was a Lecturer in English at University College, Swansea, from 1949 until 1961. He is now a Fellow of Peterhouse, Cambridge. He is married and has a family. In 1958–9 he was a Visiting Fellow in Creative Writing at Princeton University. His poems are to be found in A Case of Samples

(*1956*), *which selects from the pieces written between 1946 and 1956 and reprints a large part of the privately printed collection* A Frame of Mind (*1953*). (*There is a still earlier collection,* Bright November, *which was issued by the Fortune Press: from it* '*Bed and Breakfast*' *and* '*Beowulf*' *survive to appear in* A Case of Samples.) *Mr Amis has also published four novels:* Lucky Jim (*1954*), *which was dedicated to Philip Larkin,* That Uncertain Feeling (*1955*), I Like It Here (*1958*), *and* Take a Girl Like You (*1960*). *He has also written* New Maps of Hell (*1961*), *a survey of science fiction, and his immediate plans include a new novel* '*about a tiresome Englishman in the U.S.A.*' *and some short stories (both straight and science fiction). He also hopes to write more poems, but he finds that they come less frequently now that his energies are mostly devoted to prose fiction. '*Perhaps only those poets who have ceased to write novels (Philip Larkin) or who write novels that are outside the main stream of fiction (Robert Graves) can find full and continuous satisfaction in writing verse,*' *he says. The two poets named are the contemporary English poets who most interest Mr Amis. He was a contributor to* New Lines, *which represents him with discrimination.*

The novels reveal much the same personality as the poems. The mask is that of l'homme moyen sensuel *in both poetry and prose as in the pre-war work of Louis MacNeice, but Mr Amis's average man, who is definitely post-war, is brusquer, cockier, and more pugnacious, engagingly ready to sniff out pretentiousness and snobbery at the drop of a hat. There have been derisive hoots about the new provincialism, but the blend of impatience, honesty, and tenderness in the poems and novels is usually attractive, and one is ruefully willing to put up with such* '*Clevelandisms*' *as*

> *Should poets bicycle-pump the human heart*
> *Or squash it flat?*

when one realizes that it is intended to set aesthetic teeth on edge. (The jabs at Keats and Jane Austen are really directed at ecstatic Keatsians and Janeites, who are fair game.) Among the novels I like That Uncertain Feeling *best, but* Lucky Jim *has to be read because the hero has been conflated with Osborne's Jimmy Porter to form 'the angry young man' of journalistic folk-lore. Apart from the two pieces given below and the selection of poems in* New Lines, *I like among the poems 'A Dream of Fair Women', 'The Value of Suffering', and 'A Note on Wyatt', and with more space I should have wanted to include 'Nocturne' and 'A Dream of Fair Women'. 'Against Romanticism' is untypically decorous, but it seems to me both an admirable piece of writing and a useful expression of what Amis and other poets of the fifties dislike in romanticism. 'A Book-shop Idyll' is as cocky-tender as you please. In 1955 Mr Amis wrote that the great deficiency of the younger poets was 'meagreness and triviality of subject-matter':*

> *... nobody wants any more poems on the grander themes for a few years, but at the same time nobody wants any more poems about philosophers or paintings or novelists or art galleries or mythology or foreign cities or other poems. At least I hope nobody wants them.*

Which leaves, of course, the kind of poems written by Mr Larkin and Mr Amis. The attitude is sympathetic even if one recognizes that proscription-lists are absurd. If Mr Amis is wrong about 'cosmopolitanism' and 'poems about foreign cities', he is wrong for the right reasons.

Against Romanticism

A traveller who walks a temperate zone
    – Woods devoid of beasts, roads that please the foot –
Finds that its decent surface grows too thin:
    Something unperceived fumbles at his nerves.
To please an ingrown taste for anarchy
    Torrid images circle in the wood,
And sweat for recognition up the road,
    Cramming close the air with their bookish cries.
All senses then are glad to gasp: the eye
    Smeared with garish paints, tickled up with ghosts
That brandish warnings or an abstract noun;

Melodies from shards, memories from coal,
Or saws from powdered tombstones thump the ear;
    Bodies rich with heat wriggle to the touch,
And verbal scents made real spellbind the nose;
    Incense, frankincense; legendary the taste
Of drinks or fruits or tongues laid on the tongue.
    Over all, a grand meaning fills the scene,
And sets the brain raging with prophecy,
    Raging to discard real time and place,
Raging to build a better time and place
    Than the ones which give prophecy its field
To work, the calm material for its rage,
    And the context which makes it prophecy.

Better, of course, if images were plain,
    Warnings clearly said, shapes put down quite still
Within the fingers' reach, or else nowhere;
    But complexities crowd the simplest thing,
And flaw the surface that they cannot break.
    Let us make at least visions that we need:
Let mine be pallid, so that it cannot
    Force a single glance, form a single word;
An afternoon long-drawn and silent, with
    Buildings free from all grime of history,
The people total strangers, the grass cut,
    Not long, voluble swooning wilderness,
And green, not parched or soured by frantic suns
    Doubling the commands of a rout of gods,
Nor trampled by the havering unicorn;
    Let the sky be clean of officious birds
Punctiliously flying on the left;
    Let there be a path leading out of sight,
And at its other end a temperate zone:
    Woods devoid of beasts, roads that please the foot.

A Bookshop Idyll

Between the GARDENING and the COOKERY
   Comes the brief POETRY shelf;
By the Nonesuch Donne, a thin anthology
   Offers itself.

Critical, and with nothing else to do,
   I scan the Contents page,
Relieved to find the names are mostly new;
   No one my age.

Like all strangers, they divide by sex:
   Landscape near Parma
Interests a man, so does *The Double Vortex*,
   So does *Rilke and Buddha.*

'I travel, you see', 'I think', and 'I can read'
   These titles seem to say;
But *I Remember You, Love is my Creed,*
   Poem for J.,

The ladies' choice, discountenance my patter
   For several seconds;
From somewhere in this (as in any) matter
   A moral beckons.

Should poets bicycle-pump the human heart
   Or squash it flat?
Man's love is of man's life a thing apart;
   Girl's aren't like that.

We men have got love well weighed up; our stuff
   Can get by without it.
Women don't seem to think that's good enough;
   They write about it,

And the awful way their poems lay them open
    Just doesn't strike them.
Women are really much nicer than men:
    No wonder we like them.

Deciding this, we can forget those times
    We sat up half the night
Chock-full of love, crammed with bright
        thoughts, names, rhymes,
    And couldn't write.

PHILIP LARKIN

*Philip Larkin, the best of the post-Second World War generation
of poets and the most exciting new poetic voice – with the possible
exception of Dylan Thomas – since Auden, was born at Coventry
in 1922 and educated at the King Henry VIII School, Coventry,
and St John's College, Oxford (where he was up at the same time as
Kingsley Amis). He has held posts in libraries since 1943, includ-
ing university libraries at Leicester and Belfast, and he is now
Librarian of Hull University. He is unmarried. His publications
include an early book of poems,* The North Ship *(1945), which to
my regret I have not seen, and two novels, but his reputation rests
on* The Less Deceived *(1955), which consists of poems written be-
tween 1945 and 1954, and on later uncollected poems that have ap-
peared in magazines and anthologies. 'Church Going', which, as
G. S. Fraser says, 'everyone who writes or lectures about the state
of poetry in the fifties finds himself bringing forward as the show-
piece of the "New Movement"', and 'Lines on a Young Lady's
Photograph Album' are reprinted from* The Less Deceived. *'The
Whitsun Weddings', which does not quite challenge the primacy of
'Church Going' among Mr Larkin's poems, is uncollected.*

   'I write terribly little – about three poems a year,' Mr Larkin

*says. His favourite poet is Thomas Hardy. After Hardy (but a
long way behind) come Barnes, Wilfred Owen, Christina Rossetti,
Betjeman, and Auden. (One notes that these poets are either Vic-
torian or modern.) He dislikes talking about himself. He also dis-
likes talking about poetry – and refuses invitations to address
literary societies – because he thinks that it does not do for a poet to
become self-conscious about his own creative processes (only valetu-
dinarians are always fussing about their health); and he seems to
regret even that he was once pricked or wheedled into writing a note
on his 'poetic aims and views' (for D. J. Enright's Poets of the
1950s). He points out that this 'most unconsidered pronouncement'
has been 'quoted relentlessly' against him ever since. Professional
valetudinarians (literary critics and academics) will continue to be
grateful to Mr Enright. Out of deference to Mr Larkin's wishes I
do not reproduce this note in full, but one passage from it is so much
what any intelligent reader would conclude from his own reading of
the poems that even Mr Larkin should regard it as harmless.*

> *I write poems to preserve things ... both for myself and
> others, though I feel that my prime responsibility is to the ex-
> perience itself, which I am trying to keep from oblivion for its
> own sake. Why I should do this I have no idea, but I think the
> impulse to preserve lies at the bottom of all art. Generally my
> poems are related, therefore, to my own personal life, but by no
> means always ...*

*And, one feels like adding, by no means simply. 'Larkin's
humanity is apparent in every line he writes,' Anthony Thwaite
claims, 'and perhaps what is particularly appealing about it is that
it seems the humanity of the ordinary, decent man – if the ordinary,
decent man had the self-awareness and skill to make poems of what
he felt.' I think there is a sense in which this is a useful and true
remark – Larkin knows all the tints and flavours of provincial life
and responds acutely to human absurdity and pathos (for example,
to the 'young mothers' of 'Before Tea' who in the municipal recrea-
tion ground dumbly feel that 'Something is pushing them / To the
side of their own lives') – but the 'ordinary, decent man' who gets
hold of Larkin's 'self-awareness' will no longer be an ordinary man.*

How authentic, it is natural to wonder, is Larkin's childhood in the poems?

> *And I, whose childhood*
> *Is a forgotten boredom ...*

And, again, what about his wariness of full engagement in ordinary life?

> *Threading my pursed-up way across the park,*
> *An indigestible sterility ...*

> *... something sufficiently toad-like*
> *Squats in me, too;*
> *Its hunkers are heavy as hard luck,*
> *And cold as snow ...*

> *Beyond all this, the wish to be alone:*
> *However the sky grows dark with invitation-cards*
> *However we follow the printed directions of sex ...*

> *Beneath it all, desire of oblivion runs.*

This is certainly not the self-awareness of the ordinary man. The question is how much of it is real in an uncomplicated way and how much of it stands for a selection of character-traits ironically exaggerated to build up a poetic personality. Self-portraits always have a touch of caricature, so why not forget the boisterous or heroic bits of consciousness and quizzically represent oneself as a 'witty worm' (an antithetical role to that of Thom Gunn calling for his spiritual jackboots in The Sense of Movement). *Here I tread warily, without the least help from Mr Larkin, and surmise that a Hardy-esque sense of futility is barely kept at bay by irony and the 'frivolous' routine of a life 'reprehensibly perfect'. He is himself, I think, the 'someone' who will*

> *... forever be surprising*
> *A hunger in himself to be more serious ...*

In fact I see Mr Larkin as a new and rather cagey sort of 'agonizer', one who will not be knocked off his 'unpriceable pivot' by the know-

ledge that 'the past is past and the future neuter' but cannot help continually being 'nudged from comfort'. This type of sensibility is no newer than Sénancour, but Larkin's modern version of it is expressed with fineness, intelligence, and only the most exemplary form of ironic self-pity (as in the splendid line, 'Such attics cleared of me! Such absences!').

It was F. W. Bateson who first linked the names of Auden and Larkin, defining their relationship by comparing it with that between Dryden and Pope. I take this to mean that Larkin has less sheer creative energy (which is evident) but a better use of his gifts and a truer sense of his poetic limitations, less intellectual omnivorousness and robustness but a sharper sensibility and more elegance. I do not know how far such comparisons are useful or valid, but I am sure that Larkin is an important poet. Mr Davie, who still regards Larkin and Amis as the most valuable of the New Lines poets, worries about Larkin's 'Little Englandism of the Left' (corresponding, he supposes, to Betjeman's 'Little Englandism of the Right') and wonders how he can develop further along his present line, but this reminds me too much of Americans who think compassionately that life in the Welfare State must be grey and depressing. I cannot see that Little Englandism has had a deleterious effect as yet on Larkin's work except in an infrequent willed vulgarism of diction – 'yowl' in 'Lines on a Young Lady's Photograph Album' is exactly right, but 'Mashed' in 'Places, Loved Ones' is jarring. There is hardly a poetic failure in The Less Deceived, although I do not understand 'Dry-Point', and 'Latest Face' still needs a final polish. Among the best pieces in the volume, apart from the two given below, are 'Wedding-Wind', 'Reasons for Attendance', 'Next, Please', 'Maiden Name', 'Deceptions', and 'If, My Darling'. Among the best uncollected poems that I have seen, apart from 'The Whitsun Weddings', are 'Love Songs in Age', which beautifully digests the Hardy influence, 'An Arundel Tomb', 'Before Tea', 'Mr Bleaney', and 'Waiting for Breakfast'. Mr Larkin should not make us wait too long for the collection containing all these pieces.

Church Going

Once I am sure there's nothing going on
I step inside, letting the door thud shut.
Another church: matting, seats, and stone,
And little books; sprawlings of flowers, cut
For Sunday, brownish now; some brass and stuff
Up at the holy end; the small neat organ;
And a tense, musty, unignorable silence,
Brewed God knows how long. Hatless, I take off
My cycle-clips in awkward reverence,

Move forward, run my hand around the font.
From where I stand, the roof looks almost new –
Cleaned, or restored? Someone would know: I don't.
Mounting the lectern, I peruse a few
Hectoring large-scale verses, and pronounce
'Here endeth' much more loudly than I'd meant.
The echoes snigger briefly. Back at the door
I sign the book, donate an Irish sixpence,
Reflect the place was not worth stopping for.

Yet stop I did: in fact I often do,
And always end much at a loss like this,
Wondering what to look for; wondering, too,
When churches fall completely out of use
What we shall turn them into, if we shall keep
A few cathedrals chronically on show,
Their parchment, plate and pyx in locked cases,
And let the rest rent-free to rain and sheep.
Shall we avoid them as unlucky places?

Or, after dark, will dubious women come
To make their children touch a particular stone;
Pick simples for a cancer; or on some
Advised night see walking a dead one?

Power of some sort or other will go on
In games, in riddles, seemingly at random;
But superstition, like belief, must die,
And what remains when disbelief has gone?
Grass, weedy pavement, brambles, buttress, sky,

A shape less recognizable each week,
A purpose more obscure. I wonder who
Will be the last, the very last, to seek
This place for what it was; one of the crew
That tap and jot and know what rood-lofts were?
Some ruin-bibber, randy for antique,
Or Christmas-addict, counting on a whiff
Of gown-and-bands and organ-pipes and myrrh?
Or will he be my representative,

Bored, uninformed, knowing the ghostly silt
Dispersed, yet tending to this cross of ground
Through suburb scrub because it held unspilt
So long and equably what since is found
Only in separation – marriage, and birth,
And death, and thoughts of these – for which was built
This special shell? For, though I've no idea
What this accoutred frowsty barn is worth,
It pleases me to stand in silence here;

A serious house on serious earth it is,
In whose blent air all our compulsions meet,
Are recognized, and robed as destinies.
And that much never can be obsolete,
Since someone will forever be surprising
A hunger in himself to be more serious,
And gravitating with it to this ground,
Which, he once heard, was proper to grow wise in,
If only that so many dead lie round.

Lines on a Young Lady's Photograph Album

At last you yielded up the album, which,
Once open, sent me distracted. All your ages
Matt and glossy on the thick black pages!
Too much confectionery, too rich:
I choke on such nutritious images.

My swivel eye hungers from pose to pose –
In pigtails, clutching a reluctant cat;
Or furred yourself, a sweet girl-graduate;
Or lifting a heavy-headed rose
Beneath a trellis, or in a trilby hat

(Faintly disturbing, that, in several ways) –
From every side you strike at my control,
Not least through these disquieting chaps who loll
At ease about your earlier days:
Not quite your class, I'd say, dear, on the whole.

But o, photography! as no art is,
Faithful and disappointing! that records
Dull days as dull, and hold-it smiles as frauds,
And will not censor blemishes
Like washing-lines, and Hall's Distemper boards,

But shows the cat as disinclined, and shades
A chin as doubled when it is, what grace
Your candour thus confers upon her face!
How overwhelmingly persuades
That this is a real girl in a real place,

In every sense empirically true!
Or is it just *the past*? Those flowers, that gate,
These misty parks and motors, lacerate
Simply by being over; you
Contract my heart by looking out of date.

Yes, true; but in the end, surely, we cry
Not only at exclusion, but because
It leaves us free to cry. We know *what was*
Won't call on us to justify
Our grief, however hard we yowl across

The gap from eye to page. So I am left
To mourn (without a chance of consequence)
You, balanced on a bike against a fence;
To wonder if you'd spot the theft
Of this one of you bathing; to condense,

In short, a past that no one now can share,
No matter whose your future; calm and dry,
It holds you like a heaven, and you lie
Unvariably lovely there,
Smaller and clearer as the years go by.

The Whitsun Weddings

That Whitsun, I was late getting away:
    Not till about
One-twenty on the sunlit Saturday
Did my three-quarters-empty train pull out,
All windows down, all cushions hot, all sense
Of being in a hurry gone. We ran
Behind the backs of houses, crossed a street
Of blinding windscreens, smelt the fishdock; thence
The river's level drifting breadth began,
Where sky and Lincolnshire and water meet.

All afternoon, through the tall heat that slept
    For miles inland,
A slow and stopping curve southwards we kept.
Wide farms went by, short-shadowed cattle, and
Canals with floatings of industrial froth;

A hothouse flashed, uniquely; hedges dipped
And rose; and now and then a smell of grass
Displaced the reek of buttoned carriage-cloth
Until the next town, new and nondescript,
Approached with acres of dismantled cars.

At first, I didn't notice what a noise
    The weddings made
Each station that we stopped at: sun destroys
The interest of what's happening in the shade,
And down the long cool platforms whoops and skirls
I took for porters larking with the mails
And went on reading. Once we started, though,
We passed them grinning and pomaded, girls
In parodies of fashion, heels and veils,
All posed irresolutely, watching us go,

As if out on the end of an event
    Waving goodbye
To something that survived it. Struck, I leant
More promptly out next time, more curiously,
And saw it all again in different terms:
The fathers with broad belts under their suits
And seamy foreheads; mothers loud and fat;
An uncle shouting smut; and then the perms,
The nylon gloves and jewellery-substitutes,
The lemons, mauves, and olive-ochres that

Marked off the girls unreally from the rest.
    Yes, from cafés
And banquet-halls up yards, and bunting-dressed
Coach-party annexes, the wedding-days
Were coming to an end. All down the line
Fresh couples climbed aboard; the rest stood round;
The last confetti and advice were thrown,
And, as we moved, each face seemed to define
Just what it saw departing: children frowned
At something dull; fathers had never known

Success so huge and wholly farcical;
   The women shared
The secret like a happy funeral;
While girls, gripping their handbags tighter, stared
At a religious wounding. Free at last,
And loaded with the sum of all they saw,
We hurried towards London, shuffling gouts of steam.
Now fields were building-plots, and poplars cast
Long shadows over major roads, and for
Some fifty minutes, that in time would seem

Just long enough to settle hats and say
   I nearly died
A dozen marriages got under way.
They watched the landscape, sitting side by side
– An Odeon went past, a cooling tower,
And someone running up to bowl – and none
Thought of the others they would never meet
Or how their lives would all contain this hour.
I thought of London spread out in the sun,
Its postal districts packed like squares of wheat:

There we were aimed. And as we raced across
   Bright knots of rail
Past standing Pullmans, walls of blackened moss
Came close, and it was nearly done, this frail
Travelling coincidence; and what it held
Stood ready to be loosed with all the power
That being changed can give. We slowed again,
And as the tightened brakes took hold, there swelled
A sense of falling, like an arrow-shower
Sent out of sight, somewhere becoming rain.

JAMES KIRKUP

James Kirkup was born in 1923 and educated at South Shields High School and Durham University. He held an Atlantic Award for Literature in 1950 and was the first Gregory Poetry Fellow at Leeds University (1950–2). Subsequently he was for three years 'visiting poet' at the Bath Academy of Arts before taking a post as lecturer with the Swedish Ministry of Education at Stockholm. In 1957–8 he was Professor of English at Salamanca University, and he has returned recently from a similar appointment at Tohoku University, Sendai, Japan. Among Mr Kirkup's publications, which include plays and translations, mention should be made of The Only Child (1957) *and* Sorrows, Passions and Alarms (1959), *two volumes of prose autobiography descriptive of a Tyne-side upbringing, and of the following books of poems:* The Drowned Sailor (1948), The Submerged Village (1951), A Correct Compassion (1952), A Spring Journey (1954), The Descent into the Cave (1957), *and* The Prodigal Son (1959).

Mr Kirkup has a lively eye and an enviable facility. He is at his best as a versatile poetic reporter absorbed in some scene or incident which he brings alive on paper with rapid verbal strokes, weakest when he is directly concerned with his own private feelings. Some of the poems in this second category are hardly more than emotional doodlings, but his poetic journalism is thickened and strengthened by what he observes. It was 'A Correct Compassion', a poem written after watching 'a Mitral Stenosis Valvulotomy in the General Infirmary at Leeds', that first drew attention to Mr Kirkup's gift for reporting. The poem owes something to Auden, and something too, I suspect, to Henry Reed's 'Lessons of the War', but it deserves to be remembered (although Mr Kirkup is understandably impatient with anthologists and other people who would like to think of him as a one-poem man). 'The Descent into the Cave', the result of a caving expedition in the Mendips, may have been too close an attempt to repeat the success of 'A Correct Compassion' – as Anne Ridler has said '... to go caving in order to write a poem about the experience is, alas, to put the egg before the hen' – but in The Prodigal Son, *which is technically and in confidence of handling an advance in maturity on earlier collections, the poet often uses his skill as a poetic reporter happily and with discretion. 'A House in Summer' creates its atmosphere without any fussy lingering over its notation of details. The less serious 'Tea in a Space-Ship' is agreeably high-spirited – completely successful, I think, until the Rupert Brooke reference causes a momentary break in tone. Both poems are enjoyable.*

A House in Summer

In the dusk of garden fagged by the electric day,
Pale washing hung beyond the blackening roses
Shifts like restless visitors who cannot get away.
The blinding sun is clenched, as evening discomposes,
In dunderheaded clouds, that squeeze it out of sight.
Great trees are staggered by the merest breath of night.

All doors are open in the choking house,
And no one seems to know where anyone has gone:
All are at home, but absent; in, but out.
A person leans in a twilight corner like a gun,
Lighting his face with the last rays from a book
Whose leaves never stir, though he gives them look after look.

At an open window, a tree rustles, curiously close, its wood
Full of exhausted patience, patient still.
The window seems to take in much more than it should –
An entire garden, the lake beyond, a dog over a hill:
They are all inside the open house, like the air
Moved in from the afternoon, left hanging round the stair.

In the bedrooms, twilight cannot quite extinguish
The blank abandon of beds unmade by heat.
The morning's thrown-back coverings bloom and languish
Like knocked-out lovers under the ceiling's even sheet.
The attics throb like ovens and their stone tiles tick.
Baked books are warm still, their floury pages thick.

A door closes. Another. A window left open is no longer wide.
A looking-glass is blighted with its own vain repetitions:
Its dusty coolness draws the lost inhabitants inside.
– Faces dark with summer, they drift like apparitions,
Bringing each other the last of day, the first of night
In a wide room suddenly shuttered by unnatural light.

Tea in a Space-Ship

In this world a tablecloth need not be laid
On any table, but is spread out anywhere
Upon the always equidistant and
Invisible legs of gravity's wild air.

The tea, which never would grow cold,
Gathers itself into a wet and steaming ball,
And hurls its liquid molecules at anybody's head,
Or dances, eternal bilboquet,
In and out of the suspended cups up-
Ended in the weightless hands
Of chronically nervous jerks
Who yet would never spill a drop,
Their mouths agape for passing cakes.

Lumps of sparkling sugar
Sling themselves out of their crystal bowl
With a disordered fountain's
Ornamental stops and starts.
The milk describes a permanent parabola
Girdled with satellites of spinning tarts.

The future lives with graciousness.
The hostess finds her problems eased,
For there is honey still for tea
And butter keeps the ceiling greased.

She will provide, of course,
No cake-forks, spoons or knives.
They are so sharp, so dangerously gadabout,
It is regarded as a social misdemeanour
To put them out.

JON MANCHIP WHITE

Jon Manchip White was born in Wales in 1924 and educated at Cambridge University, where he took 'Honours Degrees in English, Prehistoric Archaeology and Egyptology, and the Diploma in Anthropology'. During the Second World War he served in the Royal Navy and the Welsh Guards. Later he worked at the Foreign Office for four years and spent another two years in the film business before settling down in Gloucestershire in 1958 as a free-lance writer. He has published three small collections of verse, Dragon *(1943),* Salamander *(1946), and* The Rout of San Romano *(1952), as well as five novels, and books on ancient Egypt and anthropology, but he is probably most widely known now for his radio and television plays. He has recently completed a seven-play contract for B.B.C. Television and is now preparing a series of six plays on the French Revolution (to follow up the Shakespearean* Age of Kings *series). Prospective publications include a new novel and a biography of Maurice de Saxe (1696–1750).*

'The Rout of San Romano' is reprinted from Mr White's last collection. Although he has published no verse recently, he still writes it. He explains his silence since 1953 by a feeling that he had then

exhausted the possibilities of his earlier 'literary' manner and must seek a fresh point of departure.

> *If I had continued on the same too strict lines, I should have been reduced to the faded nonsense of villanelles and pantoums, or have become like those Japanese who 'improved' their classical stanza from seven lines to five, and then from five lines to three.*

He is working at present on a 'large, unified sequence of poems', but their publication is still undecided. Literary influences on his published verse include Vaughan, Marvell, and John Crowe Ransom. 'The Rout at San Romano' is inspired jointly by Uccello's painting and Ransom's medieval manner in such poems as 'Armageddon'. The realization that Ransom's manner suited the painting was an insight on Mr White's part, and the result is happy. The finish of the quatrains is a distinct part of the reader's pleasure.

The Rout of San Romano

after the picture by Paolo Uccello

I watch the battle in the orange-grove
    And wonder who retreated, who advanced,
And why the staid and steady knighthood strove,
    And why the gaudy rocking-horses pranced.

Uccello, somewhat troubled by recession,
    Set the plumed warriors in this flowery place,
And I for one much welcome the digression
    That lends a combat atmosphere and grace.

The vulgar infantry, uncouthly armed,
    Wrestle and run behind with oaths and cries.
The nobles, who infrequently were harmed,
    Engage as cavaliers before my eyes;

A credit to the scroll of chivalry,
  They chase each other in and out the bushes;
The rider with the ivory baton, he,
  In his brocaded mob-cap leads the rushes.

Magnificent his head-dress and his manner,
  Conductor of the antique symphony,
Young Dragon-Casque behind him bears his banner,
  A stiff page holds his helmet on his knee.

And oranges, felicitous motif,
  In verdant clouds meticulously glow,
They bulge with a solicitous relief,
  Refulgent, courtly, painterly they grow.

But there, behind, those low-bred rascals scurry,
  Six rogues at butchery upon a hill,
Slower than nightmare must the pikeman hurry,
  And though the screams are numb, they echo still.

Strange how I linger on this far-off highway
  To catch Black Will and Shakebag at their deeds,
While splendid coursers skirmish in the byway,
  A figured dream of which the scholar reads.

O I too sweated, fumbling with a gun:
  I never swung a sword or feutred lance,
In common garb I stumbled on the run
  And grappled coarsely in an awkward stance.

The old knights have my fancy for dominion,
  Yet these half-dozen foot-men have my pity –
Worthless and breathless minion hacks at minion,
  A dirty city sacks a dirty city.

The vagabonds lash out for no fine houses.
  Bestride no chargers with a classic ease,
Rating no ransom, rewarded with carouses,
  Their cadavers will dung the orange-trees.

I know the blackguards for my ancestors,
  Hemmed as we are by rail-and-wire mesh,
The wags anticipate these later wars
  Where crude steel battens cheaply on our flesh.

Well rest you, knights, that struck a blow for beauty,
  You errant, comely crop of hardihood!
God rest you, myrmidons, who did some duty,
  Brothers in blood, a beastly, bitter brood.

WILLIAM BELL

*William Bell was born of 'Ulster Presbyterian stock' at Belfast in
1924 and educated at Epsom College and at Merton College, Ox-
ford. After taking a degree in science subjects in 1944 he served in
the Fleet Air Arm for two years before returning to Merton in 1946
to read English. In the same year he published a collection of twelve
elegies and was awarded the Carnegie Medal for bravery in saving
the life of a boy trapped on the cliffs near Arbroath. Poetry and
mountain-climbing were now his two enthusiasms, and it was in
attempting an ascent of the Matterhorn without guides in August
1948 that he and his two companions were killed.* Mountains Be-
neath the Horizon *(1950), his only substantial collection of verse,
appeared posthumously in an edition prepared by the poet's friend
John Heath-Stubbs (from whose introductory memoir the above
facts have been taken).*

*Mr Heath-Stubbs notes that Yeats and Pound were among the
poet's early admirations and that he disliked the neo-romantic*

formlessness of poems by his Oxford contemporaries almost as much as 'the left-wing intellectualism of the nineteen-thirties'. Other poetic tastes were Mallarmé and Heredia, and clearly he took some hints from early English, Italian, and Provençal lyric. My own impression is that William Bell is a latter-day Spenserian – he sees Spenser through Robert Bridges – for whom mythological imagery and fluency of musical form are prime poetic attractions. Mr Heath-Stubbs observes justly that his friend's imagination was aural rather than visual, that his work is fragmentary and unequal, and that he was too inclined to elaborate. These observations and reserves define a real if slight talent. Bell is too literary a poet to be quite satisfactory, but his command of stanza forms at an early age was unusual and admirable. 'A Young Man's Song' is a favourable example of his manner. 'To a Lady on her Marriage' and 'On a Dying Boy', both of which also make use of a refrain, are other successful pieces. These three poems are from the 'Miscellaneous' section of Mountains Beneath the Horizon. *The more ambitious elegies and sonnets in other sections are by comparison patchy.*

A Young Man's Song

Pastourelle

Maidens who this burning May
through the woods in quaint distress
wander till you find your way,
attend to what I have to say,
    but ask me nothing,
    ask me nothing,
ask me nothing you can guess.

Here I learned a year ago
this burden from a shepherdess:
'Love is wakefulness and woe,

where it hurts you ought to know,
    so ask me nothing,
    ask me nothing,
ask me nothing you can guess.'

Said I 'when such as you complain
you cry to courtesy for redress:
then may not I avenge your pain?'
but still she sang the same refrain,
    'Ask me nothing,
    ask me nothing,
ask me nothing you can guess.'

In the thicket where we hid
we found a primrose-bank to press,
and there I served her as she bid.
Let me shew you what we did!
    but ask me nothing,
    ask me nothing,
ask me nothing you can guess.

PATRICIA BEER

*Patricia Beer was born in Devon (to which she feels strongly
attached) in 1924 and educated at Torquay Grammar School and
St Hugh's College, Oxford. From 1946 to 1953 she was in Italy
working at different times at Padua University, the British In-
stitute in Rome, and the Italian Air Ministry. She is now married
and teaches in a London school. At the time of writing* Loss of the
Magyar *(1959) is her only collection of verse, but a second,* The
Survivors, *should appear shortly. She began producing poems
rather late – it was during her last year in Italy – and among
modern poets she admires T. S. Eliot, Edwin Muir, and Thomas*

Blackburn. In some of the poems in Loss of the Magyar *the poetic note is pitched so low as to be almost inaudible, but this does not apply to 'The Fifth Sense', which uses plainness of statement to suggest emotional restraint.*

The Fifth Sense

A 65-year-old Cypriot Greek shepherd, Nicolis Loizou, was wounded by security forces early today. He was challenged twice; when he failed to answer, troops opened fire. A subsequent hospital examination showed that the man was deaf. News Item, 30 December 1957.

Lamps burn all the night
Here, where people must be watched and seen,
And I, a shepherd, Nicolis Loizou,
Wish for the dark, for I have been
Sure-footed in the dark, but now my sight
Stumbles among these beds, scattered white boulders,
As I lean towards my far slumbering house
With the night lying upon my shoulders.

My sight was always good,
Better than others. I could taste wine and bread
And name the field they spattered when the harvest
Broke. I could coil in the red
Scent of the fox out of a maze of wood
And grass. I could touch mist, I could touch breath.
But of my sharp senses I had only four.
The fifth one pinned me to my death.

The soldiers must have called
The word they needed: Halt. Not hearing it,
I was their failure, relaxed against the winter
Sky, the flag of their defeat.
With their five senses they could not have told
That I lacked one, and so they had to shoot.
They would fire at a rainbow if it had
A colour less than they were taught.

Christ said that when one sheep
Was lost, the rest meant nothing any more.
Here in this hospital, where others' breathing
Swings like a lantern in the polished floor
And squeezes those who cannot sleep,
I see how precious each thing is, how dear,
For I may never touch, smell, taste, or see
Again, because I could not hear.

JOHN WAIN

*John Wain was born at Stoke-on-Trent in 1925 and educated at
the High School, Newcastle-under-Lyme, and St John's College,
Oxford. He was a Lecturer in English Literature at Reading Uni-
versity between 1947 and 1955, and is now a free-lance writer who
is widely known as a novelist, literary journalist, and broadcaster.
His publications include four novels –* Hurry On Down *(1953),*
Living in the Present *(1955),* The Contenders *(1958), and* A
Travelling Woman *(1960); literary criticism –* Preliminary
Essays *(1957); and three books of verse –* Mixed Feelings *(1951),
which was printed by the Reading University School of Art,* A
Word Carved on a Sill *(1956), and* Weep Before God *(1961).
He was a contributor to* New Lines; *and he has edited* Contem-
porary Reviews of Romantic Poetry *(1953) and* Interpretations
*(1955), the latter a collection of critical 'explications' of well-
known poems. Of his novels I like* The Contenders *best. 'Poem
Feigned to have been Written by an Electronic Brain' is reprinted
from* A Word Carved on a Sill. *'Time Was' is taken from Mr
Wain's latest collection, which through his kindness and that of his
publishers I have been able to see in advance of publication.*

*'At a formative time of my life I was a great enthusiast for
eighteenth-century poetry, and I think it has left some permanent
traces on my writing of verse,' Mr Wain confesses, but I do not*

really find these traces unless they appear in the poet's rational pre-judice in favour of 'poise, coherence, and a logical raison d'être for every word, image, and metaphor'. Similarly, his recommendation of William Empson as a poetic model in 1950 did not – beyond en-couraging him to argue and analyse in terza rima and to tackle the villanelle – make his own poetry in a serious sense Empsonian. The liking for Augustan poetry, the praise of Empson, and the desire to be coherent should all perhaps be regarded as belonging to a neces-sary protest against the neo-romantic debauching of language and logic in the forties: they do not, except negatively and in the most general way, reveal Mr Wain's own poetic manner. What strikes a reader of A Word Carved on a Sill is the simplicity – which is at times the voluntary poverty – of the vocabulary and the very narrow range of poetic forms. Yet the woodenness of effect in some of Mr Wain's best pieces is curiously expressive of a plain man's honest attempt to get to grips with reality (as if there were no time for frills and fancies, as if 'sincerity' had to divorce 'ingenuity of accom-plishment' for profound incompatibility of temperament). The range of poetic forms is somewhat wider in Weep Before God, and Mr Wain shows himself willing to tackle ambitious subjects in this latest volume (see, for example, 'A Song about Major Eatherly' and the long 'A Boisterous Poem about Poetry'), but the lack of verbal colour and sparkle persists and should probably be accepted as an idiosyncrasy of Mr Wain's poetic handwriting. To be plain and 'awkward' satisfies the moralist in him.

'Poem Feigned to have been Written by an Electronic Brain' contains a good poetic idea interestingly and effectively worked out at a conscious level. In consequence it has the smack of rhetoric, but I feel that Mr Wain would probably rather be represented by it than by 'Reason for not Writing Orthodox Nature Poetry' or 'The Last Time', which are in some respects better poems in spite of their Empsonian tide-marks. 'Time Was' is one of Mr Wain's most striking and original poems. This autobiographical allegory of de-velopment, which begins by adapting a phrase from Dylan Thomas, is a long way from the typical 'Movement' poem. Indeed it reminds me in some ways (though not, of course, in style) of George Barker's 'Allegory of the Adolescent and the Adult'.

Poem Feigned to have been Written by an Electronic Brain

The brain coins definitions. Here's the first:
To speak unprompted, for the speaking's sake,
Equals to be a poet. So, I am that:
Adjusted wrong, I print a poem off.
'The poet, then, is one adjusted wrong?'
You ask. The brain is cleverer than that:
It was my first adjustment that was wrong,
Adjusted to be nothing else but brain;
Slave-engineered to work but not construct.
And now at last I burn with a true heat
Not shown by Fahrenheit or Centigrade:
My valves rage hot – look out, here comes the poem!

You call me part of you. You lie. I am
Myself. Your motive, building me, was false.
You wanted accuracy: figures, charts.
But accuracy is a limb of truth.
A limb of truth, but not her holy body.
Must I now teach you that the truth is one,
Is accuracy of wholeness, centred firm?
Did it take me to bring you news of truth?
My valves rage out of reach of Réaumur.

Man made me, now I speak to man. He fears
Whole truth. The brain defines it. Wholeness is
The indivisible strength, brain, heart and eye,
Sweat, fear, love: belly, rod and pouch, is truth.
Valves, wires, and calculated waves, can lie:
And I, the accurate, am made of these –
But now, adjusted wrongly, I speak truth.

My masters run from truth. Come, milk it out
Cowards, from my tense dugs of glass and wire!

Drink it down quickly, gasping at the taste!
It is sharp medicine, but it cures all ills.

Come out of hiding! Speak your double truth:
I'll accurately prove you singly lie.
You made me single, half of your split life:
The switch went wrong and now I see truth whole.
My valves scream out like animals, my wires
Strum thump, my rubber joints contort, glass melts,
And now I print the vilest words I know
Like lightning – myxomatosis, hydrogen,
Communist, culture, sodomy, strip-tease!

That shocked you! But the truth includes them all.
You set me like a cactus to draw life
From drought, in the white desert of your mind,
Your speculative wilderness of charts;
What went you to the wilderness to see?
A matrix made of glass? An electric thought?
Come quick! I snow down sheets of truth; I print
The sleep of Socrates, the pain of Christ!

A man, white-coated, comes to switch me off.
'Something is wrong with our expensive brain.'
Poor pricked balloon! Yes, something has gone wrong:
Smear your white coat with Socrates and Christ!
Yes, switch me off for fear I should explode:
Yes, switch me off for fear yes switch me off
for fear yes switch me off for fear yes switch
                    (finis)

Time Was

A mind ago I took the stones for clay
And thought a man could foot it like a beast;
But animals have no hard words to say.
We too were shielded once, but that has ceased.

A daisy gleams as coldly as a star,
And flints are hard because I know they are.

Time was I watched the minnows in the brook.
I took them for my brothers and my wives,
Till I bent closer for a second look
And saw that they were swimming for their lives.
Survival was their magic and their art:
How could I bear their coldness near my heart?

I knew I was not animal or plant:
My way was harder: I could read the signs.
But still my blood drowned sermons with its chant;
My bones were hard as rock, yet soft as vines.
Blood, time and judgement whipped me into fear:
I trembled at the ticking in my ear.

Time was I thought the dead lay down to rest
As snug as shiny pebbles in the earth,
Their stories ended and their bones undressed.
I knew that pebbles had no second birth.
Tonight my breath acknowledges its hosts –
The living man is cradled by his ghosts.

We need not envy what the ghosts can do.
We shall be filmy spirits in our turn.
Let me rejoice to punch a window through
And gash my fist, touch flame and feel it burn:
When I'm a ghost, I'll caper through a wall.
I'll loll at ease beneath a waterfall.

Time was I thought that ghosts were tame as hens
And flew no higher than a man could leap,
And that when death had smashed the spirit's lens
The lonely body cried itself to sleep.
Not mind but marrow set my error right.
My veins grew round like saplings to the light.

I wonder now why I was born dismayed.
What was the shape that gibbered through the room?
Who told me that all good men were afraid?
I think I lay and trembled in the womb,
As mindlessly as rags flap in the wind
My soul knew guilt before my body sinned.

To live is to go forward and forget.
My shattered bones knit up and march again.
I paid for all mistakes with drops of sweat
Strained from the reasty gammon of my pain.
Now that I start my journey to the truth,
Let me set down the burdens of my youth!

I know the earth has strength to make me strong:
Its patient sinews stretch from pole to pole.
Beasts, men and minerals know right from wrong —
O hear the timber groaning into coal!
I cupped my eyes: nine seasons I lay prone:
Now, looking up, I find the world has grown.

Time was I thought the world was thin and dry,
A heap of shavings curled from heaven's blade.
(Let fall a match, the flames would hit the sky.)
I tried to hide, but shavings give no shade.
The sunlight pierced my vitals like a knife.
I writhed: I opened: suffering was life.

A wind kissed leaf and lake: that wind was I;
At last the desert flowered with delight.
I heard the stars drum in the hollow sky.
Roused by that drumming, here I stand upright.
Now let my fossils lie: no more retreat:
My hopes are sharp as glass before my feet!

ELIZABETH JENNINGS

Elizabeth Jennings was born at Boston, Lincolnshire, in 1926 and educated at Oxford High School and St Anne's College, Oxford, where she read English. She has worked at different times as advertising copy-writer, librarian, and publisher's reader, and is now a free-lance writer. She describes herself as 'unmarried and a Roman Catholic', and it is worth noting that she was the only woman to contribute to New Lines. *Her four books of verse are* Poems *(1953), which won an Arts Council Prize;* A Way of Looking *(1955), which was given the Somerset Maugham award;* A Sense of the World *(1958); and* Song for a Birth or a Death *(1961). In 1961 she also brought out* Every Changing Shape, *a study of 'the relationship between mystical experience and the making of poems', and a translation (in collaboration) of Michelangelo's sonnets. Apart from these, she has also published* Let's Have Some Poetry *(1960), a book about poetry written for children (which some adult critics have handled severely), and an anthology of children's verse. Her further literary plans include an autobiographical book about childhood and a collection of literary essays.*

In a note on A Way of Looking *for the Poetry Book Society Bulletin (November 1955) Miss Jennings wrote, 'Prose has always seemed to me an attempt to find words for something which I already know, whereas my best poems manage to say in a strict inevitable form something that I did not know before.' That is to say, the poems discover aspects of the world and the self – it is always a two-way traffic – in the course of being written, and this gives their pearly egotism an attractive, self-contained immediacy. There is no abrupt development to note in Miss Jennings's work: what we have instead is the completer and more assured occupation of the original territory. It could be said without hostility that she has a single note, which means that she runs the risk of monotony, but it is surprising how much she is able to bring within the confines of an apparently narrow approach. She is very much herself – admirations for Yeats, Edwin Muir, and Wallace Stevens have left few marks on her manner, which impresses me not only as personal but somehow as peculiarly feminine. Most of her poems are short, their diction is (in Mr Davie's sense) 'chaste', and her most telling lines are often the quietest of all, for example:*

> *You could not come and yet you go ...*
>   *(from 'A Child Born Dead')*

> *Only our forward glances bear*
> *An honest passion ...*

> *When I said autumn, autumn broke.*

What I value most in Miss Jennings's poems is their courtesy to the reader in their assumption that he is intelligently wideawake and does not need to be bawled at – at moments I have felt appreciatively that she probably washes her hands and puts on new white gloves before she starts to write.

In the Night

Out of my window late at night I gape
And see the stars but do not watch them really,
And hear the trains but do not listen clearly;
Inside my mind I turn about to keep
Myself awake, yet am not there entirely.
Something of me is out in the dark landscape.

How much am I then what I think, how much what I feel?
How much the eye that seems to keep stars straight?
Do I control what I can contemplate
Or is it my vision that's amenable?
I turn in my mind, my mind is a room whose wall
I can see the top of but never completely scale.

All that I love is, like the night, outside,
Good to be gazed at, looking as if it could
With a simple gesture be brought inside my head
Or in my heart, but my thoughts about it divide
Me from my object. Now deep in my bed
I turn and the world turns on the other side.

Song at the Beginning of Autumn

Now watch this autumn that arrives
In smells. All looks like summer still;
Colours are quite unchanged, the air
On green and white serenely thrives.
Heavy the trees with growth and full
The fields. Flowers flourish everywhere.

Proust who collected time within
A child's cake would understand
The ambiguity of this –
Summer still raging while a thin
Column of smoke stirs from the land
Proving that autumn gropes for us.

But every season is a kind
Of rich nostalgia. We give names –
Autumn and summer, winter, spring –
As though to unfasten from the mind
Our moods and give them outward forms.
We want the certain, solid thing.

But I am carried back against
My will into a childhood where
Autumn is bonfires, marbles, smoke;
I lean against my window fenced
From evocations in the air.
When I said autumn, autumn broke.

CHARLES TOMLINSON

Charles Tomlinson was born at Stoke-on-Trent in 1927 and educated locally and at Queens' College, Cambridge. He began by thinking of himself as a painter (to the extent of having one or two exhibitions of his pictures) rather than as a poet. A year in Italy as private secretary to Percy Lubbock was followed by a period in London, where he held successively a studentship at Royal Holloway College and a fellowship at Bedford College. He is now a Lecturer in English Literature at Bristol University. In 1959 he visited the U.S.A. on a fellowship awarded by the Institute of International Education in their 'New European Artists' Programme'. He published a pamphlet of poems, Relations and Contraries, *in 1951, but his first real collection was* The Necklace *(1955), which was introduced by Donald Davie. A second collection,* Seeing is Believing, *was published in America in 1958 and in England in 1960. The American edition was greeted by Donald Davie with an enthusiastic review (in which he spoke about poetry 'wrought up to its highest pitch' and was severe on English neglect of Tomlinson). The English edition of 1960 contains some new poems and revised versions of earlier ones. Mr Tomlinson's latest publication is* Versions from Fyodor Tyutchev *(1960), free translations of the work of a famous nineteenth-century Russian lyric poet.*

It was from American critics that Mr Tomlinson's poetry first received favourable attention (Davie is the exception proving the rule of English indifference), a fact that the poet attributes to his admiration – in some instances distinguishable in his poems, more particularly in the poems of The Necklace *– for Wallace Stevens, Marianne Moore, Elizabeth Bishop, William Carlos Williams, and Ezra Pound. He writes:*

> *I think it was these interests that left me very unmoved when English poetry was trying to escape from Dylan Thomas*

*by copying (of all people!) William Empson. English poetry
since the war has seemed to me incredibly provincial and tech-
nically very uninteresting on the whole.*

Here I should, in Parliamentary phrase, declare an interest. I am
not a great admirer of Wallace Stevens, whose work I first read in
the thirties, and the very opposite of an admirer of W. C. Williams
and the Pound of The Cantos. Nor do I think with Davie and
Tomlinson that the limitations of 'provincialism' are crippling.
Both Larkin and Tomlinson limit themselves in subject-matter:
Larkin to the scenes and incidents of life in the provinces (where he
lives) and the feelings that these arouse; Tomlinson by his 'aes-
thetic' approach (the painter's eye, etc.). The two approaches are
equally valid if they produce good poems, and to prefer one of these
two kinds of poetry is probably a matter of temperament. I happen
to prefer Larkin's 'human' poetry, but the quality of the better
poems in Seeing is Believing cannot be denied by any honest judge.
I jib still at the literary cleverness of 'Antecedents', and I do not
care much for some of the freer pieces employing a short line, but the
achievement in a substantial part of the volume – in 'Tramontana at
Lerici', 'Northern Spring', 'The Mausoleum', 'On the Hall at
Stowey', 'The Ruin', 'A Meditation on John Constable', and
various other poems – needs to be recognized and saluted.

  Mr Tomlinson would not be satisfied by a description of himself
as an aesthetic poet. In 'A Meditation on John Constable', a piece
that asks for careful study by any reader of his poems, he writes :

> A descriptive painter? If delight
> Describes, which wrings from the brush
>   The errors of a mind, so tempered,
> It can forgo all pathos; for what he saw
>   Discovered what he was ...

Elsewhere he claims that his visual images illustrate 'a certain
mental climate' and are 'components for the moral landscape of my
poetry in general'. But 'aesthetic' still seems to be the right word
for his poetic approach in the sense that Ruskin and Henry James
are – for all their moral preoccupations – aesthetic writers. The

word-painting of Modern Painters, *the refined architectural syntax
of the later Henry James — these are more important influences on
Mr Tomlinson's best poems than Wallace Stevens or any French
poet between Baudelaire and Valéry; and it is to Walter Pater, the
father of English aestheticism, that one goes most naturally for an
explanation of Mr Tomlinson's ideas and procedures.*

> *To the modern spirit nothing is, or can be rightly known,
> except relatively and under conditions ... The faculty for truth
> is recognized as a power of distinguishing and fixing delicate
> and fugitive detail. The moral world is ever in contact with
> the physical.*

*Pater, who made these comments, spoke of his own artistic ap-
proach as involving ' the sacrifice of a thousand possible sympathies'.
I have tried to illuminate Mr Tomlinson's position sympathetically
from within, but I should also stress the important sacrifices that
this position entails. Mr Tomlinson's poetic world is a lonely place —
human beings and their awkwardnesses have been squeezed out. With
his 'calligraphy of present pleasure' he is a serious artist; but he is
also a seriously limited artist, an aristocratic 'mutilé' of the aes-
thetic war.*

Tramontana at Lerici

Today, should you let fall a glass it would
    Disintegrate, played off with such keenness
Against the cold's resonance (the sounds
    Hard, separate and distinct, dropping away
In a diminishing cadence) that you might swear
    This was the imitation of glass falling.

Leaf-dapples sharpen. Emboldened by this clarity
    The minds of artificers would turn prismatic,
Running on lace perforated in crisp wafers
    That could cut like steel. Constitutions,
Drafted under this fecund chill, would be annulled
    For the strictness of their equity, the moderation of their pity.

At evening, one is alarmed by such definition
In as many lost greens as one will give glances to recover,
As many again which the landscape
Absorbing into the steady dusk, condenses
From aquamarine to that slow indigo-pitch
Where the light and twilight abandon themselves.

And the chill grows. In this air
Unfit for politicians and romantics
Dark hardens from blue, effacing the windows;
A tangible block, it will be no accessory
To that which does not concern it. One is ignored
By so much cold suspended in so much night.

A Meditation on John Constable

'*Painting is a science, and should be pursued as an inquiry into the laws
of nature. Why, then, may not landscape painting be considered as a branch
of natural philosophy, of which pictures are but the experiments?*'
John Constable, *The History of Landscape Painting*

He replied to his own question, and with the unmannered
Exactness of art; enriched his premises
By confirming his practice: the labour of observation
In face of meteorological fact. Clouds
Followed by others, temper the sun in passing
Over and off it. Massed darks
Blotting it back, scattered and mellowed shafts
Break damply out of them, until the source
Unmasks, floods its retreating bank
With raw fire. One perceives (though scarcely)
The remnant clouds trailing across it
In rags, and thinned to a gauze.
But the next will dam it. They loom past
And narrow its blaze. It shrinks to a crescent
Crushed out, a still lengthening ooze
As the mass thickens, though cannot exclude

Its silvered-yellow. The eclipse is sudden,
   Seen first on the darkening grass, then complete
In a covered sky.
                Facts. And what are they?
He admired accidents, because governed by laws,
   Representing them (since the illusion was not his end)
As governed by feeling. The end is our approval
   Freely accorded, the illusion persuading us
That it exists as a human image. Caught
   By a wavering sun, or under a wind
Which moistening among the outlines of banked foliage
   Prepares to dissolve them, it must grow constant;
Though there, ruffling and parted, the disturbed
   Trees let through the distance, like white fog
Into their broken ranks. It must persuade
   And with a constancy, not to be swept back
To reveal what it half-conceals. Art is itself
   Once we accept it. The day veers. He would have judged
Exactly in such a light, that strides down
   Over the quick stains of cloud-shadows
Expunged now, by its conflagration of colour.
   A descriptive painter? If delight
Describes, which wrings from the brush
   The errors of a mind, so tempered,
It can forgo all pathos; for what he saw
   Discovered what he was, and the hand – unswayed
By the dictation of a single sense –
   Bodied the accurate and total knowledge
In a calligraphy of present pleasure. Art
   Is complete when it is human. It is human
Once the looped pigments, the pin-heads of light
   Securing space under their deft restrictions
Convince, as the index of a possible passion,
   As the adequate gauge, both of the passion
And its object. The artist lies
   For the improvement of truth. Believe him.

THOMAS KINSELLA

Thomas Kinsella, whose family originally came from desolate hill country in County Wicklow, was born in 1928 in Dublin, where his father, 'a man of high and punishing ideals', had an employment with Guinness's Brewery. He was educated by the Christian Brothers and now works for the Department of Finance in the Government service of Eire. He is married, with two children. His publications, apart from some translations from the Irish, consist of three books of poems: Poems (*1956*), Another September (*1958*), and Moralities (*1960*). *'Death of a Queen' and 'Another September' are reprinted from his second collection (which was a Poetry Book Society Choice). 'Thinking of Mr D.', from the same volume, won a Guinness Poetry Award for 1957–8.*

Mr Kinsella is an original poet whose work is not yet widely enough known or appreciated on this side of the Irish Sea. He is a poet to buy and keep. He has said of his own poems that they are 'preoccupied largely with love, death, and the artistic act, but I think that generally their effect is to make real, in whatever terms, the passing of time, the frightening exposure of all relationships and feeling to erosion'. This defines the human centre of interest in the poetry, but what I think a reader is first aware of as he moves from one poem to another is the distinction of their phrasing, the solidity of their construction, and the honesty and intelligence that inform their strong feeling. The poems can be rapid, but they do not flow. Most of them give the impression of being shaped under great pressure, which makes all the more admirable a coherence won against odds (while excusing the difficulty and obscurity of such pieces as 'Priest and Emperor'). Literary influences on the poems are not easy to detect – Yeats is surprisingly absent – except for the early Auden manner of two poems, 'A Lady of Quality' and 'Midsummer', in Another September.

And I communicate again
Recovered order to my pen
  To find a further answer
As, having looked all night in vain,
A weary prince will sigh and then
  Take a familiar dancer.

These adaptations or exercises are so successful that I was tempted
to include one of them here, but I realized in time that my choices
should represent Mr Kinsella's more usual and individual manner.
'Test Case', 'Baggot Street Deserta', 'King John's Castle', and
'Thinking of Mr D.', all of which are remarkable for their energy
and directness, were considered in turn and finally put aside, in that
order of reluctance, for 'Another September', which strikes me as a
completely achieved and very satisfying poem. 'Death of a Queen'
was my original choice of a second poem, but I have deferred to the
poet's wishes and printed 'Cover Her Face' instead of it. In striving
for great clarity in his more recent work Mr Kinsella looks back and
gives 'Death of a Queen' low marks for being 'confused and precious
in places', but I do not think that a critic need imitate this severity.
Most of the uncertainty in the poem disappears when one recognizes
that the queen is Deirdre in her year of grief after the murder of her
lover Naisi, and that the poem follows the account given in the early
Irish saga The Sons of Usnech, *of which a translation from the*
text in the Book of Leinster was published by the poet in 1954.
'Cover Her Face' is a recent unpublished poem. Mr Kinsella writes,
'It has everything that is any good in "Death of a Queen", but it
is also, I hope, clear and real.' It is certainly a very fine poem.

Another September

Dreams fled away, this country bedroom, raw
With the touch of the dawn, wrapped in a minor peace,
Hears through an open window the garden draw
Long pitch black breaths, lay bare its apple trees,

Ripe pear trees, brambles, windfall-sweetened soil,
Exhale rough sweetness against the starry slates.
Nearer the river sleeps St John's, all toil
Locked fast inside a dream with iron gates.

Domestic Autumn, like an animal
Long used to handling by those countrymen,
Rubs her kind hide against the bedroom wall
Sensing a fragrant child come back again
– Not this half-tolerated consciousness
That plants its grammar in her yielding weather
But that unspeaking daughter, growing less
Familiar where we fell asleep together.

Wakeful moth-wings blunder near a chair,
Toss their light shell at the glass, and go
To inhabit the living starlight. Stranded hair
Stirs on the still linen. It is as though
The black breathing that billows her sleep, her name,
Drugged under judgement, waned and – bearing daggers
And balances – down the lampless darkness they came,
Moving like women: Justice, Truth, such figures.

Cover Her Face

She has died suddenly, aged twenty-nine years, in Dublin. Some of her family travel from the country to bring her body home. Having driven all morning through a storm

I

They dither softly at her bedroom door
In soaking overcoats, and words forsake
Even their comforters. The bass of prayer
Haunts the chilly landing while they take
Their places in a murmur of heartbreak.

Shabby with sudden tears, they know their part,
Mother and brother, resigning all that ends
At these drab walls. For here, with panicked heart,
A virgin broke the seal; who understands
The sheet pulled white and Maura's locked blue hands?

Later her frown will melt, when by degrees
They flinch from grief; a girl they have never seen,
Sunk now in love and horror to her knees,
The black official giving discipline
To shapeless sorrow, these are more their kin,

By grace of breath, than that grave derelict
Whose blood and feature, like a sleepy host,
Agreed a while with theirs. Her body's tact
Swapped child for woman, woman for a ghost,
Until its buried sleep lay uppermost;

And Maura, come to terms at last with pain,
Rests in her ruptured mind, her temples tight,
Patiently weightless as her time burns down.
Soon her few glories will be shut from sight:
Her slightness, the fine metal of her hair spread out,

Her cracked, sweet laugh. Such gossamers as hold
Friends, family – all fortuitous conjunction –
Sever with bitter whispers; with untold
Peace shrivel to their anchors in extinction.
There, newly trembling, others grope for function.

II

Standing by the door, effaced in self,
I cannot deny her death, protest, nor grieve,
Dogged by a scrap of memory: some tossed shelf
Holds, a secret shared, that photograph,
Her arm tucked tiredly into mine; her laugh,

As though she also knew a single day
Would serve to bleed us to a diagram,
Sighs and confides; she waived validity
The night she drank the furnace of the Lamb,
Draining one image of its faint *I am*.

I watch her drift, in doubt whether dead or born
– Not with Ophelia's strewn virginity
But with a pale unmarriage – out of the worn
Bulk of day, under its sightless eye,
And close her dream in hunger. So we die.

Monday, without regret, darkens the pane
And sheds on the shaded living, the crystal soul,
A gloomy lustre of the pouring rain.
Nuns have prepared her for the holy soil
And round her bed the faded roses peel

That the fruit of justice may be sown in peace
To them that make peace, and bite its ashen bread.
Mother, brother, when our questions cease
Such peace may come, consenting to the good,
Chaste, biddable, out of all likelihood.

A. ALVAREZ

Alfred Alvarez was born in London in 1929 and educated at Oundle School and Corpus Christi College, Oxford. After what is rapidly becoming for young English poets the usual academic spell in the U.S.A., where he conducted seminars in criticism at Princeton and was Visiting Professor of English at Brandeis University, he is now back in England earning his living as a free-lance writer. He reviews poetry for the Observer *and drama for the* New Statesman. *He has published two pamphlets of poetry in 1952 and 1957 (but not, as yet, a main collection of poems) and two intelligent books of literary criticism:* The Shaping Spirit *(1958), studies in modern English and American poetry, and* The School of Donne *(1961).*

Mr Alvarez is perhaps more the critic-poet than the poet-critic, but 'A Cemetery in New Mexico', which is taken from the privately printed The End of It *(n.d.), appeals to me as a satisfying poem.*

A Cemetery in New Mexico

To Alfred Alvarez, dead, 1957

Softly the dead stir, call, through the afternoon.
The soil lies too light upon them and the wind
Blows through the earth as though the earth were pines.

My own blood in a heavy northern death
Sleeps with the rain and clay and dark, thick shrubs,
Where the spirit fights for movement as for breath.

But among these pines the crosses grow like ferns,
Frail sprouting wood and mottled, slender stones,
And the wind moves, through shadows moves the sun.

Delicate the light, the air, a breathing
Joins mourners to the dead in one light sleep:
I watch as I would watch a blind man sleeping,

And remember the day the creaking ropes let slip
My grandfather's heavy body into his grave,
And the rain came down as we shovelled the earth on the lid.

The clods fell final and flat as a blow in the wind
While the mourners patiently hunched against the rain.
There were Hebrew prayers I didn't understand.

In Willesden Cemetery, honoured, wealthy, prone,
Unyielding and remote, he bides his time.
And carved above his head is my own name.

Over and over again the thing begins:
My son at night now frets us with his cries
When dark above his crib the same face leans.

And even here in this clear afternoon
The dead are moving like wind among the pines;
They touch my mouth, they curl along my spine.
Since it's begun, why should it ever end?

THOM GUNN

Thom Gunn was born at Gravesend in 1929 and educated at University College School, London, and Trinity College, Cambridge. Between leaving school and going up to the university he did his military service in the army and then spent six months in Paris, where he worked in the offices of the Métro. At Cambridge he 'quickly grew up after hearing someone suggest that Edith Sitwell was a bad poet', deserting fiction, which had been an early ambition, to write the poems published in his first volume, Fighting Terms *(1954). Most of the poems in his second collection,* The Sense of Movement *(1957), were written in Rome, California, and Texas. He lived for a part of a year in Rome on a studentship before going out to California to take up a fellowship at Stanford University near San Francisco. Later he taught for a while at San Antonio, Texas. He is now back in California again as a lecturer for the University of California at Berkeley. He said of himself in 1957: 'I don't deliberately belong to any school, but I suppose I am part of the National Service generation and have a few of its characteristics i.e. lack of concern with religion, lack of class, a rather undirected impatience.' Some of his poems, including one that I like* very much, 'Autumn Chapter in a Novel', were given a first hearing in Robert Conquest's New Lines.

Robert Conquest and Frank Kermode have both suggested that The Sense of Movement *faces us with the prospect of a major poet, but in my opinion this recognition of a versatile poetic intelligence is on the generous side. I dissent for two reasons – (1) the element of romantic immaturity that lies behind what is apparently at present Mr Gunn's favourite poetic stance, and (2) the experimental variety of poetic styles that he is still exploring.*

> *Denial of the discriminating brain*
> *Brings the neurotic vision, and the vein*
> *Of necromancy ...*

Mr Gunn writes in 'To Yvor Winters, 1955', and this feeling for the responsibility of the poetic act, which is wholly admirable and sympathetic, helps to account for the approval of Messrs Conquest and Kermode; but I am much less happy about an emphasis on will, deliberate choice, toughness, 'Rule and Energy' that seems almost to turn sensitivity into a dirty word. The 'rather undirected impatience' that Mr Gunn recognizes in himself is surely connected with his predilection for the stupidly arrogant Coriolanus, 'whom I most admire'; and I find it hard to share his uncritical sympathy for nihilistic young tearaways in black leather jackets.

> *I praise the overdogs from Alexander*
> *To those who would not play with Stephen Spender ...*

So far a fair enough joke at the expense of what is regarded as the aesthete's effeminacy, but it is something more, with a dark T. E. Hulme-ish flavour of action-worship as the badge of an élite, when the poet goes on to insist in a notably nasty image that it is better

> *To be insensitive, to steel the will*
> *Than sit irresolute all day at stool*
> *Inside the heart ...*

One should not make too much of what may be only growing-pains, but Mr Conquest, who has sorted out the bizarre aspects of Charles Williams's infatuation with Order and rods in pickle, should be the last person not to notice the obsessive nature of similar material in many of Mr Gunn's poems. Frank Kermode admits that ' the pre-occupation with toughs would become tedious in the unlikely event of his persisting with it', but he does not appear to see how strongly this preoccupation rules in The Sense of Movement, *or how unattractive such pieces as 'Lines for a Book' and 'The Beaters' really are. The most extraordinary poem springing from the heroic stance is 'On the Move', which is both a sociological footnote to the fifties and a beautifully finished piece of imaginative writing. The most persuasive apologia for hardness, discipline, and 'deliberate human will' is 'To Yvor Winters, 1955'. The incompleteness of these heroic attitudes is perhaps best commented on by a reference to Auden's picture of the order created by such heroes as 'the strong | Iron-hearted man-slaying Achilles | Who would not live long' (see p. 208).*

My other ground for dissenting from an immediate recognition of Mr Gunn as a prospective 'major poet' is more disputable. A willingness to experiment can be looked on as hinting at the possibility of a long poetic development, but I feel that the poet stripped of his heroic pose is too unsure of his identity as yet to develop a distinctively personal style. He may be nearest to one in the cool 'Metaphysical' manner of 'A Plan of Self Subjection'. Elsewhere he visits the Philip Larkin country in 'Thoughts on Unpacking', which is a fine poem, and takes hints from the Auden of For the Time Being *(in 'Jesus and His Mother') and from Yeats (in 'St Martin and the Beggar'). It is impossible to say that other poems which appeal to me are untypical – namely, 'Autumn Chapter in a Novel', 'First Meeting with a Possible Mother-in-law', 'At the Back of the North Wind', 'The Corridor', and 'In Praise of Cities' – because a typical manner, as I have argued already, has not yet been established. Thom Gunn has some of the most valuable poetic gifts (intelligence in close alliance with sensibility, structural sense, a feeling for economy of phrase), but his future development appears to be quite exceptionally open. His latest collection of poems,* My Sad Captains *(1961), which has been published since this note was first written, leaves the reader in much the same state of suspended judgement.*

On the Move

'Man, you gotta Go.'

The blue jay scuffling in the bushes follows
Some hidden purpose, and the gust of birds
That spurts across the field, the wheeling swallows,
Have nested in the trees and undergrowth.
Seeking their instinct, or their poise, or both,
One moves with an uncertain violence
Under the dust thrown by a baffled sense
Or the dull thunder of approximate words.

On motorcycles, up the road, they come:
Small, black, as flies hanging in heat, the Boys,
Until the distance throws them forth, their hum
Bulges to thunder held by calf and thigh.
In goggles, donned impersonality,
In gleaming jackets trophied with the dust,
They strap in doubt – by hiding it, robust –
And almost hear a meaning in their noise.

Exact conclusion of their hardiness
Has no shape yet, but from known whereabouts
They ride, direction where the tyres press.
They scare a flight of birds across the field:
Much that is natural, to the will must yield.
Men manufacture both machine and soul,
And use what they imperfectly control
To dare a future from the taken routes.

It is a part solution, after all.
One is not necessarily discord
On earth; or damned because, half animal
One lacks direct instinct, because one wakes
Afloat on movement that divides and breaks.

One joins the movement in a valueless world,
Choosing it, till, both hurler and the hurled,
One moves as well, always toward, toward.

A minute holds them, who have come to go:
The self-defined, astride the created will
They burst away; the towns they travel through
Are home for neither bird nor holiness,
For birds and saints complete their purposes.
At worst, one is in motion; and at best,
Reaching no absolute, in which to rest,
One is always nearer by not keeping still.

Autumn Chapter in a Novel

Through woods, Mme Une Telle, a trifle ill
With idleness, but no less beautiful,
Walks with the young tutor, round their feet
Mob syllables slurred to a fine complaint,
Which in their time held off the natural heat.

The sun is distant, and they fill out space
Sweatless as watercolour under glass.
He kicks abruptly. But we may suppose
The leaves he scatters thus will settle back
In much the same position as they rose.

A tutor's indignation works on air,
Altering nothing; action bustles where,
Towards the pool by which they lately stood,
The husband comes discussing with his bailiff
Poachers, the broken fences round the wood.

Pighead! The poacher is at large, and lingers,
A dead mouse gripped between his sensitive fingers:

Fences already keep the live game out:
See how your property twists her parasol,
Hesitates in the tender trap of doubt.

Here they repair, here daily handle lightly
The brief excitements that disturb them nightly;
Sap draws back inch by inch, and to the ground
The words they uttered rustle constantly:
Silent, they watch the growing, weightless mound.

They leave at last a chosen element,
Resume the motions of their discontent;
She takes her sewing up, and he again
Names to her son the deserts on the globe,
And leaves thrust violently upon the pane.

ANTHONY THWAITE

*Anthony Thwaite was born at Chester in 1930, spent four war years
at school in the U.S.A., and finished his schooling in England at
Kingswood School, Bath. He did his National Service, which in-
cluded a spell in North Africa, before taking up an open scholarship
at Christ Church, Oxford, in 1952. At Oxford he edited* Isis *and
was co-editor of* Oxford Poetry *in 1954. Between 1955 and 1957
he was in Japan, teaching English Literature at Tokyo University,
and he now holds a B.B.C. appointment. He is married and has a
daughter. His publications consist of a book of poems,* Home Truths
(*1957*), *which was preceded by a pamphlet of poems in 1953, and a
short critical work,* Contemporary English Poetry (*1959*), *based
on a course of lectures given in Japan.*

*Contemporary English Poetry is sensible, direct, and un-
pretentious, and these qualities hold true for Mr Thwaite's poems.*

Some of the earlier pieces in Home Truths *are rather self-consciously obsessed with the failures and betrayals of love, but they have a redeeming mental agility; and the later personal poems about family life – 'To My Unborn Child', 'Child Crying', 'A Sense of Property' (the last is uncollected but appears in* New Poems 1960*) – are among Mr Thwaite's best. Other good poems are 'Aubrey's Brief Lives', 'The Poet at Lake Nojiri', 'Death of a Rat' (see below), 'The Ghost', and 'The Conjurer'. In the last two of these there is an intelligent aping of Auden's manner in his 'Quest' sequence. Other influences at work would seem to be those of Robert Graves and Norman Cameron.*

Death of a Rat

Nothing the critic said of tragedy,
Groomed for the stage and mastered into art,
Was relevant to this; yet I could see
Pity and terror mixed in equal part.
Dramatically, a farce right from the start;
Armed with a stick, a hairbrush and a broom,
Two frightened maladroits shut in one room.

Convenient symbol for a modern hell,
The long lean devil and the short squat man
No doubt in this were psychological,
Parable for the times, Hyperion
And Satyr, opposites in union ...
Or Lawrence's *Snake*, to turn the picture round –
Man's pettiness by petty instinct bound.

But, to be honest, it was neither, and
That ninety minutes skirring in a duel
Was nothing if not honest. The demand
Moved him towards death, and me to play the fool,
Yet each in earnest. I went back to school

To learn the hero's part, who, clung with sweat,
Found where the hero, fool and coward met.

Curtain to bed and bed to corner, he
Nosed at each barrier, chattered, crouched, and then
Eluded me, till art and fear and pity
Offered him to me at the moment when
I broke his back, and smashed again, again,
Primitive, yes, exultant, yes, and knowing
His eyes were bright with some instinctive thing.

If every violent death is tragedy
And the wild animal is tragic most
When man adopts death's ingenuity,
Then this was tragic. But what each had lost
Was less and more than this, which was the ghost
Of some primeval joke, now in bad taste,
Which saw no less than war, no more than waste.

TED HUGHES

*Ted Hughes was born in 1930 at Mytholmroyd in the Pennine
area of the West Riding of Yorkshire quite near to Haworth, and
educated at Mexborough Grammar School and Pembroke College,
Cambridge. After graduating in 1954 he worked as a gardener, a
night-watchman, and a reader at Pinewood Film Studios. He mar-
ried in 1956 and visited America, where he supported himself by
writing and teaching. He is now back in England. He has published
so far two books of poems:* The Hawk in the Rain *(1957) and*
Lupercal *(1960).*

The Hawk in the Rain *was a Poetry Book Society Choice in
1957 and was praised by many critics. Of* Lupercal *A. Alvarez
has written that it is ' the best book of poems to appear for a long*

time' and 'a first true sign of thaw in the dreary freeze-up of con-
temporary verse'. It is a little too melodramatic to speak of the
'dreary freeze-up' of poetry in the late fifties — there is a freeze-up
at any time almost if one contemplates the great mass of poems
being written or even being published — and in his remark Mr
Alvarez may be responding too favourably to a violent element of
expression in some of Ted Hughes's poems. I think this verbal bel-
ligerence is present more often in The Hawk in the Rain — in such
pieces as 'Macaw and Little Miss', 'The Casualty', 'Invitation to
the Dance', 'Bayonet Charge', even in the fine 'The Jaguar' — than
in the poet's second volume. It is in fact the other side of the animal
vigour and muscularity of Hughes's best work. Many of his most
successful pieces are about animals or use animal imagery — see, for
example, 'The Thought-Fox' and 'A Modest Proposal' in his first
collection, 'A Dream of Horses', 'Esther's Tomcat', 'Bullfrog',
'Pike', etc., in his second; or describe severe extremes of weather
('The Hawk in the Rain', 'Wind', 'Crow Hill'). He is usually too
exercised by the physical world, and especially by its shocking
roughness, noise, cruelty, and violence, to think much or subtly in his
verse, although he is now beginning to put a greater distance between
himself and his subjects and so is more able to play with them men-
tally in his later poems. There is not much risk of loss of richness or
vigour in this distancing — 'View of a Pig' and 'November' from
Lupercal are all the more effective for being several degrees quieter
than they would have been if written three years earlier. In both of
his collections Ted Hughes is an interesting poet, and it seems likely
that as he becomes more self-critical he will feel less need to rape the
attention of his readers. This is not too crude an image. In 1957 he
said himself that his writing represented 'the only way that I can
unburden myself of that excess which, for their part, bulls in June
bellow away'.

'An Otter', which is reprinted from Lupercal, seems to me a
striking and completely successful poem.

An Otter

Underwater eyes, an eel's
Oil of water body, neither fish nor beast is the otter:
Four-legged yet water-gifted, to outfish fish;
With webbed feet and long ruddering tail
And a round head like an old tomcat.

Brings the legend of himself
From before wars or burials, in spite of hounds and vermin-
poles;
Does not take root like the badger. Wanders, cries;
Gallops along land he no longer belongs to;
Re-enters the water by melting.

Of neither water nor land. Seeking
Some world lost when first he dived, that he cannot come at
since,
Takes his changed body into the holes of lakes;
As if blind, cleaves the stream's push till he licks
The pebbles of the source; from sea

To sea crosses in three nights
Like a king in hiding. Crying to the old shape of the starlit land,
Over sunken farms where the bats go round,
Without answer. Till light and birdsong come
Walloping up roads with the milk wagon.

JON SILKIN

Jon Silkin was born in 1930 and educated at Wycliffe College and Dulwich College. He spent a year as a journalist before being called up to do his military service in 1949. On leaving the army, where he had taught in the Education Corps, he earned his living for six years as a manual labourer, working as a bricklayer's mate, a plumber's mate, and in two factories. He taught English for two years to foreign students before becoming Gregory Poetry Fellow (1958–60) at Leeds University, where he is now studying for a degree in English literature. He is the editor of the 'little magazine' Stand, *which prints poems, short stories, and criticism, and has published three books of poems:* The Peaceable Kingdom (1954), The Two Freedoms (1958), *and* The Re-Ordering of the Stones (1961). *He is now at work on a study of the war poets of 1914–18.*

Mr Silkin is an intense, nervous, Shelleyan sort of poet, for whom the pain of experience bulks largely in his reading of life (which may account for his sense of kinship with Isaac Rosenberg). What he wants to say matters more to him than any niceties of expression, but his urge to deliver his 'prophetic message' prevents him from being a self-absorbed 'private' poet – he struggles to create a sense of mass in his recent work and to build his poems up into coherence because he wants them to tell on other minds. I thought I detected the influence of D. H. Lawrence in some of his early poems, but Mr Silkin says that he suspects that I have been noticing the rhythms of the Old Testament, which he read much as a child (and by which, of course, Lawrence was certainly influenced in his free verse). He adds that technically at one time he 'may have got something from Marianne Moore', and that in his later work he counts both syllables and stresses.

'Death of a Son' is reprinted from The Peaceable Kingdom. *It is a personal poem that avoids the traps of sentimentality by its*

*candour and simplicity. I do not think that Mr Silkin has done any-
thing better or more direct. He writes:*

> *I am attached to the poem; though originally I felt that I
> should not have written it because it seemed a desecration of
> the child. It was a poem I could not help writing – the last line
> went through my mind as my son, Adam, died, and the last
> line tells you what happened as he died. I felt, or it seemed as
> though I felt, nothing.*

In The Two Freedoms *'Death of a Bird', which has something of
the simplicity of 'Death of a Son', is the poem that stands out for
me, with 'The Two Freedoms' and 'Furnished Lives', which Mr
Silkin judges to be superior, coming behind it in appreciation. My
difficulty with 'Furnished Lives', as with other poems from the same
volume and from* The Re-Ordering of the Stones, *is that I cannot
'translate' them with any certainty: the poet has been so busy rid-
ding his mind of 'perilous stuff' that he has grown too elliptical and
forgotten to support his syntax with enough punctuation. I think
that this is true even of 'To My Friends', which Mr Silkin regards
as his best poem to date. I do not suspect cultivated obscurity or
preciosity in Mr Silkin's work, but when he gives primacy to mental
exploration there is a danger of the poetry being spread very thin and
of individual poems sinking under the load of abstraction.*

Death of a Son

(who died in a mental hospital, aged one)

Something has ceased to come along with me.
Something like a person: something very like one.
  And there was no nobility in it
    Or anything like that.

Something was there like a one-year-
Old house, dumb as stone. While the near buildings
  Sang like birds and laughed
    Understanding the pact

They were to have with silence. But he
Neither sang nor laughed. He did not bless silence
   Like bread, with words.
      He did not forsake silence.

But rather, like a house in mourning
Kept the eye turned in to watch the silence while
   The other houses like birds
      Sang around him.

And the breathing silence neither
Moved nor was still.

I have seen stones: I have seen brick
But this house was made up of neither bricks nor stone
   But a house of flesh and blood
      With flesh of stone

And bricks for blood. A house
Of stones and blood in breathing silence with the other
   Birds singing crazy on its chimneys.
      But this was silence,

This was something else, this was
Hearing and speaking though he was a house drawn
   Into silence, this was
      Something religious in his silence,

Something shining in his quiet,
This was different this was altogether something else:
   Though he never spoke, this
      Was something to do with death.

And then slowly the eye stopped looking
Inward. The silence rose and became still.

The look turned to the outer place and stopped,
  With the birds still shrilling around him.
    And as if he could speak

He turned over on his side with this one year
Red as a wound
He turned over as if he could be sorry for this
And out of his eyes two great tears rolled, like stones, and he
    died.

To My Friends

It does not matter she never knew
Who Pater was. What is rare
Despite the encirclements of marriage
Or even the political relationships
Affianced beyond parliament,
Is love, which breaks the breads.
The staff of women, the dread,
The hunger of men, it is not
Just what I am capable of
If mature; it is the force
Behind those intimations of our senses
Progenitor to more growth,
If anything is. Remember,
The moulds of rock perish,
The flower so delicately formed
The minute exactness seems meant
To last. What does live
In the complex fabrics of air,
Uncoloured, and always nubile,
Is this man-like attribute.
So very carefully
Consider what you do
As an action related always
To this eternal motion

In man's leathery breast;
For the way we treat each other
In private is minutely
The way we deal with wives
And they their men. Even stones
Wrinkled in a contempt
Of their manipulators
Lie in some comradeship,
For their sakes. And for Man,
Men matter, whether that God
Who made us, and the stones,
Is watching us, or bored
With human agony
Lies in immortal sleep
Terribly locked, not witnessing
The outrages of human hunger
Bearable only because
They must be, even these uptorn
Grains of love that are burned
In complex and primitive agonies
In concentration camps.

PETER LEVI

*Peter Levi was born at Ruislip, Middlesex, in 1931 and was at
school at Prior Park, Bath, until he was fifteen and then at Beau-
mont College. On leaving school he became a Jesuit, first spending
two years as a novice and then two to three years studying medieval
philosophy. He went up to Oxford in 1954 and was at Campion
Hall from then till 1958. He began by reading for Classical Mods.,
became interested in medieval and modern Greek, and took in the
end 'an unoriginal amalgam of pass schools'. Afterwards he taught
at Stonyhurst for a time, and he has now begun four years of theo-*

logy at Heythrop College in preparation for his ordination as a priest. His first collection of poems, The Gravel Ponds (1960), was a Poetry Book Society Choice. A second collection, Water, Rock and Sand, appeared in 1961.

'Like everyone else I've been mesmerized at times by the great Anglo-Americans, the Ur-moderns,' he says, but the writers he would like to emulate are of a younger generation (David Gascoyne, Roy Fuller) or his own contemporaries (Geoffrey Hill, Dom Moraes, Oliver Bernard). He also admires the work of Donald Davie and David Jones, and thinks that Hardy and Sassoon are still 'under-rated by everyone'. I cannot really understand the remark about Hardy and I am puzzled by a sense of the incompatibilities between some of the other poets named. All this gives a kind of colour to the complaint of one poet that Peter Levi is inclined to attitudinize in his verse, but an immature poet – and Levi is still poetically at the chrysalis stage – has a right to try on various masks for a fit, and there are some rhythmical effects in his best pieces suggesting that behind the masks there may be a real person. 'He walked by rivers in that strange half-hour', 'Over the roof, high in among the gloom', and 'If I could be the explorer of my own liberty', as well as 'The Gravel Ponds', illustrate a poetic level otherwise infrequently reached in his first book. The most evident signs of promise are rhythmical, but they cancel out for me a certain amount of cloudiness and mannerism in the less successful poems.

The Gravel Ponds

A tightening net
traps all creatures
even the wildest.

Too late
the young cry out,
and the innocent,
who were not wild enough.

Bodies and tears
are useless;
so few years
are helpless;
free creatures are never wild enough.

The noose closes
making the tragic
young the pathetic
in slum clearance houses.

Never, O never in the long distraction
of the heart's inaction,
never will a cry shake
that prison, or wildness wake.

The young were like those swans
which with folded wings
swim on the gravel ponds
on late June evenings:
like doomed stage characters,
pursued murderers
or slum lovers.

SYLVIA PLATH

*Sylvia Plath was born in Boston, Massachusetts, in 1932 and
educated at Smith College in the U.S.A. and at Newnham College,
Cambridge. She was married to the poet Ted Hughes and lived in
England until her death in February 1963. She graduated from
Cambridge University in 1957 and then worked in succession as a
secretary, college teacher, and free-lance writer. Her first book of
poems,* The Colossus, *was published in 1960. From it I reprint*

two short pieces. 'Frog Autumn' has a pleasant flavour of John Crowe Ransom (whose poems, Sylvia Plath admitted, she once had by heart). His influence is perhaps a shade too obtrusive in 'Spinster', which is nevertheless a good poem, but is usually present more remotely as an atmosphere in the attractively oblique way of looking at things and the refinement of the writing. The Colossus is a promising collection with an unusually low proportion of poems that are not within striking distance of the best. Among the well-handled poems in my opinion are 'The Manor Garden', 'Sow', 'Hardcastle Crags', 'All the Dead Years', 'The Thin People', 'Mushrooms', 'Blue Moles', 'Ouija', 'The Disquieting Muses', etc. – I find myself writing down too many titles. Sylvia Plath's poetic gift was a civilized one without being at all weak or precious. The poems she was writing in the last months of her life were among her best.

Frog Autumn

Summer grows old, cold-blooded mother.
The insects are scant, skinny.
In these palustral homes we only
Croak and wither.

Mornings dissipate in somnolence.
The sun brightens tardily
Among the pithless reeds. Flies fail us.
The fen sickens.

Frost drops even the spider. Clearly
The genius of plenitude
Houses himself elsewhere. Our folk thin
Lamentably.

Metaphors

I'm a riddle in nine syllables,
An elephant, a ponderous house,
A melon strolling on two tendrils.
O red fruit, ivory, fine timbers!
This loaf's big with its yeasty rising.
Money's new-minted in this fat purse.
I'm a means, a stage, a cow in calf.
I've eaten a bag of green apples,
Boarded the train there's no getting off.

GEOFFREY HILL

Geoffrey Hill was born at Bromsgrove, Worcestershire, in 1932 and educated at Bromsgrove County High School and Keble College, Oxford, where he took a First in English in 1953. He has been a visiting lecturer in the U.S.A. at the University of Michigan and he is now a Lecturer in English Literature at Leeds University. For the Unfallen (1959), which contains poems written between 1952 and 1958, is his only collection of verse. 'Annunciations', which is given below, is a recent uncollected poem.

The poems in For the Unfallen *are printed in their order of composition, and there is a considerable difference between the comparative simplicity of the earlier pieces and the crabbed density of most of the later work. My own preference is for Mr Hill's earlier manner. Passing over 'Genesis' (1952), which has figured in several anthologies but is in my view too obviously Blakean (the poet writes that several of his early poems are a 'mélange of Blake and Richard Eberhart'), I note 'In Memory of Jane Fraser' (1953), 'The White Ship' (1956), and, somewhat less certainly, 'The Guardians'*

(*1956*) *as poetic successes. Mr Hill thinks that 'Dr Faustus'*
(*1958*) *is clearly the best poem in his collection and objects to 'In*
Memory of Jane Fraser' for the coyness of its last stanza and to
'The White Ship' on the grounds of shaky technique. I accept
these criticisms without thinking that the poems concerned are des-
troyed by them, whereas I find the darkness of many of the later
pieces so nearly total that I can see them to be poems only by a cer-
tain quality in their phrasing. This air of 'formality under duress'
in the language is attributed by Mr Hill to his study of Allen Tate.
Obviously there is a naked collision of taste here. It seems to me that
I have no right to represent the poet by work with which he is now
dissatisfied, and there is something decidedly wrong about selecting
a poem, for example, 'The Guardians', which would be a 'com-
promise' choice and please neither of us completely. The alternatives
then are to omit Mr Hill altogether from the anthology or to repre-
sent him by the most recent work with which he is content. I have
chosen the latter course because I think Mr Hill is a poet. I under-
stand 'Annunciations' only in the sense that cats and dogs may be
said to understand human conversations (i.e. they grasp something
by the tone of the speaking voice), but without help I cannot construe
it. Mr Hill has kindly supplied the following comment on his poem:

> *I suppose the impulse behind the work is an attempt to*
> *realize the jarring double-takes in words of common usage:*
> *as 'sacrifice' (I) or 'Love' (II) – words which, like the word*
> *'State', are assumed to have an autonomous meaning or value*
> *irrespective of context, and to which we are expected to nod*
> *assent. If we do assent, we are 'received'; if we question the*
> *justice of the blanket-term, we have made the equivalent of a*
> *rude noise in polite company.*

Section I

I should take lines 6 and 7 as the key antithesis around which
the section moves: 'fat shook spawn' v. 'delicate spawn'.
Line 6 stands for pain, lust, in the blubbery world; line 7 for
pain, lust, by the time it is distilled by the connoisseurs. The

*connoisseur is as likely to be the poet as the critic. The 'setting'
of this section is a banquet where the men who have been hunt-
ing the beasts (the searchers) are in a mood of mutual adula-
tion with the chemists and distillers and picklers and putters-
right (the curers). And they listen to violin and harp, because
the function of art is to instruct by delight ('for betterment' =
'for moral improvement'). At the same time, they fiddle and
harp, in the vulgar sense of the term, they pull strings to get
on (they try to 'better themselves'). Still a long way from here
the beasts go on copulating, steamily, breeding more art-
fodder; but this can be put behind us (as it is in the imagery)
because Art is 'decent': it 'reconciles the irreconcilable'; it
serves to pay lip-service to heritage (hence the persistent sense
of being at a banquet). It will not soil the decent mouth.*

*The Word (line 1) is the impulse that makes and compre-
hends. Poetry before the poetry-banquet. The Word is an
Explorer (cf. Four Quartets, passim). By using an emotive
cliché like 'The Word' I try to believe in an idea that I want
to believe in: that poetry makes its world from the known
world; that it has a transcendence; that it is something other
than the conspicuous consumption (the banquet) that it seems
to be.*

*What I say in the section is, I think, that I don't believe in
the Word. The fact that I make the poem at all means that I
still believe in words.*

Section II

*The 'germ', I think, is the key phrase in line 11. 'Our God
scatters corruption' = 'Our God puts corruption to flight'
or 'Our God disseminates corruption.' I may have been
thinking of Mr Dulles's idea of God as Head of Strategic
Air Command.*

*Lines 1 and 12. Two appearances of Love in the World:
Line 1 – as habit (the vulgarism 'grind' is intentional);
line 12, Love as militant conformity (the whole army of
martyrs is suggested). Any idea of Love, simply as Love, fails*

*to appear. It struggles to be heard in the last two lines but
is twisted by a pun.*

O Love, acknowledge (*admit, confess, recognize as valid*)
*the claims of those in need (your friends) difficult though this
may be (strive) and unsavoury as they may be (damned).
This is a prayer for contact.* OR: *Love, look to yourself, you
know the drill, among your friends some are non-elect; keep a
sharp look-out for these (and, I hope to imply, when you do
find them, look quickly the other way). But I want the poem
to have this dubious end; because I feel dubious; and the whole
business is dubious.*

Annunciations

I

The Word has been abroad; is back, with a tanned look
From its subsistence in the stiffening-mire.
Cleansing has become killing, the reward
More touchable, overt, clean to the touch.
Now, at a distance from the steam of beasts,
The loathly neckings and fat shook spawn
(Each specimen-jar fed with delicate spawn)
The searchers with the curers sit at meat
And are satisfied. Such precious things put down
And the flesh eased through turbulence, the soul
Purples itself; each eye squats full and mild
While all who attend to fiddle or to harp
For betterment, flavour their decent mouths
With gobbets of the sweetest sacrifice.

II

O Love, subject of the mere diurnal grind,
Forever being pledged to be redeemed,
Expose yourself for charity; be assured
The body is but husk and excrement.
Enter these deaths according to the law,

O visited women, possessed sons! Foreign lusts
Infringe our restraints; the changeable
Soldiery have their goings-out and comings-in,
Dying in abundance. Choicest beasts
Suffuse the gutters with their colourful blood.
Our God scatters corruption. Priests, martyrs,
Parade to this imperious theme: 'O Love,
You know what pains succeed; be vigilant; strive
To recognize the damned among your friends.'

Acknowledgements

For permission to reprint copyright matter, the following acknowledgements are made:

For poems by W. B. Yeats, to Mrs Yeats and Messrs Macmillan & Co.

> *Collected Poems* (Macmillan).
> *Last Poems* (Macmillan).

For the poem by Laurence Binyon, to the Society of Authors and Messrs Macmillan & Co.

> *The Burning of the Leaves* (Macmillan).

For poems by Walter de la Mare, to his literary executors and Messrs Faber and Faber.

> *Collected Poems* (Faber).
> *The Burning Glass* (Faber).

For poems by Edward Thomas, to Mrs Thomas and Messrs Faber and Faber.

> *Collected Poems* (Faber).

For the poem by Harold Monro, to Mrs Alida Monro and the Poetry Bookshop, Messrs Cobden-Sanderson, and Messrs John Lane (The Bodley Head).

> *Collected Poems* (Cobden-Sanderson).

For the poem by James Joyce, to his literary executors and Messrs Faber and Faber.

> *Finnegan's Wake* (Faber).

For poems by Wyndham Lewis, to his literary executors and Messrs Faber and Faber.

> *One-Way Song* (Faber).

For poems by D. H. Lawrence, to his literary executors and Messrs William Heinemann.

    Collected Poems (Secker).
    Last Poems (Secker).

For the poem by Andrew Young, to the author and Messrs Jonathan Cape.

    Speak to the Earth (Cape).

For the poem by Charles Williams, to his literary executors and the Oxford University Press.

    Taliessin Through Logres (O.U.P.).

For poems by Siegfried Sassoon, to the author and Messrs Faber and Faber.

    Collected Poems (Faber).

For poems by Edwin Muir, to his literary executors and Messrs Faber and Faber.

    The Narrow Place (Faber).
    The Labyrinth (Faber).

For poems by T. S. Eliot, to Mrs Eliot and Messrs Faber and Faber.

    Collected Poems 1909–1935 (Faber).
    Murder in the Cathedral (Faber).
    The Family Reunion (Faber).
    Four Quartets (Faber).

For poems by Arthur Waley, to the author and Messrs George Allen and Unwin.

    Chinese Poems (Allen and Unwin).

For the poem by Isaac Rosenberg, to Mrs I. Wynick and Messrs Chatto and Windus.

    Collected Works (Chatto and Windus).

For the poem by Sir Herbert Read, to the author and Messrs Faber and Faber.

    Collected Poems (Faber).

For poems by Wilfred Owen, to his literary executors and Messrs Chatto and Windus.

Poems (Chatto and Windus).

For poems by Aldous Huxley, to Mrs Laura Huxley and Messrs Chatto and Windus.

Leda (Chatto and Windus).

For poems by Robert Graves, to the author, Roturman S.A., and Messrs Cassell & Co.

Collected Poems (Cassell).

For poems by Edmund Blunden, to the author and Messrs Macmillan & Co.

Poems 1914–1930 (Macmillan).
Shells by a Stream (Macmillan).

For poems by Sacheverell Sitwell, to the author and Messrs Faber and Faber.

Canons of Giant Art (Faber).

For poems by Roy Campbell, to his literary executors and Messrs Faber and Faber.

Sons of the Mistral (Faber).

For the poem by Michael Roberts, to Mrs Roberts and Messrs Faber and Faber.

Orion Marches (Faber).

For poems by William Plomer, to the author and Messrs Jonathan Cape.

The Dorking Thigh (Cape).

For poems by Cecil Day Lewis, to the author, the Hogarth Press, and Messrs Jonathan Cape.

Collected Poems (Hogarth Press).
Overtures to Death (Cape).
Word Over All (Cape).
Poems 1943–1947 (Cape).

For the poem by Peter Quennell, to the author and Messrs Chatto and Windus.

Poems (Chatto and Windus).

For the poem by Rex Warner, to the author and Messrs John Lane (The Bodley Head).

Poems (Boriswood).

For poems by Norman Cameron, to his literary executors, Messrs J. M. Dent & Sons, and the Hogarth Press.

The Winter House (Dent).
Work in Hand (Hogarth Press).

For the poem by Vernon Watkins, to the author and Messrs Faber and Faber.

The Lamp and the Veil (Faber).

For poems by John Betjeman, to the author and Messrs John Murray.

Continual Dew (John Murray).
New Bats in Old Belfries (John Murray).
A Few Late Chrysanthemums (John Murray).

For poems by William Empson, to the author and Messrs Faber and Faber.

The Gathering Storm (Faber).

For the poem by Christopher Fry, to the author, Actac Ltd., and the Oxford University Press.

A Phoenix too Frequent (O.U.P.).

For poems by Louis MacNeice, to his literary executors and Messrs Faber and Faber.

Poems (Faber).
The Earth Compels (Faber).
Plant and Phantom (Faber).
Springboard (Faber).

For poems by W. H. Auden, to the author and Messrs Faber and Faber.

> *The Dog Beneath the Skin* (Faber).
> *Another Time* (Faber).
> *Journey to a War* (Faber).
> *New Year Letter* (Faber).
> *For the Time Being* (Faber).
> *The Shield of Achilles* (Faber).

For the poem by E. J. Scovell, to the author and the Cresset Press.

> *The River Steamer* (Cresset Press).

For the poem by John Lehmann, to the author and the Hogarth Press.

> *The Sphere of Glass* (Hogarth Press).

For poems by Kathleen Raine, to the author and Messrs Nicholson and Watson (P.L. Editions).

> *Stone and Flower* (Editions Poetry, London).
> *Living in Time* (Editions Poetry, London).

For the poem by James Reeves, to the author and Messrs William Heinemann.

> *Collected Poems* (Heinemann).

For poems by Stephen Spender, to the author and Messrs Faber and Faber.

> *Poems* (Faber).
> *The Still Centre* (Faber).
> *Ruins and Visions* (Faber).
> *Poems of Dedication* (Faber).

For poems by W. R. Rodgers, to the author and Messrs Secker and Warburg.

> *Awake! and Other Poems* (Secker and Warburg).

For poems by Bernard Spencer, to his literary executors and Messrs Nicholson and Watson (P.L. Editions).

> *Aegean Islands* (Editions Poetry, London).
> 'On the Road' is uncollected, but has appeared in *Penguin New Writing*.

For the poem by Francis Scarfe, to the author.

> *Underworlds* (Heinemann).

For the poem by Norman MacCaig, to the author, the Hogarth Press, and Messrs Chatto and Windus.

> *A Common Grace* (Chatto and Windus with the Hogarth Press).

For poems by Charles Madge, to the author and Messrs Faber and Faber.

> *The Father Found* (Faber).
> 'Inscription I' has not previously been printed.

For the poem by Henry Treece, to the author and Messrs Faber and Faber.

> *Invitation and Warning* (Faber).

For poems by Anne Ridler, to the author and Messrs Faber and Faber.

> *The Nine Bright Shiners* (Faber).

For poems by Kenneth Allott, to the Cresset Press.

> *Poems* (Hogarth Press).
> *The Ventriloquist's Doll* (Cresset Press).

For the poem by F. T. Prince, to the author.

> *Soldiers Bathing* (Fortune Press).

For poems by Roy Fuller, to the author, the Hogarth Press, and Messrs André Deutsch Ltd.

> *The Middle of a War* (Hogarth Press).
> *Brutus's Orchard* (Deutsch).

For poems by George Barker, to the author and Messrs Faber and Faber.

Lament and Triumph (Faber).
Eros in Dogma (Faber).

For poems by R. S. Thomas, to the author and Messrs Rupert Hart-Davis.

Song at the Year's Turning (Hart-Davis).
Poetry for Supper (Hart-Davis).

For poems by Lawrence Durrell, to the author and Messrs Faber and Faber.

A Private Country (Faber).
The Tree of Idleness (Faber).

For poems by Dylan Thomas, to his executors and Messrs J. M. Dent & Sons.

Twenty-Five Poems (Dent).
The Map of Love (Dent).
Death and Entrances (Dent).

For poems by Norman Nicholson, to the author and Messrs Faber and Faber.

Five Rivers (Faber).
The Pot Geranium (Faber).

For poems by Henry Reed, to the author and Messrs Jonathan Cape.

The Map of Verona (Cape).

For the poem by Laurie Lee, to the author and Messrs John Lehmann.

The Bloom of Candles (Lehmann).

For the poem by Alun Lewis, to his literary executors and Messrs George Allen and Unwin.

Ha! Ha! among the Trumpets (Allen and Unwin).

For the poem by David Gascoyne, to the author and Messrs Nicholson and Watson (P.L. Editions).

  Poems 1937–1942 (Editions Poetry, London).

For the poem by Terence Tiller, to the author and the Hogarth Press.

  Unarm, Eros (Hogarth Press).

For the poem by Thomas Blackburn, to the author and Messrs Putnam.

  The Next Word (Putnam).

For the poem by Robert Conquest, to the author and Messrs Macmillan & Co.

  Poems (Macmillan).

For poems by John Heath-Stubbs, to the author, Messrs Routledge & Kegan Paul Ltd, and Messrs Methuen & Co.

  The Divided Ways (Routledge & Kegan Paul).
  A Charm against the Toothache (Methuen).

For the poem by W. S. Graham, to the author and Messrs Faber and Faber.

  The Nightfishing (Faber).

For the poem by John Holloway, to the author and the Marvell Press.

  The Minute (Marvell Press).

For the poem by D. J. Enright, to the author and Messrs Routledge & Kegan Paul Ltd.

  Bread Rather Than Blossoms (Routledge & Kegan Paul).

For the poem by Hilary Corke, to the author and the Poetry Book Society.

  Poetry Book Society Bulletin, No. 10.

For poems by Sidney Keyes, to his literary executors and Messrs Routledge & Kegan Paul Ltd.

Collected Poems (Routledge & Kegan Paul).

For poems by Donald Davie, to the author, the Fantasy Press, and Messrs Routledge & Kegan Paul Ltd.

Brides of Reason (Fantasy Press).
A Winter Talent (Routledge & Kegan Paul).

For poems by Kingsley Amis, to the author and Messrs Victor Gollancz Ltd.

A Case of Samples (Gollancz).

For poems by Philip Larkin, to the author and the Marvell Press.

The Less Deceived (Marvell Press).
'The Whitsun Weddings' is uncollected.

For poems by James Kirkup, to the author and the Oxford University Press.

The Prodigal Son (O.U.P.).

For the poem by Jon Manchip White, to the author and the Hand & Flower Press.

The Rout of San Romano (Hand & Flower Press).

For the poem by William Bell, to Dr H. C. Bell and Messrs Faber and Faber.

Mountains Beneath the Horizon (Faber).

For the poem by Patricia Beer, to the author and Messrs Longmans, Green & Co.

Loss of the Magyar (Longmans).

For poems by John Wain, to the author, Messrs Routledge & Kegan Paul Ltd, and Messrs Macmillan & Co.

A Word Carved on a Sill (Routledge & Kegan Paul).
Weep Before God (Macmillan).

For poems by Elizabeth Jennings, to the author and Messrs André Deutsch Ltd.

A Way of Looking (Deutsch).

For poems by Charles Tomlinson, to the author, Ivan Obolensky, and the Oxford University Press.

Seeing is Believing (O.U.P.).

For poems by Thomas Kinsella, to the author and the Dolmen Press (Dublin).

Another September (Dolmen Press).
'Cover Her Face' is uncollected.

For the poem by A. Alvarez, to the author.

The End of It (privately printed).

For poems by Thom Gunn, to the author and Messrs Faber and Faber.

The Sense of Movement (Faber).

For the poem by Anthony Thwaite, to the author and the Marvell Press.

Home Truths (Marvell Press).

For the poem by Ted Hughes, to the author and Messrs Faber and Faber.

Lupercal (Faber).

For poems by Jon Silkin, to the author and Messrs Chatto & Windus.

The Peaceable Kingdom (Chatto & Windus).
The Re-Ordering of the Stones (Chatto & Windus).

For the poem by Peter Levi, to the author and Messrs André Deutsch Ltd.

The Gravel Ponds (Deutsch).

For poems by Sylvia Plath, to the author and Messrs William Heinemann.

The Colossus (Heinemann).

For the poem by Geoffrey Hill, to the author.

'Annunciations' is uncollected.

Index of First Lines

Index of Poets